POWER AND THE PULPIT

IN PURITAN NEW ENGLAND

EMORY ELLIOTT

Power and the Pulpit in Puritan New England

PRINCETON UNIVERSITY PRESS, PRINCETON, NEW JERSEY

Copyright © 1975 by Princeton University Press
Published by Princeton University Press
Princeton and London

All Rights Reserved

Library of Congress Cataloging In Publication Data
will be found on the last printed page of this book

Composed in Linotype Baskerville and printed
in the United States of America by
Princeton University Press at
Princeton, New Jersey

F O R

Georgia

PREFACE

RECENT STUDIES of early American history and culture have indicated the need for an understanding of the role that Puritan writings played in expressing the emotional lives of the people of early New England communities. Ever since Perry Miller proposed that Puritan sermons must be studied as works of literary art—as a "way of conceiving the inconceivable, of making intelligible order out of the transition from European to American experience"—students of the period have sought to explain what it was in these writings that gave them their remarkable appeal for New England readers and caused Miller to raise them to the level of artistic expression. For me the key question has long been this: how can we understand the powerful hold that the sermon had upon the imaginations of the New England Puritans?

Until the last decade we possessed neither the methodology nor the historical information to probe the conscious and unconscious responses of Puritan audiences to the sermons they heard and read. However, during the last few years the methodologies of structuralism and psychohistory and the demographic data compiled in important new histories of New England towns have given us a basis for constructing a tentative answer. These developments in scholarship have provided the foundation for the analysis of

Puritan society and language that I set forth in this book. Though my primary interest has remained that of a student of language and literature, I have tried to recreate some of the patterns of experience of Puritan readers and audiences. At the same time, through an examination of the intricate interrelationships between the society and the literature of the early colonial period and through a close analysis of Puritan writing, I have attempted to show how the Puritan sermons provided the myths and metaphors that helped the people express their deepest feelings, emotions created by their peculiar cultural situation and aroused by crucial social events of the seventeenth century.

The first two chapters focus upon the corporate character of New England's first generations and upon such aspects as the family, the church, and the economy in order to understand how social institutions and events shaped the emotional lives of the people. Then, within this context, the last three chapters examine the themes and language of the Puritan sermon as that form developed during the course of the last four decades of the century. Though I have tried not to insist upon necessary cause-and-effect relationships between the nature of the society and the literature, I do believe that the juxtaposition of these inquiries reveals many significant and striking connections between the two and thus may deepen our understanding and appreciation of the minds and hearts of the American Puritans.

For my purposes I have defined the "first generation" to include all of those settlers who came to New England between the years 1630 and 1650. By 1670 many of these long-lived founders, who then ranged in age between fifty and seventy years, still controlled the land and power of the colonies. The "second generation," as I have defined it, was composed of those who were born during New England's first two decades. By 1670 these sons and daughters were in their twenties and thirties, but they did not inherit full control of the society until the late 1670's and the 1680's.

To some degree, however, my terms "first" and "second" generations become metaphors, as in the case of the Winthrop family with the second-generation founder and patriarch, John Jr. (b. 1607), considered a member of the "first generation." Also, the generational conflict that I define in this book must be understood to have existed in broad terms. That is, when the collective fathers of the first generation and the ministers who acted as their spokesmen looked upon the "rising generation," they foresaw disaster, but each of these fathers as individuals were not necessarily cruel or unfeeling toward their own children. For example, although Increase Mather spoke most harshly to the young from the pulpit in his public pose, he was an understanding father in his own home. However, a wealth of evidence indicates that within the society there was a high degree of tension between the generations thus broadly defined and that my terms do reflect the general conflict as it actually existed in Puritan New England.

Because Puritan spelling and punctuation are frequently inconsistent and sometimes confusing, I have modernized some spellings and made occasional alterations in punctuation when the original may have been misleading or distracting. While I have tried to remain faithful to the precise meaning of the texts, my purpose has also been to recapture for the modern reader the original vitality and excitement of the writings.

My debts to those who have contributed to this study are deep and lasting. I would like to begin by thanking my wife, Georgia Carroll Elliott. Her perceptive insights and stimulating criticisms of my ideas and writings have had considerable influence upon this study and upon all my work. Her contribution is gratefully acknowledged in the dedication. To my father, Emory B. Elliott, Sr., who, regretfully, was unable to see this work completed, and to my mother, Virginia L. Elliott, I am grateful for their enduring encouragement, humanity, and faith. Three of my former teachers deserve special mention: Henry St. Clair Lavin, S.J., whose continued counsel and friendship I value highly; Francis E. Hodgins, in whose exciting seminar at the University of Illinois I first undertook this study; and Edward H. Davidson, my dissertation director. Professor Davidson has given superb guidance at every stage of the writing, and in his intellectual vitality and true professionalism as a teacher-scholar, he stands as a model for all of his students.

Although I accept full responsibility for any errors that may be present here, the book has benefited from the advice of scholars and friends who have read and commented upon the manuscript. I have valued the suggestions of Michael D. Bell and Richard M. Ludwig of Princeton, U. Milo Kaufman and Winston U. Solberg of the University of Illinois, and G. Howard Miller of the University of Texas. I owe a special thanks to Sacvan Bercovitch of Columbia University for his insightful reading, helpful comments, and kind encouragement. Albert J. Rivero, my research assistant, diligently checked my quotations and notes, and I also received gracious assistance from Janet Miller and Marilyn Walden and from the staffs of the American Antiquarian Society and Massachusetts Historical Society and of the Harvard University, Princeton University, and University of Illinois libraries, in particular, Eva Fay Benton, Norman Frederick Nash, and Mary C. Ceibert of the Illinois library. Finally, I wish to express my gratitude for financial assistance I received from the Woodrow Wilson National Fellowship Foundation, the American Council of Learned Societies, and the Princeton University Committee on Research in the Humanities and Social Sciences.

EMORY ELLIOTT

Princeton, N.J.
August, 1974

CONTENTS

POWER AND THE PULPIT

IN PURITAN NEW ENGLAND

INTRODUCTION

In 1679 Increase Mather stood before his congregation at a time when church membership had as yet shown no sign of decline and put forth this analogue for New England: "Yea, it is a sad Truth, that Religion hath seldom been upheld in the power of it, for above one or two Generations together . . . [History] maketh it very manifest that that most corrupt Generation were the grand-Children of those that were first embodied as a peculiar People; when the Lord . . . did build up the Children of Israel . . . the *third Generation* among that People proved degenerate and apostate."[1] Frequently Mather took up the same theme addressing the children of his congregation, using an image of family separation that was a favorite for New England ministers in the period from 1660 to 1680: "What a dismal thing will it be when a Child shall see his Father at the right Hand of Christ in the day of Judgment, but himself at His left Hand: And when his Father shall joyn with Christ in passing a Sentence of Eternal Death upon him, saying, *Amen O Lord, thou art Righteous in thus Judging*: And when after the Judgment, Children shall see their Father going with Christ to Heaven, but themselves going away into Everlasting Punishment!"[2]

[1] Increase Mather, *A Discourse Concerning the Danger of Apostasy* (Boston, 1679), pp. 57-58.

[2] Increase Mather, *An Earnest Exhortation to the Children of New England* (Boston, 1711), pp. 35-36.

3

Such words to children and young people may seem harsh to us, but they become nearly inexplicable in the light of the recent study by Robert G. Pope, *The Half-Way Covenant*, which gives convincing evidence that there never really was a decline of religion in late seventeenth-century New England. Pope observes that the people and ministers of New England seemed to need the idea of a decline and thus they unwittingly created, in Pope's phrase, "a myth of the decline."[3] Only after the myth was well established did a falling away actually occur in the early eighteenth century. Therefore, the notion of the degeneracy of the "Rising Generation" was not a reflection of an historical event, but an expression of inner fear and insecurity in the society, a sense of impending doom. The myth of the declining generation was a metaphor for expressing those inner feelings. Of course, the need for myth and metaphor for understanding and expressing inner fears, doubts, and insecurities is great in every culture, but this need was especially acute for the second and third generations of New England Puritans.

The one metaphor in early American Puritan writing that held the greatest imaginative power in the minds of the first-generation founders was that of a holy quest, a sacred errand that they were leading for God into the howling and barren wilderness. The controlling image of such works as Edward Johnson's *Wonder-Working Providence* and Puritan sermons from John Cotton to Samuel Danforth was the dream that God had commissioned this small band of colonists to fulfill the special mission of creating a new Jerusalem in a barbarous land.[4]

---

[3] Robert G. Pope, *The Half-Way Covenant* (Princeton, N.J.: Princeton University Press, 1969), *passim*.

[4] For commentary on the function of the errand myth in Puritan American writings, see the following studies: Sacvan Bercovitch, "The Historiography of Johnson's *Wonder Working Providences*," *Essex Institute Historical Collections*, 104 (1968), 138-161; and "Horologicals to Chronometricals: The Rhetoric of the Jeremiad," *Literary Mono-*

The Puritan founders perceived the story of the exodus of the Jews out of Egypt in search of the promised land as the "type" or prefiguring of their own journey: they were the saints, the newly chosen people of God, and their "city upon a hill" would be the sacred ground where the pure worship of God would be preserved throughout the final days of the anti-christ's rule in the world. In such typo-

---

graphs (Madison, Wisc.: University of Wisconsin Press, 1970), in particular pp. 3-26; Kenneth B. Murdock, "Clio in the Wilderness: History and Biography in Puritan New England," *Church History*, 24 (1955), pp. 221-238, revised and reprinted in *Early American Literature*, 6 (Winter, 1971-1972), pp. 201-219, and "William Hubbard and the Providential Interpretation of History," *Proceedings of the American Antiquarian Society*, 52 (1942), pp. 15-37; Alan E. Heimert, "Puritanism, the Wilderness and the Frontier," *NEQ*, 26 (1953), pp. 361-382; Peter N. Carroll, *Puritanism and the Wilderness: The Intellectual Significance of the New England Frontier, 1629-1700* (New York, 1969), and Perry Miller, *The New England Mind: From Colony to Province* (Boston: Beacon Press, 1953 reprinted 1966), pp. 1-39, and *Errand Into the Wilderness* (New York: Harper & Row, 1956), Chapter I.

For studies of the continuing presence of the Puritan or Christian errand myth in the American imagination that are helpful in any study of the Puritan mind, see Loren Baritz, *City on a Hill, A History of Ideas and Myths in America* (New York: Wiley, 1964), and "The Idea of the West," *American Historical Review*, 66 (1961), pp. 618-640; Roderick Nash, *Wilderness and the American Mind* (New Haven: Yale University Press, 1967), in particular p. 353; Charles Sanford, *The Quest for Paradise: Europe and the American Moral Imagination* (Urbana: University of Illinois Press, 1961), pp. 83-90; and Ernest L. Tuveson, *Redeemer Nation: The Idea of America's Millennial Role* (Chicago: University of Chicago Press, 1968).

For studies of the power of the quest in religious thought that are valuable for understanding the American Puritan imagination, see: Norman Cohn, *The Pursuit of the Millennium* (New York: Oxford University Press, 1970), in particular his comments on the psychological and social implications of the myth of the quest, pp. 35-36, 84-85, 176 and 201; Mircea Eliade, "The Yearning for Paradise in Primitive Tradition," *Daedalus*, 88 (1959), pp. 255-267; and George H. Williams, *Wilderness and Paradise in Christian Thought* (New York: Harper & Row, 1962). Williams studies "the paradise-wilderness motif [as] a powerful religio-psychological force" (p. 7); see in particular Chapter I.

logical terms the first-generation settlers conceived of themselves, and these are the metaphors that helped them to understand and interpret their trials and successes. Their metaphor of the quest-errand has been sustained through three centuries by historians from Cotton Mather to Perry Miller as capturing the spirit of adventure and intellectual tenacity that characterized the early years.[5]

But historians have also tended to portray the questing spirit of the Puritans as ending with the passing of the founders, the errand unfulfilled, the original ideal of purity and perfection unachieved. Such a delineation of the process of development of early American thought and culture echoes the bitter charges of the aging first-generation settlers against their sons. Unfortunately, it is an interpretation that fails, as the fathers failed, to understand and appreci-

---

[5] For studies of the importance of typological interpretation of Scripture to the Puritan literary imagination, see Sacvan Bercovitch, "Horologicals to Chronometricals," pp. 13-17; and "Typology in Puritan New England: The Williams-Cotton Controversy Reassessed," *American Quarterly*, 19 (1967), pp. 166-191; for a collection of essays on typology edited by Bercovitch, see *EAL*, 5 (Spring, 1970) and *Typology and Early American Literature* (Amherst: University of Massachusetts Press, 1972); also see Ursula Brumm, *American Thought and Religious Typology* (New Brunswick, N.J.: Rutgers University Press, 1970), Chapters I and II; and Perry Miller, "Introduction" to *Jonathan Edwards, Images and Shadows of Divine Things*, ed. Miller (New Haven: Yale University Press, 1948), pp. 1-51. Three important dissertations on this subject are Joy Gilsdorf, "The Puritan Apocalypse: New England Eschatology in the Seventeenth Century," Yale University, 1965; Mason Lowance, "Images and Shadows of Divine Things: Puritan Typology in New England from 1660-1750," Emory University, 1968; and Richard Reinitz, "Symbolism and Freedom: The Use of Biblical Typology as an Argument for Religious Toleration in Seventeenth Century England and America," University of Rochester, 1967.

For historical studies of the development of typological interpretation of the Scriptures in Christian thought, see Rudolf Bultmann, *The Presence of Eternity: History and Eschatology* (New York: Harper & Row, 1957); and Jean Daniélou, *From Shadows to Reality: Studies in the Biblical Typology of the Fathers*, trans. D. W. Hibberd (London: Burns and Oates, 1960).

ate the deeper meaning of the lives of the second and third generations of New England that is exposed in their private and public writings.

From those writings we may begin to define the psychological needs of the second- and third-generation Puritans that arose from the generational conflict between the founders and their sons and from the methods of child-rearing and religious education used in Puritan New England. The generational conflict between America's first generations involved much more than the usual family tensions. The particular character of the founding fathers, the problems of cultural adjustment to the new land, and the special economic and religious forces that were present in seventeenth-century New England heightened the normal stresses upon the young to an extraordinary degree and helped to create a unique crisis.

During the second half of the century the society also underwent a series of crucial events: specifically, the establishment of the Half-Way Covenant, the Indian Wars, fires and plagues, the revocation of the charter, and the witchcraft delusion. These events affected the second and third generations in ways both conscious and unconscious. Consciously, they feared that the errand begun by their fathers was being destroyed by acts of Divine Providence; they needed an explanation of the reasons for God's wrath and a means for regaining God's favor. But diaries, biographies, and autobiographies reveal that these members of the second and third generations also possessed deeper fears about themselves and their relationship to society and to God. Because of the intimate nature of the Puritan family, the patterns of child-rearing and education, and the deep desires of young adults to live up to the demanding, often perplexing, expectations of their illustrious fathers and grandfathers, the young adults of this period interpreted external events inwardly as personal failures. Some suffered severe psychological illnesses while many were possessed by a confused sense of guilt, melancholy, shame, and nostalgia

7

that they had no way of understanding except as it could be translated into symbolic language.

The writings of the later generations reveal that they too were venturing upon an errand into the wilderness—a journey into the terrible wilderness of their own inner selves to overcome severe feelings of inadequacy and insecurity in order to survive in their rapidly changing world. To be sure, the second-generation Puritans were neither recluse nor mystical; they were men who struggled to carry forward the errand of their fathers in spite of the attacks of hostile Indians, the constant threat of the revocation of the Massachusetts Bay Charter and subsequent loss of property rights, and a series of droughts, fires, and plagues that threatened their efforts. Yet, the people of the second generation reacted to such events with an extraordinary degree of irrational fear and uncertainty and with a deep sense that they were failing to live up to certain expectations of their parents and their God. The first-generation fathers had prolonged the dependency and undermined the confidence of their sons and daughters by teaching them that the solution to external difficulties must be sought through excruciating self-examination, for inner corruption was the secret cause of all trials.

Thus, the errand of the second generation was all the more difficult because it was not an external quest across the Atlantic to a new land or westward into the frontier. The years from 1665 to 1685 were a critical period of personal and corporate searching—a quest involving a separation from the past, an initiation in the fires of self-doubt, and an ultimate return to the faith of the fathers. The quest was completed for the people of the second generation only when they found new meaning and power in their religion that enabled them to make sense of their special cultural situation.

Puritan poetry provides little testimony of this quest for personal and corporate identity because poetry was not the usual literary vehicle for the expression of powerful personal emotion.[6] The Puritan who sought to express and understand his unconscious self turned naturally to the diary or the spiritual autobiography as the proper literary form for private feelings. The diaries and autobiographical writings of the Mathers, Sewall, Shepard, Wigglesworth,

[6] By no means am I suggesting that Puritan poetry was austere or lacking in aesthetic value, but I believe that it was rhetorical more often than personal, that it turned outward to an audience and involved a degree of separation between the poet and his *persona* like the dramatic detachment we find in the poetry of John Donne. See N.J.A. Andreasen, *John Donne: Conservative Revolutionary* (Princeton, N.J.: Princeton University Press, 1967), and my essay, *"Persona* and Parody in John Donne's *The Anniversaries," The Quarterly Journal of Speech*, 58 (Feb., 1972), pp. 48-57. For another view of Puritan poetry that emphasizes its rhetorical nature, see Kenneth Silverman's "Introduction" to *Colonial American Poetry*, ed. Silverman (New York: Hafner, 1968). For example, Silverman finds "the Puritan elegy was not a personal cry but a communal exercise" (p. 13). See also Edwin S. Fussell, "Benjamin Thompson, Public Poet," *NEQ*, 26 (1953), 501.
I also believe that the poetry of Edward Taylor is similar to Donne's in the use of a *persona*: Taylor assumes different roles to examine the doctrines of religion in different kinds of language, just as the speaker of Michael Wigglesworth's *Day of Doom* changes his dramatic pose frequently throughout the poem. One critic who has traced the poetic strains from John Donne to early American writers is Austin Warren, *Connections* (Ann Arbor: University of Michigan Press, 1970); in particular see his essays on Donne and Cotton Mather.
For the traditional interpretation of Puritan poetry as meditation, see Louis L. Martz, "Foreword," *The Poetry of Edward Taylor*, ed. Donald Sanford (New Haven: Yale University Press, 1960); Norman S. Grabo, *Edward Taylor* (New York: Twayne Publishers, 1962) and Grabo's "Introduction" to Edward Taylor's *Christographia*, ed. Grabo (New Haven: Yale University Press, 1962), pp. i-xlviii; and Harrison T. Meserole, "Introduction," *Seventeenth-Century American Poetry*, ed. Meserole (New York: W. W. Norton & Company, Inc., 1968). Although Meserole states that "These poets were not writing for audiences but for themselves and their God . . ." (p. xxi), he shows that "seventeenth-century Americans had a great fondness for exercising their poetic wit, particularly in the anagram, the acrostic, and the epigram" (p. xxix). Thus he suggests the tendency toward the emotional detachment and intellectual exercise that I believe to be the most dominant characteristics of seventeenth-century Puritan poetry.

and many others testify to the burden of the soul that these men carried.[7] These writings also reveal the intimate connection the Puritans perceived between their own personal internal struggles and external events. But while the diaries tell us of the deep inner struggles men endured, it was the sermon that provided the outlet for public expression of the deepest tensions of the society, and it was in the sermon literature of the period that the record of the inner quest of the second generation was written.[8]

[7] Daniel B. Shea, Jr., *Spiritual Autobiography in Early America* (Princeton, N.J.: Princeton University Press, 1968), *passim.*

[8] For studies of the American Puritan sermon that focus upon the rhetorical arts of the ministers, see the following works: Babette Levy, *Preaching in the First Half-Century of New England History* (Hartford, Conn., 1945, reprinted New York: Russell Reprints, 1967), especially Levy's comments on the development of the sermon and the discrepancy between the theme of decline and the facts in reality, pp. 44-46; see also A. W. Plumstead, ed., *The Wall and the Garden: The Massachusetts Election Sermons, 1670-1775* (Minneapolis, Minn.: University of Minnesota Press, 1969), in particular Plumstead's "Introduction," pp. 3-37; David D. Hall, *The Faithful Shepherd: A History of the New England Ministry in the Seventeenth Century* (Chapel Hill: University of North Carolina Press, 1972); Wayne C. Minnick, "The New England Execution Sermon, 1639-1800," *Speech Monographs*, 35 (1968), pp. 77-89; and Lindsay Swift, "The Massachusetts Election Sermons," *Publication of the Colonial Society of Massachusetts, Transactions*, 1 (1892-1894), pp. 388-451. For a broader study of the importance of the Puritan sermon as literature, see Kenneth Murdock, *Literature and Theology in Colonial New England* (Cambridge: Harvard University Press, 1949), and Josephine K. Piercy, *Studies in Literary Types in Seventeenth Century America* (New Haven: Yale University Press, 1939), in particular, pp. 155-167.

Three recent dissertations valuable for analysis of the sermons are Marvin X. Lesser, "All for Profit: The Plain Style and the Massachusetts Election Sermons of the Seventeenth Century," unpublished dissertation, Columbia University, 1967; Robert M. Benton, "The American Puritan Sermon before 1700," unpublished dissertation, University of Colorado, 1968 (Benton's dissertation has a valuable bibliography that has been issued as "An Annotated Check List of Puritan Sermons Published in America before 1700," *Bulletin of the New York Public Library*, 74 (1970), pp. 286-337; and Kenneth J. Spencley, "The

In sermons on subjects as diverse as the execution of a murderer, the election of an artillery commander, or the controversy over a particular religious doctrine, the ministers orchestrated recurrent motifs and imagery that possessed powerful appeal for a generation of listeners and readers who made the sermon the most popular writing of the period. In their sermons the ministers provided the symbolic keys whereby the deepest psychological needs of their society could be touched, and eventually exposed, understood, and released or appeased. Sensitive to the changing moods of the people, the ministers created a literature continuous with human experience, constantly in the process of reconciling objective observation with subjective experience.[9]

Rhetoric of Decay in New England Writing, 1665-1730," unpublished dissertation, University of Illinois, 1967.

The problem of defining an aesthetic for Puritan writings has received recent attention in essays by John T. Frederick, "Literary Art in Thomas Hooker's *The Poor Doubting Christian*," *American Literature*, 40 (1968), pp. 1-8, and "Literary Art in Thomas Shepard's *The Parable of the Ten Virgins*," *Seventeenth Century News*, 26 (1968), p. i, item 7; and in Norman Grabo, "John Cotton's Aesthetic: A Sketch," *EAL*, 3 (1968), pp. 4-10, and "The Veiled Vision: The Role of Aesthetics in Early American Intellectual History," *William and Mary Quarterly*, 3rd ser., 19 (1962), pp. 493-510. In this essay Grabo uses Susanne Langer's definition of popular art as a basis for viewing the Puritan writings as artistic expressions (p. 497).

[9] While Perry Miller recognized the ritualistic function of those sermons he termed the "jeremiad," there have been no previous attempts to examine in any detail the psychosocial functions of Puritan sermons. However, there have been several studies of the psychological function of religious language and investigations of the dynamics of audience response to literary expression that have formed the basis for the present analysis and interpretation.

On the psychological function of religious language, see Amos N. Wilder, *The Language of the Gospel: Early Christian Rhetoric* (New York: Harper & Row, 1964); Maud Bodkin, *Archetypal Patterns in Poetry: Psychological Studies of Imagination* (London: Oxford University Press, 1934, reprinted, 1965); *Religious Symbolism*, ed. F. Ernest

In the first two chapters of this study I have defined the conscious and unconscious needs of the second- and third-generation Puritans and demonstrated how the natural and social disasters in the later years combined with psychosocial elements in the nature of the society to produce the crisis I shall describe. For example, the revoking of the charter and the subsequent rule and overthrow of the Andros regime renewed the ever-nagging need in New England for self-identity, both for individuals and for the community—were they still true Englishmen, were they still

Johnson (New York and London: Harper and Brothers, 1955), in particular see Paul J. Tillich, "Theology and Symbolism," Nathan A. Scott, Jr., "Religious Symbolism in Contemporary Literature," and Goodwin Watson, "A Psychologist's View of Religious Symbols"; Joseph Campbell, ed., *Myths, Dreams, and Religion* (New York: E. P. Dutton, 1970), and *The Masks of God* (New York: Viking Press, 1959); Kenneth Burke, *The Rhetoric of Religion* (Boston: Beacon Press, 1961, reprinted, Berkeley, Calif.: University of California Press, 1970). Also see the writings of Walter J. Ong, especially "The Lady and the Issue," in *In the Human Grain: Further Explorations of Contemporary Culture* (New York, 1967), and *Ramus: Method and the Decay of Dialogue* (Cambridge, Mass.: Harvard University Press, 1958). For an interesting study of the ritualistic function and formulaic structure of sermons in contemporary America, see Bruce A. Rosenberg, *The Art of the American Folk Preacher* (New York: Oxford University Press, 1970).

On the emotional complexities of religious experience, see Howard M. Feinstein, "The Prepared Heart: A Comparative Study of Puritan Theology and Psychoanalysis," *AQ*, 22 (1970), pp. 166-176; William Sargant, *The Battle for the Mind: A Physiology of Conversion and Brainwashing* (Garden City, N.Y.: Doubleday & Co., 1957), in particular chapters on "Techniques of Religious Conversion" and "Applications of Religious Techniques." See also William James, *The Variety of Religious Experience* (New York: Longmans & Green, 1902); less helpful are Edwin D. Starbuck, *The Psychology of Religion* (New York: C. Scribner's Sons, 1903) and Elmer T. Clark, *The Psychology of Religious Awakening* (New York: The Macmillan Co., 1929).

I am also indebted throughout to two important studies of literary response, Norman Holland, *The Dynamics of Literary Response* (New York: Oxford University Press, 1968) and Simon O. Lesser, *Fiction and the Unconscious* (Boston: Beacon Press, 1957).

12

Puritans, or were they now Americans perhaps? In 1679 Increase Mather lamented: "Blessed Puritans (for there was a time when the Saints were known by that honorable Nickname) that are gone before us." The whole question of church membership and the Half-Way Covenant touched those ever-present inner doubts and fears about God's favor in the covenant and toward the individual. The need for unity and order against the fear of destruction from without and religious disintegration within is reflected in public and private statements. Also, there is a need to feel a continuity between the past, the present, and the future in order to defend against that terrible sense that God had abandoned New England.

In the later chapters I show that the ministers responded to the crisis in their society by constructing in their sermons a religious language that helped to fulfill the deepest psychological needs of their people. In the 1660's and the early 1670's when the patriarchs still maintained control of New England, the ministers touched the needs of both generations with their lament of the doom and decay of New England. Their common theme was that humility, discipline, and obedience were the only means for restoring the favor of an angry God, but that theme also helped to articulate and objectify the inner feelings of decline and abandonment of the young people. For example, the figure of the eternal separation of the child from his parents became a symbol for the sense of disintegration and failure the younger people felt.

In the late 1670's and early 1680's as the younger people gradually took over the roles of responsibility in the colony, the ministers struggled to redefine the doctrines and meaning of religion. They presented a new message of assurance and hope that gave strength to the younger generations during the trials of the late 1680's and early 1690's. The process of development of the Puritan sermon from the 1660's to the 1690's is the process of the exchange of one dominant archetype—the image of the angry and wrathful God the

Father—to another archetype—the figure of the gentle, loving, and protective Christ. The transition from the first image to the second occurred as the second generation came into power. Through their sermons the ministers acted as the literary artists of their day, helping the society to move from the sense of disorientation and alienation that marked the years of separation from the fathers (1665-1675) through the transition years of frustration and social malaise (1670-1682) to the final years of assurance and confidence (1680-1695). The metaphors and themes of men like Increase Mather and John Wilson, whose writings dominate the early 1670's, express the bitterness of the aging first generation and voice the sense of inadequacy and of inevitable failure among the young people. By the late 1680's and 1690's the new message of assurance and the language of exuberance, even rapture, of the writings of Cotton Mather and Samuel Willard demonstrate the intensity of the new vision of cultural and spiritual identity of the second generation's mature years.[10]

[10] As Sacvan Bercovitch shows in his "Horologicals to Chronometricals," the preachers of the jeremiads frequently tempered their warnings of doom with some words of hope, but most important for the effect the sermon had upon the audience was its central theme and dominant language. The development I define here is evident in the shifting of the central focus and imagery of the sermons between 1630 and 1720. The pattern is clear in the ministers' choices of texts for their sermons: before 1650 passages from the New Testament concerning mercy and grace predominate; between 1650 and 1680 there were fifty-seven published sermons based on Old Testament texts and only fifteen on texts from the New Testament; from 1681 to 1695 verses from the Gospel served as the texts for eighty-nine sermons while there were fifty-six texts from the Old Testament.

For studies related to the development of Puritan thought and theology in this period, see Joseph Haroutunian, *Piety Versus Moralism: The Passing of the New England Theology* (New York: H. Holt and Co., 1932); Clifford K. Shipton, "The New England Clergy of the 'Glacial Age,'" *Pub. of the Col. Soc. of Mass., Transactions*, 32 (1933), pp. 24-54; Miller, *From Colony to Province, passim*; Hall, *Faithful Shepherd*, Chapters 9-10; and James W. Jones, *The Shattered Synthesis:*

14

Many of the changes the ministers introduced in the Puritan sermon in these years were conscious shifts in rhetoric designed to embolden the young. At the same time, however, and perhaps without being aware of exactly what they were accomplishing, the preachers also gave powerful literary expression through their metaphors and imagery to the unconscious emotions of the new generations. Because they were acutely sensitive to the nuances of symbolic language and to the needs of their people, the ministers gave their society the symbolic keys for achieving a cultural unity and identity that enabled the younger generations to adapt and accommodate to the rapidly changing world of a new age.

New England Puritanism before the Great Awakening (New Haven: Yale University Press, 1973), *passim*.

For an approach to the transition period through a study of the development of the concept of the covenant, see Peter Y. DeJong, *The Covenant Idea in New England Theology, 1620-1847* (Grand Rapids, Mich.: William B. Eerdmans Publishing Co., 1945), in particular Chapters 3-6; and H. Richard Neibuhr, "The Idea of the Covenant and American Democracy," *CH*, 23 (June 1954), pp. 126-135, reprinted in *Puritanism and the American Experience*, ed. Michael McGiffert (Reading, Mass.: Addison-Wesley, 1969), pp. 219-225.

BUILDING THE PATRIARCHY

The first ideas of religion arose not from a contemplation
of the works of nature, but from a concern with regard to
the events of life, and from the incessant hopes and fears,
which actuate the human mind.

David Hume, *The Natural*
Origin of Religion

IN BOSTON in 1707 the Reverend Samuel Willard was laid
to rest. At the age of sixty-seven Willard was one of the
oldest and most prominent ministers and citizens of New
England, and the congregation assembled for his funeral
might well have expected the Reverend Ebenezer Pemberton to echo the traditional formula for eulogizing passing
ministers by portraying Willard as a father who had
brought paternal guidance and church discipline to his
flock. But the symbolic importance of Willard's ministry
derived from his rejection of the traditional role of the
minister as a father figure at a crucial period in New England's history when the people needed to think of the
Church, of the minister, and of God in new ways. Thus
Willard presented himself in the image of an equal—a son
and member of the second-generation of Puritans—and
Pemberton paid him the highest compliment by lauding
him not as a father, but as a son: "In Natural Endowments,
he appeared as the *Elder Son* among many Brethren. . . .
He applied himself to *Wounded Consciences* with great
Skill, Faithfulness, and Tenderness. . . . And he knew how
to be a *Son of Thunder* to the Secure and Hardened; and a
Son of Consolation to the Contrite and Broken in Spirit."[1]

---

[1] Ebenezer Pemberton, "Funeral Sermon Preached upon the Occasion
of the Death of Reverend Samuel Willard," reprinted in *A Compleat
Body of Divinity*, eds. Thomas Prince and Joseph Sewall (Boston,
1726), pp. 1-2.

When Willard began his ministry in the Old South Church in 1678, the second generation had begun to inherit the land and the society the first generation had tightly controlled for fifty years. In their childhood and youth the people of Willard's congregation had been severely repressed by their parents and accused of inadequacy by their elders; consequently, they needed a young minister who would give them assurance of their worth and confidence in their ability to lead New England during an age of revolutionary change. The people of the second and third generations did not need a minister who would act as yet another patriarch in his role as pastor. Willard filled his people's needs.

Pemberton underlined this changing attitude toward the generations when he said of Samuel's father, Major Simon Willard, that in spite of Simon's eminence as a founder of Concord, nothing "could be more Honorable than in being the FATHER of such a SON."[2] Samuel Willard would be remembered in these terms in Boston for many years after his death. When the energetic young ministers, Thomas Prince and Joseph Sewall, edited and published his *A Compleat Body of Divinity* in 1726, then the largest book ever to be printed in the colonies, the image of Willard as the comforting son remained prominent in their Preface, where they praised him as the model minister. Moreover, they noted Willard's significant place in history in observing that "our Author chiefly flourished when we were but just emerging out of those Obscurities"[3] which had marked the age of their fathers and grandfathers. Willard was the symbol of their victory over that past age.

The long period of struggle between the generations had begun in the 1650's when the first sons of the second generation began to reach maturity and to desire families and homes of their own. When they looked to their fathers for

[2] *Ibid.*, p. 1.
[3] Sewall and Prince, "Preface" to *A Compleat Body of Divinity*, p. iii.

17

the land necessary for independent lives, however, they met with firm resistance. The first settlers had labored courageously for what they possessed and were not going to give it up easily, not even to their sons. What first appeared as an unwillingness to yield to demands for land was only the most apparent feature of a general repression of the younger generation that influenced every aspect of New England thought and culture for the rest of the century. The founders themselves were uncertain of exactly what role they expected their children to play in the errand into the new world. The fathers instructed their sons that great tasks lay before them, but at the same time they also demanded strict obedience in the home and repressed the young wills to the point of undermining any sense of self-confidence and individualism. Thus they left their children bewildered as well as insecure. The effects of their methods were aptly summarized by thirty-two-year old Eleazar Mather, when in 1671 he described the mood of confusion and uncertainty of the second generation: "[We are] like a company of Children in a Boat that is driven out to Sea, may be it may come to shore, but in greater danger to sink or drown than otherwise. . . . What think you of a Vessel at Sea that springs a leak, and takes in water apace, and Mariners some dead, many sick, a few left to keep Pump going, Are they not in danger to sink and perish in the waters?"[4] Even as Samuel Willard at thirty-one was preparing himself to assume the spiritual leadership of the Third Church, Eleazar was wondering: "What will become of poor Children when Heads of Families die? what will become of unskilful Passengers, when Pilot and able Steerman is taken away? *What will become of this generation?*"[5]

It has become traditional for historians to dismiss the second and third generations of New Englanders in the same words that the first-generation ministers used in their

[4] Eleazar Mather, *A Serious Exhortation to the Present and Succeeding Generation in New England* (Cambridge, 1671), p. 17.

[5] *Ibid.*, p. 26.

sermons to reject them; the common epithet of the old preachers of the 1660's that the young people were a "corrupt and degenerate Rising generation" is echoed in modern studies. Perry Miller, for example, called the second generation "a newly arisen, American-born tribe of pragmaticals."[6] Similarly, in his examination of the first three generations of the Winthrop dynasty, Richard S. Dunn finds a "gradual deterioration" in the family with each generation; he describes a decline from public interest to private interest and from religious conviction to indifference.[7] The recent biographer of John Winthrop, Jr. confirms Dunn's view by finding the second-generation Winthrop restless, wayward, and irresponsible, and unable to take hold of anything permanently until his father's death in 1649,[8] while Dunn goes on to condemn the Winthrop grandsons as "half-ludicrous, uncertain of their values, and always chiefly absorbed with fashion, status and the accumulation of real estate."[9] The latter characteristic is hardly surprising in view of the first generation's tight control of the lands.

But the pattern repeated in the lives of these men demands careful and sympathetic consideration. Fitz-John Winthrop, son of John, Jr., was a troubled and unsettled youth who disappointed his family: he landed in jail for drunkenness, insulted his sister's fiancé, and seemed to shirk his responsibilities in New England religion and politics. Similarly, his younger brother Wait Still Winthrop left Harvard without a degree and skirted community responsibilities. Yet after the death of their father, the lives of these two brothers, like that of John Winthrop, Jr. before them,

[6] Miller, *From Colony to Province*, p. 111.

[7] Richard S. Dunn, *Puritans and Yankees: The Winthrop Dynasty of New England, 1630-1717* (Princeton, N.J.: Princeton University Press, 1962), p. vi.

[8] Robert C. Black, III, *The Younger John Winthrop* (New York: Columbia University Press, 1966), *passim*.

[9] Dunn, *Puritans and Yankees*, p. vi.

19

suddenly underwent a striking transformation as they began
to fill key positions in the society in the closing decades of
the century. In his middle years Fitz-John became a defender of the Connecticut charter that his father had established; Wait joined himself into full communion in Willard's church at the age of forty-five and was a champion
of Massachusetts' liberty.[10] This pattern in the lives of the
second- and third-generation Winthrops, involving a
lengthy period of irresponsibility and confusion followed
by a sudden reversal, raises questions about the relationship between the generations and the availability of roles
for sons to fill in the New England society before the deaths
of their fathers. Of course, we cannot understand the sons
of New England without knowing their fathers.

THE PATRIARCHS

Most of the men who founded the many towns of New
England established by 1650 came to New England in their
twenties and thirties in the two decades following the
founding of Massachusetts Bay in 1630. They were some of
the toughest and most ambitious men of England's most
aspiring generation.[11] The fact that they were Puritans tells
us much about their strength, for in the early seventeenth
century Congregational Puritanism was a religion that
posed a radical new life style. The ideas of St. Paul and the
European reformers, as interpreted by the English theologians William Ames, William Perkins, and John Preston,

[10] *Ibid.*, see section on the grandsons, pp. 191-356.

[11] Anthony Esler, *The Aspiring Mind of the Elizabethan Younger
Generation* (Durham, N.C.: Duke University Press, 1966), *passim*. I am
indebted to Esler not only for his information on the kind of men
who became New England settlers but also for his demonstration of
the methodology of generational history. See also David C. McClelland,
The Achieving Society (Princeton, N.J.: Van Nostrand, 1961), who
demonstrates that in England "achievement (need for achievement)
level was high from 1500 through 1625," p. 140.

were fresh, exciting, and particularly well suited for the social and psychological needs of the vigorous people who felt themselves on the vanguard of a new age.[12]

The men who embraced the spirit of early Puritanism, the Pauline Renaissance, and who dared to venture into the wilderness to put their ideas of society into practice were independent and aggressive and felt that the traditional patterns of community life in England had grown too rigid for them. They sought an outlet for their creativity and energy and desired relief from an England that they felt was adhering to a corrupted European heritage.[13] Their resistance to the Anglican compromise with the past tradition of the Roman Church was inspired by the message of Paul that declared them "new men" freed by Christ's sacrifice to create a new world; with St. Paul they believed: "That we henceforth be no more children, tossed to and fro, and carried about with every wind of doctrine, by the sleight of men, and cunning craftiness, whereby they lie in wait to deceive" (Eph 4:14). Determined to create their own world, where they could speak "the truth in love" and

[12] John S. Coolidge, *The Pauline Renaissance in England: Puritanism and the Bible* (Oxford: Clarendon Press, 1970); see in particular Chapter II, "Christian Liberty and Edification," pp. 23-54.

[13] These qualities of the first generation are presented most vividly in Sumner Chilton Powell, *Puritan Village, The Formation of a New England Town* (Middletown, Conn.: Wesleyan University Press, 1963), p. 19. Works that describe these traits in the Puritans in New England include Darrett B. Rutman, *Winthrop's Boston* (Chapel Hill, N.C.: University of North Carolina Press, 1963) and *American Puritanism: Faith and Practice* (Philadelphia: Lippincott and Co., 1970). For a similar portrait of the ambitious merchant class, see Bernard Bailyn, *The New England Merchants in the Seventeenth Century* (Cambridge: Harvard University Press, 1955). For studies of the sixteenth- and seventeenth-century English roots of the first-generation character, see Carl Bridenbaugh, *Vexed and Troubled Englishmen, 1590-1642* (New York: Oxford University Press, 1968), William Haller, *The Rise of Puritanism* (New York: Columbia University Press, 1938) and Christopher Hill, *Society and Puritanism in Pre-Revolutionary England* (London: Secker and Warburg, 1964).

"grow up into Him in all things," they announced to parents and friends, as well as to the land-owning aristocracy and crown, that they must have the freedom to use their talents to the fullest: "This freedom have all Christians that they consider what is lawful and what is profitable . . . and in no case be brought under the power of any thing, as Paul teacheth us. Whatsoever doth most edify, that must we choose, and avoid the contrary: and whatsoever is most expedient, that must be done, and so we must apply ourselves all unto all, that notwithstanding we hold our liberty. For if either Magistrate or other would take that from us we must not give place by yielding unto them, no, not for an hour, and this liberty is the free use of our callings and gifts, as we see most agreeing to the word of God, and expedient for his glory."[14] John Cotton captured this independent spirit when he sent out his call in 1634 for more men to come to New England: "*When a man's Calling and Person are free* and not tied by Parents, or Magistrates, or other people that have an interest in him . . . [God] opens a door there and sets him loose here, inclines his heart that way, and outlooks all difficulties. . . . In such a case God tells them, he will appoint a place for them."[15]

THE ORIGINAL PAULINE SPIRIT

The religious spirit of the settlers when they arrived in New England was not the narrow exclusiveness into which it evolved under the pressure of massive emigration from England in the 1640's and 1650's. The vital force of early Puritanism was its confidence and openness to growth.[16]

[14] Robert Browne, "A Treatise of reformation without tarying for any," in *The Writings of Robert Harrison and Robert Browne*, eds. Albert Peel and Leland H. Carlson (London, 1953), p. 158.

[15] John Cotton, *God's Promise to his Plantations* (London, 1634, reprinted Boston, 1686), p. 11.

[16] While there is still controversy about the idea of a pure church in Puritan thought, recent historians have found that the notion of

Men who felt a sense of their own importance and who
believed that they were somehow in a special position in
world developments joined together with others who shared
these convictions to form congregations. Each group then
elected spiritual and political leaders and called upon a
minister whose preaching and interpretation of Scripture
they admired. In the early years of the colony the minister
preached, instructed, and advised, but the laymen defined
the laws of the congregation and imposed church discipline
upon themselves. The concept of ministerial control was
still so foreign to the men of Sudbury, Massachusetts, in
1652 that when a group of "Reverend Elders" came to investigate a land dispute involving the local pastor, the Reverend Edmund Brown, the town simply ignored the outsiders; their presence was not even recorded by the clerk
in the Town Book.[17] When the good English Puritan,
Thomas Lechford, visited New England in the 1640's, he
was shocked by the self-importance and power of the laymen, who, he observed, had established themselves as equals
with the ministers on church matters.[18]

These early Puritans were inclined to assume themselves
and their community worthy of God's special favor and
grace. Therefore, for them the word "discipline" meant
self-discipline; it defined the personal toughness and self-

purity developed only in New England and only after the establish-
ment of the first churches. See Morgan, *Visible Saints* (New York: New
York University Press, 1963), and Norman Pettit, *The Heart Prepared:
Grace and Conversion in Puritan Spiritual Life* (New Haven: Yale
University Press, 1966), Chapter I; for membership in English and
early American Puritanism, see Coolidge, *Pauline Renaissance*, "Intro-
duction"; Perry Miller, "The Marrow of Puritan Divinity," *Pub. of the
Col. Soc. of Mass., Transactions*, 32 (1935), pp. 247-300; and John von
Rohr, "Covenant and Assurance in Early English Puritanism," *CH*, 34
(June, 1965), pp. 195-203.

[17] See *Tensions in American Puritanism*, ed. Richard Reinitz (New
York: Wiley, 1970), p. 183.

[18] Thomas Lechford, *Plain Dealing or, NEWS from New-England*
(London, 1642), "To the Reader," p. A3.

control the settlers felt they needed for overcoming weaknesses not conducive to the formation of an exemplary society.[19] Similarly, they conceived of self-examination as a practical method for improving the individual and the society, not as a way of fostering an undue sense of guilt and doom.[20] Such a conception of corporate Christian experience served to strengthen in each church member the sense of individual identity that comes about through social relationships. These qualities of personal conviction and determination made the first settlers outstanding pioneers, but they would also make them resisting fathers.

In the beginning the churches of New England followed the pattern of open membership that had been established in the Puritan churches of England. New members were accepted into full membership with relative ease. As John Cotton assured his congregation: "God accepts at our hands a willing mind, and of child-like endeavors; if we come with child-like service, God will spare us."[21] There were no rigorous tests for membership, for most believed, as Thomas Hooker was to continue to hold even after the mood had changed, that a man should not "search into 'the heart of another' which 'no man can know.' "[22] Although there was to be no compromise with the dead things of the world, isolationism and absolute perfectionism were not the original goals of the early Christian or the early Puritan movement.[23] The later effort to make the visible church on earth reflect the invisible church of the saved in heaven became part of the New England way only in the decades after settlement and emerged as a solution to problems that were not wholly religious in nature.

[19] Alan Simpson, *Puritanism in Old and New England* (Chicago: University of Chicago Press, 1955), p. 6.

[20] Coolidge, *Pauline Renaissance*, pp. 60-61.

[21] John Cotton, *Covenant of God's Free Grace* (London, 1645), p. 19.

[22] Thomas Hooker, *The Souls Implantation* (London, 1637), as quoted in Pettit, *The Heart Prepared*, p. 101.

[23] Morgan, *Visible Saints*, particularly pp. 36-47, 77-93, and Coolidge, pp. 60-63.

The system of personal and social ethics taught by the early Puritan theologians was also particularly suited to the aspiring men of the first generation. The writings of John Robinson were designed to instill in men a sense of self-importance by emphasizing that no matter how menial a man's work may seem to him or others it had great significance in the eyes of God as long as the laborer were a true Christian.[24] In 1641 in his *The Way of Life*, John Cotton showed the intimate connection between one's practical calling and his spiritual calling. Cotton argued that every Christian's spiritual calling charges his earthly vocation with such dignity that God sees no real difference between a minister and a laborer.[25] The Puritan ministers preached that as long as a person lived a good life, felt himself saved in Christ, and was not idle in his calling, he could expect a greater reward than many of the rich and powerful who were wicked.

This religion also strengthened a man's importance as a father, for election into God's covenant was a gift that could be passed on to others. The father was the spiritual as well as practical head of his household. By teaching his children the message of the Gospel as he learned it from the preacher and the Bible, the Puritan father could leave his offspring an inheritance more valuable than earthly wealth. Thus Cotton urged: "Every righteous Householder and Parent, to take more care to leave a good covenant to their children and servants than anything else. If they have but this portion left to them, they still do well, whether they grow and prosper in the things of the world or not, God hath made a Covenant with Parents and Householder."[26]

[24] John Robinson, *Observations of Knowledge and Virtue* (London, 1625), pp. 149-154. See also *Tensions in American Puritanism*, Reinitz, p. 70.

[25] John Cotton, *The Way of Life* (London, 1641), p. 104; see also "Christian Calling" in *The Puritans*, eds. Perry Miller and Thomas Johnson (New York: Harper & Row, reprinted 1963), pp. 319-327.

[26] John Cotton, *God's Free Grace*, p. 19.

Because Puritanism was a religion that encouraged men
to take such pride in themselves and their work, it touched
the hearts of those Englishmen who became the New England colonists: Puritanism was a religion that attracted men
who possessed a competitive and aggressive nature, as Governor Bradford discovered when he tried a plan of communal farming: "The taking away of property and bringing in community into commonwealth . . . was found to
breed much confusion and discontent and to retard employment." But Bradford was quick to recognize the value of
this spirit and to defend it: "Let none object this . . . God
in His wisdom saw another course fitter for them."[27]

Generations in Conflict

In the last few years we have learned much about the
actual nature of early New England society from the work
of those historians who have made intensive studies of the
individual town records.[28] The portrait of the founders to
emerge from these studies is one of a generation of unusually healthy, long-lived men of determination and vigor who
established and maintained a strong patriarchy in New
England for over forty years. In fact, the presence of so

[27] William Bradford, *Of Plymouth Plantation, 1620-1647*, ed. Samuel Eliot Morison (New York: Alfred A. Knopf, 1952), p. 121.

[28] In particular see the following: John Demos, *A Little Common-
wealth: Family Life in Plymouth Colony* (New York: Oxford University
Press, 1970), "Notes on Life in Plymouth Colony," *WMQ*, ser. 3, 22
(1965), pp. 264-286, and "Families in Colonial Bristol, R.I.," *WMQ*, 25
(1968), pp. 40-57; Philip J. Greven, Jr., *Four Generations: Population,
Land and Family in Colonial Andover, Mass.* (Ithaca, N.Y.: Cornell
University Press, 1970); Kenneth A. Lockridge, *A New England Town:
Dedham, Mass., 1636-1736* (New York: Norton Co., 1970), and "The
History of a Puritan Church, 1637-1736," *NEQ*, 40 (1967), pp. 399-424;
and Powell, *Puritan Village*. For two valuable reviews of the work of
the demographic historians, see John M. Murrin, "Review Essay," *His-
tory and Theory*, 11 (1972), pp. 226-275, and Richard S. Dunn, "The
Social History of Early New England," *AQ*, 24 (1972), pp. 661-679.

many strong personalities in the first generation caused much contention and disorder during the years of settlement when imaginations and ideas clashed over issues of division of the lands and establishment of the rules of town governments.[29] Local economic squabbles were intensified during the years of economic depression in the 1640's; but, ingenious and persevering men that they were, the first settlers managed to create a relatively stable society by the 1650's. Indeed, once they had the original difficulties worked out, their society became even more traditional and rigid than the one they had abandoned in England. Isolationism, exclusiveness, and intolerance became the characteristics of the first settlers in their middle and declining years. Proud of their achievement, they wished to witness no changes in this social structure.

The town of Sudbury, Massachusetts, is a case in point.[30] There the men who joined together to form the town had come from widely diverse sections of England and had lived under four different kinds of economic systems. In the process of devising a new system that would be acceptable to all, the founders completely abandoned the methods, the vocabulary, and even the calendar of the courts-barron and bailiff of England. Over the course of about six years, initial misunderstandings and disagreements were eventually overcome. The major portions of the town's land were divided by rank among the freemen, and sections of additional lands

[29] Darrett B. Rutman has emphasized this early instability, contention, and disruption of Puritan ideals in his works; he summarizes his thesis in "The Mirror of Puritan Authority," in *Law and Authority in Colonial America*, ed. George A. Billias (Barre, Mass.: Barre Publishers, 1965), pp. 149-167. Cf. Miller, *From Colony to Province*, who views the early years as relatively stable and ordered with disruption coming only in the last half of the century. See also Richard L. Bushman, *From Puritan to Yankee: Character and the Social Order in Connecticut, 1690-1765* (Cambridge, Mass.: Harvard University Press, 1967), who finds little social disorder in Connecticut before the end of the century.

[30] Data on Sudbury is drawn from Powell, *Puritan Village, passim.*

27

were set aside for later arrivals or for the subsequent plans of the town's founders. However, no land was ever granted to a new arrival. As the founders reached middle age in the 1650's, they were no longer open to emigrants. After all, they reasoned, they had endured the initial hardships, why should a late-comer reap the benefits? Yet there was one threat to their stability that they had not foreseen.

By 1650 there were at least twenty-six sons who had grown to manhood, yet none had been granted a portion of the available open lands. Without land they could not marry and begin lives of their own, for in the towns outside Boston farming was the only effective way of earning enough to support a family. There was no need yet for skilled laborers, and manual labor paid only enough to support a single person. Indentured servants were prohibited by law from marriage. The sons of Sudbury had no choice but to challenge their fathers' claims to the unused lands. Sudbury's historian, Sumner Powell, summarized the events of the early 1650's: "As the younger sons matured and began to take part in town meetings, the elder generation was shocked into the realization that their sons could use political power to demand far more than their fathers were prepared to give."[31]

The generational conflict that raged openly for five years in Sudbury became increasingly frustrating to the young men as fathers who had become protective of their land rights against outsiders now found the requests of their sons unreasonable. The minister, the Reverend Thomas Brown, became involved in the fight when discussion arose about the possibility of giving his land to the sons since his property had been granted to him as a gift by the founders. Brown seems to have recognized that his strength lay with the first generation. In his sermons he began to attack the immorality, degeneracy, and Sabbath-breaking of the younger generation. Also neither Brown nor the great

[31] *Ibid.*, p. 96.

28

majority of the original church members were disposed to the admission of the younger men into church membership. Soon the young men found that the church of their fathers had become an institution that offered little meaning to their lives and problems.

As the situation grew volatile in 1655, one young man expressed the thinking of his peers at a town meeting when he burst out: "If you oppresse the poore, they will cry out; and if you persecute us in one city, wee must fly to another."[32] If they were going to have homes of their own before their fathers passed away, the young men had only one course of action: they decided to leave Sudbury. As they made plans, the elders tried to create legislation that would prevent any single young man from moving outside the parish, but the controls that would eventually be quite effective for this purpose throughout New England had not yet been established. In 1656, therefore, John Ruddock, an elder spokesman who had supported the claims of the young, presented the town officials with a formal statement: "God has been pleased to increase our children, which are grown to man's estates. . . . [Their fathers] should be glad to see them settled before the Lord take us away from hence. . . . Some of us having taken some pains to view the country, we have found a place which lyeth westward."[33] The American pattern of generational migration of children away from parents began with episodes like this one when the members of the second generation of Sudbury moved fifteen miles to the west to establish the town of Marlborough.

This example represents only the first phase of conflict that would continue to tear New England families apart during the first generation's remaining twenty years. The first group of second-generation sons, perhaps because they were usually the first sons in their families, seemed to have possessed a spirit of rebellion and independence that would

---

[32] As quoted in Powell, p. 124.   [33] *Ibid.*, p. 131.

appear to be lacking in the young men who would grow to maturity during the next two decades. In the later years the New England churches and courts under the control of the first generation devised effective methods for keeping the young people under legal controls and reducing the possibilities of confrontations such as had occurred in Sudbury.[34] Through legislation and more subtle emotional restraints employed in the home, the first generation seems to have effectively repressed or destroyed any sense of personal autonomy in their sons. Only partially was this a conscious process on the part of the elders, but their drive to retain their patriarchal control had deep and lasting effects in the formation of the personalities of their children. The founders created a model patriarchy.[35] Having once planned to form a new society that their children would gratefully inherit, the older generation let their own dominant personalities and desire to maintain control alter their original design.

The Power over Land and Life

The powerful control that the fathers of the first generation held over their sons through the manipulation of land inheritance is reflected in the extremely high marriage age for the second generation.[36] Throughout the second half of the seventeenth century the average age at marriage was between twenty-six and twenty-eight years for men and be-

[34] See Demos, *Little Commonwealth*, p. 78. For discussion of possible underlying causes of these restrictions, see Alan E. Heimert, "Puritanism, the Wilderness and the Frontier," *NEQ*, 26 (1953), pp. 361-382, and Michael Walzer, *The Revolution of the Saints* (Cambridge: Harvard University Press, 1965), in particular his chapter "Puritan Repression and Modernization."

[35] For the qualities of the patriarchal family, see Clifford Kirkpatrick, *The Family as Process and Institution* (New York: The Ronald Press Co., 1963), pp. 81-82.

[36] The data for my discussion of the land control is drawn from the various works of the demographic historians.

tween twenty-four and twenty-six years for women, with marriage ages for first marriages of both sexes often reaching into the middle thirties. If a young man desired to marry, his only hope was that he remain a dutiful son and laborer on his father's land. In those towns recently studied by the demographic historians' there are no instances in which a son was permitted to marry and live with his wife in his parent's home; in early New England the extended family was a rarity, with the settlers favoring the nuclear arrangement of one generation only under one roof.[37] Within this system the single sons became an integral part of their father's income, and parents used their sons' labors to their own interests. It was commonplace for sons to work off the father's debts on other men's lands, as in Andover, where the pastor, the Reverend Thomas Barnard, was frequently paid in this manner.[38]

When the land grant finally did come to the son, it usually carried certain obligations. Often the son was given a permission only to use the land with no formal title passed on to him until after the father's death. In such instances the father might recall the land anytime he should become dissatisfied with his son's behavior. Some fathers extended their control beyond the grave by including provisions in their wills that granted local authorities the right to disinherit the son who failed to comply with certain requests of the father. It is no wonder that after such early episodes of generational conflict as had occurred at Sudbury there appears to be little open conflict between the generations in the middle decades of the century.[39]

[37] See especially Demos, "Notes on Life in Plymouth Colony," p. 279, and "Families in Colonial Bristol," p. 40; Greven, *Four Generations*, pp. 14-17; and Bernard Bailyn, *Education in the Forming of American Society* (Chapel Hill: University of North Carolina Press, 1960), pp. 15-16.

[38] Greven, *Four Generations*, pp. 69-70.

[39] Demos, *Little Commonwealth*, p. 186, and Greven, *Four Generations*, pp. 98-99.

To prevent the westward migration from being a means for the second generation to establish autonomy and thereby undermine the power of the patriarchy, the fathers developed various tactics. The founders had been fortunate in being able to claim large areas of wilderness that they divided among themselves and settled, but they deprived their sons of that opportunity. Many fathers bought up large tracts of western land so that their sons would find it more advantageous to wait for the inheritance of such lands rather than attempt to venture farther into the wilderness to find open, unpurchased land in unknown territory. Once these lands were claimed, the sons were forced to await inheritance or, in those cases in which the father himself did not have enough land to give his sons, to rely upon their fathers for a gift of money to purchase western land. When it was necessary for the sons to move away because the father did not have enough land to divide among his sons, arrangements were usually made for the young man to move to a new area where an uncle or friend of his father would be nearby to assist and to control the son.[40] And there was also the effective psychological hold of natural family affection that parents had upon the son who desired to leave home in his early twenties. Surely, there were many cases of sons who postponed their own lives to serve their parents out of the motive of natural affection or guilt. The westward migration of the second and third generations had a profound psychological effect, particularly upon the young people torn between the desire to establish their own homes and to remain near their parents.[41] In at least one

[40] Demos, *Little Commonwealth*, pp. 120-121. Of course, for children who had been raised to be particularly dependent upon their elders, this practice also provided comfort to the young people far from home as well as control by the elders; for such beneficial aspects of the firm control of the patriarchy over the frontier, see Charles E. Clark, *The Eastern Frontier: The Settlement of Northern New England, 1610-1763* (New York: Knopf, 1970), in particular his chapter on "Growing Pains, 1660-1713."

[41] Greven, *Four Generations*, pp. 120, 270. Greven notes the prob-

instance maternal love was turned against a resisting father when the mother threatened to move west with her son unless the husband granted him some of the nearby family land holdings. The father conceded.[42]

Ultimately, laws were passed that extended the paternal control over departing sons by making the ruling elders of the other New England towns into substitute fathers who would investigate the background of any young man who arrived in their district and put him under surveillance, usually by placing him in the home and under the control of one of the elders. Enforcement of such laws, as that established by the Massachusetts Bay Colony, made leaving home an ineffective method for a young person to establish his independence:

"It is Ordered, That the Select Men in each Town shall immediately upon the receipt of this Order, and so from time to time apply themselves with all diligence to take a particular account of all Persons and Families so coming unto them, requiring them if need be to appear before them that they may be fully informed of their state and way of living, and how they dispose of themselves: And the said respective Select Men are further impowered and required to take effectual care that the Incomers aforesaid settle themselves, or be by them settled in some orderly and diligent way of Imployment and Government, especially single and younger persons, who are all of them hereby required to yield Obedience unto the Disposal and Order of the Select Men accordingly."—By the COUNCIL[43]

---

ability of a connection between the anxiety caused by separation and the effects of the Great Awakening since "many of the people who left Andover moved to towns . . . which later were caught up in the revivals," p. 279. See also Bushman, *From Puritan to Yankee*, Chapters 4 and 5.

[42] The case of Samuel Ryder that occurred in 1679 is reported in Demos, "Notes on Life in Plymouth Colony," pp. 281-282.

[43] *Publication of the Council of the Massachusetts Bay Colony* (Boston, 1676), see Evans, *American Bibliography*, number 215.

Similar laws were passed that prevented a young man from establishing himself in a trade until he had reached a minimum age, received parental consent, and spent seven years in apprenticeship.[44] It is only fair to say that many parents probably had a genuine fear that without such firm controls over their sons they might be left helpless in old age by ambitious, heartless children. However, their efforts to keep their children at home unmarried for such a long period seem extreme.

LATE MARRIAGE AND EVOLVING SEXUAL MORES

The combination of a scrupulous Puritan morality regarding premarital sex and the system of economy that kept the young adults unmarried until so late in their lives posed serious moral and emotional difficulties for the young people of the second generation and many of the third generation as well. The records reveal that for the middle part of the century premarital sex was seldom practiced among second-generation couples; normal behavior in towns like Andover reflected a period of abstinence that was unduly prolonged.[45] As a result, many second-generation youths who were convinced that secret sins of self-pollution were a sign of certain damnation suffered bitter anxieties. In their diaries Michael Wigglesworth and Cotton Mather have left records of such misery.[46]

[44] *Boston Records*, VII, p. 39. See also Robert F. Seybolt, *Apprenticeship and Apprenticeship Education in Colonial New England and New York* (New York: Columbia University Press, 1917), p. 26.

[45] Greven, *Four Generations*, pp. 113, 116; Demos, "Notes on Life in Plymouth Colony," pp. 273-274. Cf. Edmund S. Morgan, "The Puritans and Sex," in *Pivotal Interpretations of American History*, Vol. I, ed. Carl N. Degler (New York: Harper & Row, 1966), p. 7. In contrast to Greven and Demos, Morgan believes illicit sexual intercourse to have been fairly common.

[46] Specific passages from these diaries will be discussed in the following chapter.

Early Puritanism had valued marriage highly for its role in relieving sexual frustration and thus cutting down on perversion.[47] The first-generation parents were certainly conscious of the sexual difficulties they caused their children, for such prohibition on the normal sexual outlet that marriage could provide was completely contrary to the spirit of their religion. The Reverend Thomas Cobbett noted this contradiction between Puritan ideals and the restrictions placed on the young when in 1657 he urged parents to make earlier arrangements for the marriages of their children for fear that the young people "not being able to contain . . . [would be guilty of] unnatural pollutions and other filthy practices in secret; and too oft of horrid Murders of the fruit of their bodies."[48] Warning the parents at length, Cobbett tried to appeal to family pride as well as affection by reminding the parents of the biblical story of Lot's daughters, who "seeing no man like to come into them in a conjugal way . . . they plotted that incestuous course, whereby their Father was so highly dishonored."[49] William Bradford, always an acutely sensitive observer of the emerging difficulties of his people, recognized that the combination of late marriages and strict laws governing premarital sex may have been responsible for a sudden outbreak of sexual misdemeanors in Plymouth: "It may be in this case as it is with waters when their streams are stopped or damned up. When they get passage they flow with more violence . . . so wickedness being here more stopped by strict laws . . . so as it cannot run in a common road of liberty as it would and is inclined, it searches everywhere

[47] Morgan, "Puritans and Sex," p. 13, and *The Puritan Family; Religion and Domestic Relations in Seventeenth-Century New England* (New York: Harper & Row, New Edition, 1966); see chapter on "Husband and Wife," pp. 29-64.

[48] Thomas Cobbett, *A Fruitful and Useful Discourse touching the Honour due from Children to Parents and the Duty of Parents towards Children* (London, 1656), p. 174.

[49] *Ibid.*, p. 177.

and at last breaks out where it gets vent."[50] In spite of such warnings, however, the first-generation parents did not weaken their stand on late marriages. They would not yield their control of the land and of the lives of their children simply because of the sexual frustrations of the young.

Surprisingly, what developed instead in New England was a gradual relaxation of the moral code on premarital sex. By the last quarter of the century the penalty for premarital sex for betrothed couples was comparatively mild and was only a fraction of the penalty for unengaged single people.[51] There is also disputed evidence that the parental condoning of the practice of bundling that permitted a courting couple to spend an evening together in bed, fully clothed or separated by a board, may have provided ample opportunity for sexual outlet.[52] Also, parents may have developed a more lenient attitude toward masturbation; at least Cotton Mather seemed to think that young people had when in 1690 he complained: "Beware of having light thoughts about some sorts of *Uncleanness* wherein many young people have been so infatuated as to excuse themselves. There are abominable *self-pollutions* which many, that would be loath to commit other kinds of *Uncleanness*, look upon as little, venial, easy *peccadillo*'s."[53] The very fact that Mather felt free to speak out openly on the subject and even to preach an entire sermon on it at a later

[50] Bradford, *Plymouth Plantation*, pp. 316-317.

[51] Demos, "Notes on Life in Plymouth," pp. 273-274. For the case of a young couple accused of fornication before marriage whose parents were brought before a Massachusetts court to show cause why they were denied the marriage so long after the couple was betrothed, see Arthur W. Calhoun, *A Social History of the American Family* (Cleveland: The Arthur H. Clark Co., 1917-1919), I, 56.

[52] For the question of the relationship between bundling and permissiveness, compare Dana Doten, *The Art of Bundling* (New York: Farrar & Rinehart, 1938) and Henry R. Stiles, *Bundling* (Mount Vernon, N.Y.: Peter Pauper Press, 1937).

[53] Cotton Mather, *Addresses to Old Men, Young Men, and Little Children* (Boston, 1690), p. 73.

date indicates a more open atmosphere of discussion of the problem that in itself probably helped young people.[54]

The evidence all seems to indicate, therefore, that the parents of the first generation were more inclined to alter their Puritan moral code than to provide their children with the means to earlier marriage and independence. Subtly and most likely unconsciously, first-generation parents used sex as a powerful incentive for their sons to remain dutiful and obedient until they could be married. A particularly hard-working son might be permitted to marry earlier; a young man whose efforts were not satisfactory could wait until his early thirties. The power over sex rested with the patriarchy.

THE NEW ENGLAND CHURCHES

Besides the family, the most powerful institutional tool for controlling the young people of the second generation and undermining their self-confidence came to be the Puritan church as it developed in mid-century New England. The original Puritan spirit had been conducive to the growth of the church and open to the relatively smooth acceptance of new members, including in particular the children of the church members. Thus between the years 1630 and 1650 the proportion of the colonists who were church members gradually increased.[55] In the first years most churches required only that candidates for membership declare that they felt the presence of Christ's grace in their hearts; rigorous tests or threatening examinations of religious experiences came later.[56] The emphasis in the sermons during the early years was upon the New Dispensation of salvation that Christ had won for men through his death. With assurance of salvation almost assumed for

[54] See Cotton Mather, *The Pure Nazarite* (Boston, 1723).

[55] Kenneth A. Lockridge, "Puritan Church," pp. 408-410.

[56] See Morgan, *Visible Saints*, pp. 66-73; Coolidge, *Pauline Renaissance*, pp. 64-66, 147; Pettit, *Heart Prepared*, pp. 101ff.

the majority of their congregations, the ministers sought to build upon grace with moral instructions. But as the first settlers began to feel more and more threatened by the newcomers to the colony who sought lands and political power, the mood changed and with it the New England churches evolved a system of exclusiveness and isolationism.

The development of this new exclusiveness stemmed from two factors: economic and religious. First of all, from the political and economic point of view of the first settlers, the choice of church members became important because in the original plan only church members would have the power of the vote in local affairs. If too many late arrivals were to gain church membership, they could vote themselves sections of land or other powers and privileges reserved for the founders. The original landholders were inclined to feel that if the local church would become more demanding in its requirements for church membership, some immigrants might be discouraged from coming to their community.[57] Without question rigorous public examinations of the state of one's soul did discourage some would-be entrepreneurs. Such was the effect upon Thomas Lechford, who returned to London after his unsuccessful attempt to settle in New England. In his exposé, *Plain Dealing from New England*, he reported on the dangerous practices of the New England churches: "Many chose rather to go without the Communion than undergo such public confessions and trials. . . . [I wonder] whether these public confessions be not extremes."[58] Unlike Lechford the established church members in New England seemed to have approved the idea of perfecting the church by keeping out the hypocrites. When the Cambridge Platform was written in 1648, it endorsed the practice of having tests for membership.[59]

[57] Darrett B. Rutman, "God's Bridge Falling Down: Another Approach to New England Puritanism Assayed," *WMQ*, ser. 3, 19 (1962), pp. 408-421.

[58] Lechford, *Plain Dealing*, p. 7.

[59] There is controversy about the severity of the tests approved by

In contrast to the subtle and practical motivations of the laymen, the desires of the ministers in changing membership requirements were the result of genuine religious concerns. As a result of the Antinomian episode involving the excommunication of Mrs. Anne Hutchinson in the late 1630's, many of the ministers of the New England churches were receptive to a policy of exclusion on theological grounds.[60] Mrs. Hutchinson had demonstrated how the doctrines of Puritanism could be interpreted to lead to what the ministers began to feel was a bit too much assurance of one's own salvation and personal favor by God.

Puritanism had always been open to Mrs. Hutchinson's kind of interpretation. A sermon that played upon the main theme of backsliding and impending doom could have as its minor theme the millennial optimism of God's chosen people; trials and calamities could be used as a sign of God's wrath or as proof of God's special attention and a notice of final victory to come.[61] In fact, it had been John Cotton's emphasis upon the Gospel and Christ's salvation that had mislead Mrs. Hutchinson; she became convinced that the

the Platform which hinges upon the interpretation of the words of the Platform, "the weakest Christian, if sincere, may not be excluded or discouraged." Pettit, *Heart Prepared*, p. 168, believes that these words endorsed individual interpretation by the local minister and, therefore, led to severe tests, while R. P. Stearns and D. H. Brawner believe that the Platform was trying to modify such tests with their phrasing: See "New England Church 'Relations' and Continuity in Early Congregational History," *Proceedings of the American Antiquarian Society*, 75 (1965), pp. 13-45.

[60] For a penetrating analysis of the Antinomian affair, see Emery Battis, *Saints and Sectaries: Anne Hutchinson and the Antinomian Controversy in the Massachusetts Bay Colony* (Chapel Hill: University of North Carolina Press, 1962). On Cotton's interpretation of Paul, see p. 35; and for the relationship between Mrs. Hutchinson's own emotional instability and her need for a doctrine of inner assurance, see pp. 51ff.

[61] A discussion of these qualities of the sermons will be taken up in Chapters 3-5 of this study.

other ministers preached too much upon the need for following laws and practicing good works in order to merit heaven. She argued that after Christ's death the laws of the Old Testament were dead laws, and good works no longer mattered for salvation. For her, predestination was a joyous doctrine, for Christ had done all that is needed for His believe through His suffering. Cotton's fellow ministers recognized that such over-emphasis upon the Pauline spirit of assurance and the new man could destroy the authority of the ministers themselves and create a society of people who possessed such inner conviction that they might be rebellious. Therefore, in reaction to an early stress upon the assuring side of Puritan doctrines, the ministers sought to regain control by stressing uncertainty. They observed that in view of the absolute corruption that men inherited from Adam there were probably few who were predestined to heaven. They argued that, even if a man thinks he is saved, he is probably wrong. Candidates for church membership were urged to look within, to search out secret wickedness and proof of damnation. Upon such examination many began to find themselves unworthy of election. Such was the ominous message of the New England ministers that those who arrived from England in the 1640's and 1650's would hear when they sought church membership.

The unforeseen, if perhaps eventually welcomed, effect of this process of excluding new members from the churches was upon the children of the first generation themselves. In their infancy these young people had been baptized by virtue of their parentage and upon the assumption that at maturity they would declare themselves believers in Christ and become full church members. With the change in admission procedures these children would be required to undergo tests for membership and exhibit evidence that they had passed through complex stages of religious experience—such examinations their parents had never had to endure in the churches in England. For accompanying their new policy of exclusion, the ministers evolved the doctrine

40

of the preparation of the heart, a New England innovation in Puritan thought. Works like John Norton's *The Orthodox Evangelist* and Thomas Shepard's *The Sincere Convert* elaborated the steps of the valid conversion that were to be used as the standard for examining a candidate for membership.[62] As a way of insuring against another Antinomian crisis, the ministers were careful to point out that even a successful relation of the conversion experience could not provide real assurance of election: one must always doubt and search the heart. They warned that even the confusion of a young man about his temporal calling could be evidence that he was deceiving himself about his spiritual life. Thus, instead of building self-esteem, the ministers even transformed the idea of the calling into an effective tool for creating doubt and, incidentally, lessening the spiritual value of one's practical life.

In all, the theological developments of the 1640's and 1650's in New England bred "uncertainty of outcome [which] could lead and often did lead to an inner tension and agony of soul disruptive in a new society."[63] Indeed, nervous breakdowns and suicides were not uncommon. The kind of anguish that could result from such uncertainty is described by John Winthrop in 1642: "A cooper's wife of Hingham, having been long in a sad melancholic distemper near to phrensy, and having formerly attempted to drown her child, but prevented by God's gracious providence, did now again take an opportunity, being alone, to carry her child, aged three years, to a creek near her house, and stripping it of the clothes, . . . threw it in so far as it could not get out; but then it pleased God, that a young man, coming that way, saved it. She would give no other reason for

[62] John Norton, *The Orthodox Evangelist* (London, 1657) and Thomas Shepard, *The Sincere Convert* (London, 1650). For examples of the kind of relation required, see those recorded by Michael Wigglesworth in *The Diary of Michael Wigglesworth: 1653-1657*, ed. Edmund S. Morgan (New York: Harper & Row, 1965), pp. 107-125.

[63] Pettit, *Heart Prepared*, p. 19.

41

it, but that she did it to save it from misery, and withal that she was assured, she had sinned against the Holy Ghost, and that she could not repent of any sin."[64]

William Adams recorded another example in his diary in 1673 of a Mrs. Thomas Whitteridge who felt herself in great danger over the state of her soul: "Mr. Richard Hubbard gave her several scriptures to consider of. When he was gone she turned the Bible the best part of an hour. . . . At night she told her son, a youth of about 12 or 13 years at the most, . . . *He is come!* The door . . . being opened with great violence she ran out. And being presently followed, no sight could be had of her, but a shrieking or moaning or both was heard. The next morning there was to be seen a path made thro the thickest places of weeds and briars as if a great timber log had been drawn there which, being followed, her coat was found therein, and she a little further with her face thrust into a little puddle of water not sufficient to cover all her face, lying dead."[65] And in 1675 Increase Mather told in one of his sermons about the young boy Abraham Warner, who had drowned himself in 1660 and had left the following note to his father: *"O Father, I have kept my soul as long as ever I could; My ruin was, the pride and stubbornness of my tender years, which should have been fetched out with sharp corrections. . . . I have a young brother that follows my steps, he is going the wide way to destruction. I beseech you to take pains with him and correct him as well as counsel him, that he may not be undone soul and body as well as I."[66]

The political result of the exclusion of new members from the churches was that few young people became full church members; therefore, at mid-century few of the sec-

[64] John Winthrop, *History of New England*, ed. James Savage (Boston: Little, Brown and Company, 1853), II, 79.

[65] "Memoir of the Reverend William Adams of Dedham, Massachusetts," in *Collections of the Massachusetts Historical Society*, 4th series (Boston, 1852), I, 17-18. This incident occurred in 1673.

[66] Increase Mather, *The Wicked Man's Portion* (Boston, 1675), p. 19.

ond generation had the power of the vote in most New England towns. The young adults remained as inferior church members, and it is not surprising that the ministers complained of their sabbath breaking. The church, as the institution of the fathers, had little or no immediate value to the lives of their sons and thus failed in the middle years to provide the young with any spiritual comfort or identification with the local community.

THE HALF-WAY COVENANT

During the development of the policy of exclusion and the changes in the theology that would intimidate the young church members, some of the New England ministers like Richard Mather and James Allin grew concerned about what would happen to the churches when the first settlers passed away. Few members of the second generation would be full church members; and since baptism in infancy was a privilege reserved only for the children of full communicants, none of their children would even have received baptism. By the late 1650's controversy had begun about the possibility of baptizing these third-generation infants even if their second-generation parents were not full members. After years of heated debate over the issue, the ministers of New England met in March 1662 and devised a policy of church membership that came to be called scornfully by the laymen the Half-Way Covenant. It provided that the children of baptized church members could also receive baptism even if their parents were not full members.[67] Thus the ministers insured the continuance of the churches without violating the political privilege of the first-generation patriarchy.

[67] For the best discussion of the Half-Way Covenant, see Pope, *The Half-Way Covenant*; for its impact on the churches, cf. Perry Miller, "The Half-Way Covenant," *NEQ*, 6 (1933), pp. 676-715 and *From Colony to Province*, Chapters 4-7.

The dissent that arose from the first-generation elders shook all of New England, and in the case of the First Church of Boston it tore the church apart. Having become quite well satisfied with things as they were, the elders cried out against the synod: "That practice that exposeth the blood of C[hris]t to contempt, and bap[tism] to p[ro]fanation, the Church to pollution and the Commonwealth to confusion is not to be admitted."[68] John Davenport was the champion of the first fathers until his death in 1670 at the age of seventy-three; he strongly resisted the synod's proposals as he cried out, "The *Porter* look well unto the Doors *of the Lord's House*."[69] In the course of their objections to the synod's solution, the church members even argued that instead of letting the third-generation infants into the church, the ministers should expel the second-generation members since they had proved their sinfulness by not presenting themselves for full membership; they had deserted the covenant and were not capable of passing membership to the next generation. The elders declared that "it remains to be proved that the Parents in question are children of the Covenant."[70] Nicholas Street spoke for many when he observed that "these Parents . . . are under very great sin & offence."[71]

Some of the ministers struggled heroically against their congregations and in favor of the younger generation. Richard Mather, who led the ministers at the synod of 1662, could not get his church at Dorchester to accept the innovation, but he persistently brought up the question each year for review. At Dedham James Allin, who composed one of

[68] "Judgement of the Dissenting Brethren," MS at Yale Library, p. 29 quoted in Pope, *Covenant*, p. 57.

[69] John Davenport, *Another Essay for the Investigation of the Truth, In Answer to Two Questions* (Cambridge, 1663), p. 15.

[70] *Ibid.*, p. 28.

[71] Nicholas Street, "Considerations upon the seven propositions," MS at Yale Library, quoted in Pope, *Covenant*, p. 69.

the major publications defending the synod, met strong opposition from his church.[72] Even though there had been no new members admitted to the church for nine years, the members would not permit alteration of their policy on membership. After Allin's death they waited for five years before they could find a minister who sympathized with their position; their eventual choice, the Reverend William Adams, must have pleased them with his attacks on the rising generation: "A giddy flighty generation that can scarce be serious or fixed on anything, that cannot get their hearts fixed seriously to think of things, especially of a spiritual nature. . . ."[73] As a result of Dedham's resistance, the town's modern historian has observed that "the spiritual and political leadership of the town came to rest largely in the hands of a small group of ageing men."[74] For at least ten years after the synod met, the ministers would complain with John Woodbridge, Jr. that "many of the Ministers would launch out farther [for new members] but . . . the Churches are such a heavy stone at the ministers' legs that they cannot fly at their own Course."[75] Others would express confusion over the motives of the first-generation members: "Neither can I understand why the question about adult Children of the Church should make any estrangement, since all godly men have the same scope to fetch in to Christ the young generation."[76] Searching for an answer, Thomas

[72] James Allin, *Animadversions Upon the Antisynodalia Americana* (Cambridge, 1664). For Allin's struggle with the church see Lockridge, "Puritan Church," p. 411. Perry Miller, *From Colony to Province*, pp. 83-104, also argues that the ministers were in general ahead of the flock on widened church membership.

[73] William Adams, *The Necessity of Pouring Out of the Spirit from on High upon a Sinning Apostatizing People* (Boston, 1679), p. 43.

[74] Lockridge, "Puritan Church," p. 17.

[75] "The Correspondence of John Woodbridge, Jr. and Richard Baxter," ed. Raymond P. Stearns, *NEQ*, 10 (1937), p. 574.

[76] John Oxenbridge, *New England Freemen Warned and Warmed To Be Free Indeed* (Cambridge, 1673), p. 43.

Walley concluded in 1669 that this *"Fire of Contention . . .* comes from pride and self-love."[77]

The motives of the grandfathers in refusing to allow their own grandchildren to be baptized needs examination, for initially the synod seems not to have been any threat to their power as rulers of New England. In fact, by increasing the proportion of the population made up of church members while at the same time keeping the leadership of the church in the hands of the first generation, the synod's proposal would seem such as might have pleased the elders by making the churches of which they were the leaders even more powerful institutions. But again the resistance of the founders appears to have been based on a fear that any change might initiate a gradual and subtle erosion of their authority. The elders suspected that the ministers would not stop at baptism of the younger generation children but that they would soon bring all the baptized members of the second generation into full membership without the requirements of public relation of the conversion experience.[78] The elders were right in sensing that such a development was in the air in the 1660's, for as early as 1672 Solomon Stoddard would propose such a policy in Northampton, and in the late 1670's and early 1680's other New England churches would greatly modify membership requirements.[79] Such changes would have to be made in order to accept the younger generations into the churches. The tragic crisis of the Half-Way Covenant demonstrated how far the first-generation members had wandered from their original Pauline ideas of the church as a growing vine. In 1671 Eleazar Mather believed that he had found the real cause of the failure of so many of the younger people to present themselves for full church members, and he laid the blame on the older men in the congregation: "Nay, are

[77] Thomas Walley, *Balm in Gilead to Heal Sions Wounds* (Cambridge, 1669), pp. 8-9.

[78] Pope, *Covenant*, pp. 56-57.

[79] Miller, *From Colony to Province*, p. 135.

46

there not many that lay stumbling blocks in their way? I
know men are apt to complain against the Rising Generation . . . but I beseech you consider whether you give not
too much occasion thereunto. . . . Therefore improve your
little time for the good of them that are to come after
you."[80] Undoubtedly, his words met the approval of the
growing numbers of second-generation members of the
congregation.

A FAILURE IN EDUCATION

One feature of the relationship between the generations
that came to the attention of the ministers and the General
Courts during the years of dispute surrounding the Half-
Way Synod was a general failure on the part of parents to
provide adequate education for the young beyond instilling
the most fundamental fear of God and sense of sin and
corruption. In the first years of settlement there had been
a great emphasis upon education demonstrated by the establishment of Harvard College by 1636, but by the 1670's the
college had nearly crumbled for lack of funds.[81] As early
as 1642 Massachusetts had to enact a law requiring heads
of families to teach their children to read at a minimum
level: "[Let no one] suffer so much barbarism in any of
their families as not to endeavor to teach by themselves or
others, their children and apprentices so much learning as
may enable them perfectly to read the English tongue, and
knowledge of the Capital laws, upon penalty of twenty
shillings for each neglect therein."[82] In 1668 this law had
to be amplified: "This court taking notice, upon good information and sad complaints, that there are some persons

80 Eleazar Mather, *A Serious Exhortation*, p. 17.

81 See Samuel Eliot Morison, *Harvard College in the Seventeenth
Century* (Cambridge: Harvard University Press, 1936), in particular,
I, 328-334 and II, 415-445.

82 Massachusetts Laws of 1648, p. 11, quoted in Morgan, *The Puritan
Family*, pp. 87-88.

in this jurisdiction, that have families to provide for, who greatly neglect their callings. . . . Such neglectors of families are comprehended among [such idle persons as are subject to the house of correction]."[83] Throughout the next thirty years the courts met strong resistance in trying to get each of the towns to establish some form of public education. By 1700 only a few had complied with the order.[84]

This apparent contradiction between the high educational ideals of the first generation and the apparent ignorance of the second and third generations has puzzled historians. Louis B. Wright, for example, has the greatest admiration for the educational aims of the founders, but he admits that the second generation seems to have been particularly ignorant in comparison with their fathers; after considering this fact, he hesitantly concludes: "The second generation of Americans, even in such literate spots as Boston, appeared to be less cultivated than their elders, but perhaps, as Samuel Eliot Morison has suggested, they merely reflect a prosaic period."[85] Edmund S. Morgan notes that the original settlers failed completely to catechize the children of the non-church members of the community.[86] From the 1650's through the 1670's and even into the 1690's the ministers were constantly returning to the issue of the re-

[83] Quoted in Calhoun, *American Family*, I, 77.

[84] See Bailyn, *Education*, pp. 73-84; Demos, *Little Commonwealth*, pp. 142ff; Morgan, *Puritan Family*, pp. 87-108; and Samuel Eliot Morison, *The Intellectual Life of Colonial New England* (New York: New York University Press, 1956, reprinted 1965, 1970), pp. 66-75. Morison finds the last half of the century particularly poor for education.

[85] Louis B. Wright, *Culture on the Moving Frontier* (Bloomington, Ind.: Indiana University Press, 1955), p. 43 and see Morison, *Intellectual Life*, p. 149.

[86] Cf. Morgan, *Puritan Family*, pp. 87-108 and pp. 161-186. Morgan's argument on education hinges upon his theory of "Puritan Tribalism," that is, that the first settlers, when threatened from without by new arrivals to New England, turned in upon their own families and educated their children only. I believe that they failed their own children as well.

luctance of the first two generations to educate even the children of the elect.

In his *Farewel-Exhortation* in 1657 Richard Mather imagined the children of the first settlers addressing a rebuke to their parents in heaven on Judgment Day: *"All this that we here suffer is through you: You should have taught us the things of God, and did not. . . . You were the means of our Original Corruption and guiltiness, and yet you never showed any competent care that we might be delivered from it . . . and now we are damned for it. . . . Woe unto you that had no more Compassion and pity to prevent the everlasting misery of your own Children."*[87]

In 1669 Thomas Walley offered the suggestion that the parents hire someone to teach the children since it had become apparent that education in the home was not successful: "Let not the Kids of the Flock be forgotten. . . . It will be necessary to get the help of some able Christian in the work of Teaching the Children of the Congregation."[88] Significantly, he suggested this course of action as a way of overcoming the objections of the elders that the young people be denied membership because of their ignorance. Apparently, the elders would neither admit to the churches the young nor see that they were educated in religious doctrines. In 1674 Samuel Torrey complained "how much both Civil and Religious Education is neglected,"[89] and in 1673 Urian Oakes, acting president of Harvard College during four of its darkest years, sought out the underlying social causes for the elders' lack of interest in the education of their sons. He observed that the frustration that even an educated young man encountered in New England society effectively discouraged any desire for higher education:

[87] Richard Mather, *A Farewel-Exhortation To the Church and People of Dorchester* (Cambridge, 1657), pp. 10-11.

[88] Walley, *Balm in Gilead*, p. 16.

[89] Samuel Torrey, *An Exhortation unto Reformation* (Cambridge, 1674), p. 16.

"Consider what will be the Latter End of the neglect of the Encouragement and Advancement of Learning among us. It is the Observation of wise men . . . that the Schools languish. . . . Parents will have no heart to breed their children to Learning. Rich men will not, because they have better ways before them to provide for the comfortable subsistence of their Children; and persons of meaner condition cannot, or at least are discouraged from expending all they can upon their Children's Education, because when that is done, and they are ready for service, there is no Encouragement. . . . I have nothing to offer by way of Advice."[90]

Although President Oakes did not have a solution to this complex problem, he did know where to lay the blame: "We make very solemn Complaints to God, and one to Another of the Degeneracy of the Rising Generation. But are not we to blame? Do we not greviously neglect them? to instruct them, to cherish and promote any good in them? . . . But alas! *What good do we do them?* Our Children are little beholden to us. We own them so far as to baptize them: But then Fare ye well, Children, we have nothing more to do with you."[91]

Perhaps it would be taking the argument against the members of the first generation too far to suggest that as part of their general effort to retain control of the church and society they consciously, or even unconsciously, became lax about educating their own sons and daughters, that they found an uneducated young man to be more content to work on his father's farm well beyond his maturity. Yet the cries of the ministers and the courts against the ignorance of the second and third generations and the sad condition of Harvard College in the middle decades of the century indicate that the education of the young was slighted by the first generation. At any rate, modern educators who

90 Urian Oakes, *New-England Pleaded With* (Cambridge, 1673), pp. 56-57.
91 *Ibid.*, p. 58.

struggle against the annual failures of tax bills for the support of education can have much sympathy with Cotton Mather's question to his congregation in Boston: "Is it not also possible to Settle and Endow *Schools* in all our *Plantations?* . . . Doubtless, men of ingenuity might instruct us how . . . [we might] fill the Country with a *Liberal Education*, the want of which has a more *Threatening Aspect* on us than the worst of our other circumstances."[92]

THE THIRD CHURCH

An important development of the controversy over the Half-Way Covenant was the emergence of a natural alliance between the men of the second generation and the rising merchant class.[93] During the first four decades of the colony's history, the political power had rested in the hands of the farmers and landowners who also made up the majority of the full church members. While this situation continued to prevail in the churches and local governments of outlying farming communities throughout the century, the scene in Boston was beginning to change by the middle of the century.[94]

Unlike their landed brethren, the Puritan merchants of Boston did not become intolerant isolationists in their middle years. Because they did not feel threatened by new settlers, the merchants retained some of the original Pauline spirit of openness and growth. Also, they found no advantage in keeping a young man under thumb in his father's house when the boy might serve himself and his father by getting out on his own and establishing new contacts and markets in the business world. Similarly, there was no

[92] Cotton Mather, *The Serviceable Man* (Boston, 1690), p. 51.
[93] Bailyn, *New England Merchants*, pp. 106-107.
[94] For a thorough examination of the differing developments of the urban and rural areas, see Carl Bridenbaugh, *Cities in the Wilderness: The First Century of Urban Life in America, 1625-1742* (New York: The Ronald Press Co., 1938).

reason for a merchant father to want to have his son excluded from church membership; indeed, the more members of the second generation of merchants to participate in the church and local affairs, the sooner the merchants might begin to have a stronger voice in community affairs. Some of these men, like Robert Keayne and John Hull, were deeply troubled and confused by the isolationist attitudes among their landholding brethren.[95] Therefore, during the decades of the 1660's when the synod's decision creating the Half-Way Covenant caused dissension within the First Church of Boston, the merchant members tended to side with the younger generation's claim to church membership.[96] The result was the separation of a group of merchants from the First Church in 1669 and their formation of the Third Church, later known as the Old South. The man who led the separation was John Hull, the richest merchant in New England who would also be the father-in-law of Samuel Sewall.

Hull had long sympathized with the young people of Boston who desired to be church members. In his diary in 1661 he noted "a great willingness [which] appeared in both youths, maids and women," and he was delighted when a few of these second-generation people were admitted to the First Church: "Being called on by their names, in the face of the whole congregation [they] did openly manifest their desire to acknowledge their relation to the church."[97] He

[95] For a dramatic example of the confusion the merchants had over the increasing narrowness and patriarchal authority of the church, see "The Apologia of Robert Keayne," ed. Bernard Bailyn, in *Publications of the Colonial Society of Massachusetts, Transactions*, 42 (1954), pp. 243-341; see also Bailyn, *Merchants*, p. 43.

[96] For occupations and names of the men who made up the Old South, see Hamilton A. Hill, *History of the Old South Church, 1669-1884* (Boston and New York: Houghton Mifflin and Co., 1890), I, 113-122.

[97] "The Diaries of John Hull," in *Transactions and Collections of the American Historical Society*, 3 (1857), p. 198.

also sadly recorded that some of the elder church members were outraged by the admission of these new members: "Mr. Edward Hutchinson, though he had before promised to rest silent . . . (yet turned his back upon the church), as soon as they began this solemn and publick performance, he desired a dismission from the church. Mr. Anthony Stodered seemed also not a little offended; but the church, with general satisfaction and cheerfulness, attended this work."[98] Hull's concern over the welfare of the young caused him to consider what might be the motives of men like Hutchinson who rejected young church members and failed to encourage the young people to present themselves for membership; he concluded that "self-interest is too predominant in many."[99]

After enduring this situation for another eight years, Hull felt strongly enough about the issue of church membership in 1669 to lead the rebellion. For deeply religious men like Hull, merchants or landowners, the thought of separating from one's church was not to be taken lightly. Years afterward young Samuel Sewall, who would become an important member of the Old South, worried over the validity of the Third Church in the eyes of God: "I have been exceedingly tormented in my mind sometimes lest the Third Church should not be in God's way in breaking off from the old."[100] But with the expansionist spirit of a merchant, Hull was convinced that the doors of the church needed to be opened wide and that youth needed more encouragement. Such convictions would reshape the church and religious writings of the 1680's and 1690's.

Under the first minister of the Old South, the Reverend Thomas Thatcher, the initial policy on admission of candidates provided that those candidates with scruples need not read their relation before the whole congregation; instead,

[98] *Ibid.*   [99] *Ibid.*, p. 211.
[100] *The Diary of Samuel Sewall, 1674-1729, Collections of the Massachusetts Historical Society*, ser. v, vol. v (Boston, 1878-1882), p. 46.

they could submit it in writing or present it orally to the elders in private. After 1678 under Thatcher's young successor, Samuel Willard, the church developed even more liberal policies on membership. Though he would stop short of Stoddard's radicalism, Willard was most gentle and reassuring with candidates for membership. Willard did not openly oppose Increase Mather, who became a powerful spokesman of the dying patriarchy in the 1670's, but Samuel Sewall noted about Willard's relationship to Mather: "One might gather by Mr. Willard's speech that there was some Animosity in him toward Mr. Mather."[101] When the General Court of Massachusetts finally yielded to Mather's six-year plea that they appoint a synod to discover the reason of the degeneracy of the rising generation, the Old South did not send a representative to the synod. The members of Willard's congregation saw no reason for such a synod since their church was in a period of extraordinary growth.[102]

The second- and third-generation members of the Old South Church needed a new spiritual message, and Willard's theme of assurance and Christian love was a response to their needs. Ministers like Giles Firmin had detected this changing mood in the people in the early 1670's when he wrote *The Real Christian* in England after returning disillusioned from New England. Firmin attacked the gloomy exclusionists of New England like Thomas Shepard. He argued in his Preface that all "stumbling blocks" should be removed from the path of a professing Christian, for "a man

[101] *Ibid.*, p. 30. For the moderate position of Willard on Church matters, see also John G. Palfrey, *History of New England* (Boston, 1875), IV, 317, and George W. Dollar, "The Life and Works of The Reverend Samuel Willard, 1640-1707," unpublished dissertation in modern history, Boston University Graduate School, 1960, pp. 20-25.

[102] Pope, *Covenant*, pp. 220-223. Pope's graph on membership in the Old South shows an increase of full communicants from fifteen to forty per year between 1673 and 1675 and a jump in the number of new members baptized from five in 1669 to ninety-one in 1680 and sixty in 1685.

[must] be allowed to have assurance at all costs." In New England Firmin had found that his ideas had received a warm reception from the people for the psychological health that they afforded: "*A Gentleman and a Scholar meeting me some time after gave me thanks. . . . I asked him why. He told me he had a Maid-servant who was very godly, and reading of that particular in Mr. Shepherd's Book, which I opposed, she was so cast down and fell into such troubles that all the Christians that came to her could not quiet her spirit. . . . I have met with several Persons who . . . could not be resolved that ever their faith was true because of that which he had written.*"[103]

Similarly, in his sermons of the 1680's Willard tried to restore the sense of identification between the inner man and the external social and spiritual institution. Willard reintroduced the figure of Christ as a loving Son of God who had already paid for the sins of His believers, and he began preaching of the Covenant as the Covenant of Redemption. Turning to parents, Willard urged them to love their children as well as discipline them, to aid them in the matter of finding a calling, even to provide them with financial assistance if necessary.[104] His *A Compleat Body of Divinity* represents his attempt to recapture and reiterate the original spirit that New England had lost.

Thus with the institution of the Half-Way Covenant and with movements like the formation of the Third Church, the people of the second generation finally began to integrate into the church and society and to recreate the institutions to fit their special needs. Social maturity had come at a rather late age for many of the second generation who

---

[103] Giles Firmin, *The Real Christian* (London, 1670), "Introduction," pp. 1-3, and "To the Christian Reader."

[104] Willard, *Compleat Body*, for Christ as redeemer, see pp. 12-35, 275-287, 353, 421-432, 487, 504, 511-515; on the duty of parents, see second series of pp. 604-644 (note that page numbers 581-666 are repeated although the text of the second series differs). Further discussion of Willard's message will be included in Chapter IV.

were already by the 1670's in their forties and fifties, and it would be their children who would reap the benefits of the changes that they would bring about. The face of God that Willard turned toward the children of the third generation was a more merciful one, and the person of Christ that he stressed was a more human deity who could be thought of as a brother or a husband or a son:

"If we believe in him, he then stands to answer for us to our Judge, and all his earnings are made over to us upon our *believing* and placed to our account. . . . What strains of thankfulness can be thought too high for him [a believer] to raise his heart up unto, in the solemnization of this unspeakable gift? Had he the Oratory of the Angels, he could never find out expressions full enough to give it its deserved encomium, but must at length, finding of words to fail, lose himself in an ecstasy of silent admiration."[105]

THE SOCIETY, THE CHURCH, AND WOMEN

One interesting change to occur during the latter half of the century as the patriarchy gradually lost its hold upon New England was the increasing importance women began to have in the church and in the society. By the 1670's women had gained in matters of courtship and marriage an independent position that had been unprecedented during the first decades of the colony's existence. With permission by the courts, women were now allowed to own property, to conduct the family business for the husband when need be. As John Demos notes, they were given "considerable freedom to move on roughly the same terms with men even into some of the darker byways of Old Colony life."[106]

[105] Samuel Willard, *A Brief Discourse on Justification* (Boston, 1686), pp. 95 and 115.

[106] Demos, *Little Commonwealth*, p. 90. See also Calhoun, *American Family*, I, pp. 52-55; for a thorough treatment of this aspect of the society, see Herbert Moller, "Sex Composition and Correlated Culture Patterns of Colonial America," *WMQ*, ser. 3, 2 (1945), pp. 113-153.

Some of the literary works present in the Boston book-
stores in the 1680's suggest a self-conscious liberation movement of sorts was attracting women readers. Two titles indicate the trend: *Wonders of the Female World, or A general
History of Women, Wherein many hundreds of Examples
is showed what Woman hath been from the first Ages of
the World to these Times in respect to her Body, Senses,
Passions, Affections, her Virtues and Perfections, her Vices
and Defects . . . To which is added a Discourse of Female
Pre-eminence.* The theme of female superiority is the central theme of another work: *Her and His, or The Feminine
Gender more worthy than the Masculine, Being a Vindica-
tion of that ingenious and innocent Sex from the biting
Sarcasms, bitter Satires, and opprobrious Calumnies where-
with they are daily, though undeservedly, aspersed by the
virulent Tongues and Pens of malevolent Men; with many
examples of the rare Virtues of that noble Sex in which
they have not only equalled but excelled most of the other
Sex.* Also available for women were accounts of the lives
of virtuous women who died in their youth. Metaphors
describing Christ as the lover appeared frequently in sermons; Willard described death as a time "to lye in Christ's
Bosom, and be ravished with his dearest love, and most
intimate Embraces."[107] The sermons of English preacher
John Flavel that were particularly sensuous and sentimen-
tal in their handling of the suffering of Christ and his marriage to His church also seem to have been popular.[108]

In Boston ministers began in the last quarter of the century to take more notice of the women in their churches.
By 1699 the Brattle Street Church gave women the power
of franchise, declaring: "We cannot confine the right of
choosing a minister to the male communicants alone, but we

107 Samuel Willard, *The High Esteem Which God Hath of the Death
of His Saints . . . Occasioned by the Death of the Worshipful John
Hull* (Boston, 1683), p. 15.

108 See Worthington Chauncey Ford, *The Boston Bookmarket: 1679-
1700* (Boston: The Club of Odd Volumes, 1917), pp. 135-137.

think that any baptized adult persons who contributed to the maintenance should have a vote."[109] Nine years before this Cotton Mather had confirmed the recent statistical evidence that in the 1690's the women church members in New England outnumbered men by more than two to one: "There are far more *Godly Women* in the World than there are *Godly Men*; and our *Church Communions* give us a Little Demonstration of it. I have seen it without going a Mile from home, That in a Church of between *Three* and *Four* Hundred *Communicants*, there are but few more than *One* Hundred *Men*; all the Rest are *Women*. . . . It seems that the *Curse* in the Difficulties both of *Subjection* and of *Child-bearing*, which the *Female Sex* is doom'd unto, has been turned into a *Blessing*. . . . God . . . makes the *Tenderness* of their Disposition a further *Occasion* of Serious Devotion in them."[110] In another sermon Mather also indicated that the mother had replaced the father as the spiritual leader of the household: "You that are *Mothers* have a special Advantage to instill the Fear of God into the Souls of them that sit upon your knees . . . [and] may insinuate Religion into your Children earlier and easier than their *Fathers* can."[111] It appears the passing of the first-generation patriarchy brought a new freedom and importance for the women of subsequent generations.

[109] Quoted in Moller, "Sex Composition," p. 153. For data on the ratio of women to men in the churches, see Pope, *Covenant*, pp. 213-214, 217-218, 225; for an analysis of the possible causes for these changes, see Moller, "Sex Composition," pp. 151-153, and Cedric B. Cowing, "Sex and Preaching in the Great Awakening," *AQ*, 20 (1968), pp. 624-644. For an interesting psychological discussion of the rise and fall of Puritanism as related to the acceptance and rejection of women in society, see Walter J. Ong, "The Lady and the Issue," in *In the Human Grain* (New York: Macmillan Company, 1967).

[110] Cotton Mather, *Ornaments for the Daughters of Zion, or the Character and Happiness of A Virtuous Woman* (Cambridge, 1692), pp. 44-45.

[111] Cotton Mather, *Small Offers Toward the Savior of the Tabernacle in the Wilderness* (Boston, 1689), p. 44.

THE DECLINE OF THE PATRIARCHY

The founding of the Old South Church marked an important turning point in the generational conflict and in the social affairs of New England. While in the west the control over the land and the absence of a merchant class would keep the patriarchal agrarian economy alive, in the east the lack of available land and the necessary movement toward a commercial economy were rapidly bringing an end to the rule of the fathers in the 1660's and 1670's. Incensed over the inevitable changes that were coming to New England with the new generation, the elders often vented the same kind of intolerance and animosity upon the rising generation that they had upon the Quakers, the English government, and any other group that had threatened the established forms. In 1670 the House of Deputies published an official summary of two decades of Puritan sermons; the statement voiced both the bitterness and gloom of the passing generation and the sense of helplessness of many of their sons: "Declension from the primitive foundation work, innovation in doctrine and worship, opinion and practice, an invasion of the rights, liberties and privileges of churches, an usurpation of a lordly and prelatical power over God's heritage, a subversion of gospel order, and all this with a dangerous tendency to the utter devastation of these churches, turning the pleasant gardens of Christ into a wilderness, and the inevitable and total extirpation of the principles and pillars of the congregational way; these are the leaven, the corrupting gangerene, the infecting spreading plague, the provoking image of jealousy set up before the Lord, the accursed thing which hath provoked divine wrath, and doth further threaten destruction."[112]

But what the old New England fathers could not realize was that they were to be among the last men of their cul-

[112] Quoted in Thomas Hutchinson, *The History of the Colony and Province of Massachusetts Bay*, ed. Lawrence S. Mayo (Cambridge, Massachusetts: Harvard University Press, 1936), I, 232.

tural epoch to cling to a notion of patriarchate that was already giving way in western thought to a notion of sonship, that is, to the philosophical view that a society is formed by the free choice of a leader from among the group of sons who make up its people. The greatest symbol of the patriarchy—the monarchy—was being sapped of its power by the movement toward parliamentary rule and ultimately toward democracy. This shift in the current of ideas was receiving its clearest expression in the change in political and social thought from Hobbes to Locke.[113] In Hobbes the power of the father was absolute and permanent while in Locke it would be conditional and temporary. Similarly, religious toleration that had come even with the Cromwellian regime and had accelerated with the Restoration and the shift from agrarian to capitalistic economy served to undermine the position of the father. No longer the dominant figure whose presence was felt in all aspects of family life, the father now went off to work for another man in the city each day, and his choice of religious beliefs was not crucial as it had once been. Therefore, when the fathers of the first generation of New Englanders felt that they were resisting the impatience and rebelliousness of their own ungrateful sons, they were really feeling the weight of historical developments that have left a lasting impression on the nature of the family down to our own time. But the fathers could only sense this change; they could not intellectualize it.

Their reaction was to create a myth about themselves even before their own passing and to repress their sons in

113 For discussion of this philosophic shift in western thought, see R.W.K. Hinton, "Husbands, Fathers, and Conquerors: Patriarchalism in Hobbes and Locke," *Political Studies*, 16 (1968), pp. 55-67. For a more general overview of these cultural developments in seventeenth-century thought, see H. R. Trevor-Roper, *The Crisis of the Seventeenth-Century: Religion, the Reformation and Social Change* (New York: Harper & Row, reprinted, 1968) in particular pp. 125-130 on the fear of social change; and Christopher Hill, *Society and Puritanism*, p. 503, on the father's loss of authority.

society and in the family. The founders came to believe that their motives for coming to New England were purely religious, that they had risked all for the sake of their God and their children. Thomas Shepard spoke for the fathers when he addressed the sons in 1673: "[Do you think your] Fathers in their coming over to these ends of the Earth was it only for themselves? Oh no, they had an eye to their poor Children also that they might remove them far from the temptations and snare of Superstition and Prophaness."[114] In fact, their fathers' motives had been quite mixed. Also the elders remembered that their New England society had been an ideal city on a hill, free from contention and disorder until their sons began to inherit the power; at the age of sixty-two John Oxenbridge looked back from 1671 upon the golden past and warned the young men: "The first worthy Planters they professed to erect and administer according to God. . . . But the Bastard Son will needs break to the ruine of himself and his partakers; if a degenerate and spurious Generation will not stand by the intendments and engagements of their faithful Ancestors, but in their giving and exercising rule neglect the Lord, he will ruin them and their helpers."[115]

In reality the early society had been wracked with contention, and the first settlers themselves had drifted from their original ideals. Similarly, the fathers decided that their sons had no religious interest; Increase Mather found a "lamentable decay in New-England as to the power of Godliness. This Generation is far short of the former."[116] But history shows that the younger generation was actually quite religious and needed only a little encouragement to be brought into the churches.

The discrepancy between the facts and the rhetoric, between the reality and the ideals, that has puzzled historians

114 Thomas Shepard, Jr., *Eye-Salve, or a Watch-Word . . . to Take Heed of Apostasy* (Cambridge, 1673), p. 24.

115 John Oxenbridge, *Freemen Warned*, pp. 21-22.

116 Increase Mather, *Renewal of Covenant* (Boston, 1677), pp. 16-17.

was created by the fathers of New England themselves in their attempt to construct an imaginative vision of the way their society had been and to impose that vision upon the reality they rejected. Cotton Mather's *Magnalia Christi Americana* is a third-generation man's supreme effort to make this vision supplant the reality; the illusion is so convincing that only recently have we seen that his history is really an epic, a work of imaginative expression and power.[117] The truly remarkable thing about the sons of the first settlers was that they were eventually able to emerge from their confusion and insecurity and to lead the society into a new age, remarkable especially in view of the kind of child-rearing and religious training they had endured.

[117] See Sacvan Bercovitch, "New England Epic: Cotton Mather's *Magnalia Christi Americana,*" *English Literary History,* 33 (1966), pp. 337-350, and for a more thorough treatment, see his "New England Epic: A Literary Study of Cotton Mather's *Magnalia Christi Americana,*" unpublished dissertation, Claremont Graduate School, 1965.

SHAPING THE PURITAN
UNCONSCIOUS

*Freud's myth of the rebellion of the sons against the father
in the primal, prehistoric horde is not a historical explanation of origins, but a super-historical archetype; eternally
recurrent; a myth; an old, old story.*

Norman O. Brown, *Love's Body*

A RECOGNITION of the social pressures and frustrations that
encumbered the people of New England's second and third
generations enables us to understand better the meaning
of later Puritan writings. Puritan literature, particularly
the sermon, received its fundamental vitality and meaning
from the deepest feelings of the individuals who listened to,
purchased, read, and reread those writings. To appreciate
fully the imaginative power of this people's popular literature, we must do more than simply place those writings
in their historical and social context. We must also try to
probe, even if in the most tentative and experimental way,
the underlying unconscious forces of their culture. Of
course, it is most difficult to construct a useful hypothesis
about the formation of the unconscious lives of an entire
generation of people who lived three hundred years ago.
However, the Puritans were an unusually introspective people and their diaries and autobiographies reveal much
about their inner lives.

CHILD-REARING METHODS

The methods of child-rearing employed in Europe and
America in the sixteenth and seventeenth centuries were
aptly described in Thomas Becon's advice to parents in
England in 1560: "Laugh not with thy son, lest thou have

sorrow with him, and lest thou gnash thy teeth in the end. Give him no liberty in his youth, and wink not at his follies. Bow down his neck while he is young, and beat him on the sides while he is a child lest he wax stubborn, and be disobedient unto thee, and so bring sorrow to thine heart."[1]

The seventeenth century produced a wealth of child-rearing literature that echoed Becon, such as Daniel Rogers' *Matrimonial Honour* (1642), in which he encouraged mothers to give fathers full cooperation in the matter of discipline: "[She] holds not his hand from due strokes, but bares their skins with delight, to his fatherly stripes."[2] During these two centuries which have been called "an epoch of systematic brutality toward the young,"[3] England produced some of its most aggressive men. In seventeenth-century America, however, the results were strikingly different, for suppression of children seems to have caused abnormal uncertainty and guilt in the young. The peculiar form that Puritanism took in the colonies reinforced the repressive child-rearing methods, and the dominance of the first-generation patriarchs blocked the integration of the young adults into the society. Thus in New England the pattern of child-rearing appears to have had crucial psychological effects upon the people who reached adulthood in the last half of the seventeenth century.

[1] Thomas Becon, *The Catechism of Thomas Becon* (London, 1650), as quoted in Levin L. Schucking, *The Puritan Family: A Social Study from the Literary Sources*, trans. Brian Battershaw (New York: Schocken Books, 1970), p. 74. Schucking's work focuses upon the Puritan family in Europe. For similar studies on the state of the child in Europe in the period, see Phillippe Ariès, *Centuries of Childhood* (New York: Knopf, 1962); Ivy Pinchbeck, "The State and the Child in Sixteenth Century England," *British Journal of Sociology*, 7 (1956), pp. 273-285 and 8 (1957), pp. 59-74; and Hill, *Society and Puritanism*, pp. 124-144, 219-258, and 443-481.

[2] Daniel Rogers, *Matrimonial Honour* (London, 1642), p. 299.

[3] Katherine Anne Porter, *The Collected Essays and Occasional Writings of Katherine Anne Porter* (New York: Delacorte Press, 1970), p. 314.

Nearly every scholar who has studied the place of the child in the early New England family has emerged from the records and scattered diaries dismayed by the severe psychological difficulties he finds in the young people. Barrett Wendell observed that in early New England "as soon as children could talk they were set to a process of deliberate introspection, whose mark is left in the constitution of melancholy and frequent insanity" of young adults.[4] Arthur Calhoun's study of the American family also revealed a tendency toward "pathological abnormalities" in early New England children. He attributed these problems to the fact that "home discipline was relentless": "stern and arbitrary command compelled obedience, submissive and generally complete."[5] In his work, *Children and Puritanism*, Sanford Fleming found in the children of the second and third generations "a condition of melancholia leading to insanity and suicide"; and he observes that when children did manifest a conversion experience "it was the result of pressure brought to bear upon them, and was wholly abnormal and therefore deplorable."[6] He goes on: "Children suffered cruelly from the fear of sin's consequences. Sometimes their distress continued over a long period, during which they could get no peace. Apparently they were not helped very much by their elders, the latter being able only to counsel submission. They could not declare the

[4] Barrett Wendell, *Cotton Mather, The Puritan Priest* (New York: Dodd, Mead, and Company, 1891), p. 29.

[5] Calhoun, *American Family*, p. 112. See also Bailyn, *Education*; Willystine Goodsell, *A History of the Family as a Social and Educational Institution* (New York: Macmillan Co., 1915); Alice M. Earle, *Child Life in Colonial Days* (New York: Macmillan Co., 1899), and *Home Life in Colonial Days* (New York: Macmillan Co., 1898).

[6] Sanford Fleming, *Children and Puritanism: The Place of Children in the Life and Thought of the New England Churches, 1620-1847* (New Haven: Yale University Press, 1933), pp. 45 and 65. It is Fleming's thesis that "the child as such had no place in the thought and life of the churches" (p. 68) and that the treatment of children "constitutes a serious indictment of the message and methods of those churches" (p. 45).

assurance of salvation, the doctrine of election precluding such assurance" (p. 153).

There is also ample first-hand evidence of these early American attitudes toward children in much of the children's literature, which featured an emphasis upon shame, guilt, and early death. Michael Wigglesworth's popular *Day of Doom* is, of course, the most famous example. He captured the essence of many Puritan sermons to children in his vision of the shame of the Last Judgment:

> All filthy facts, and secrets acts, however closely done,
> And long conceal'd, are there reveal'd before the
>   mid-day Sun.
> Deeds of the night shunning the light, which darkest
>   corners sought
> To fearful blame, and endless shame, are there most
>   justly brought.[7]

But Wigglesworth is mild in comparison to some of the sermons of Increase Mather, who on one occasion unleashed images of an angry God the Father and a murderous band of Indians to shame the young girls of his congregation: *"The Lord saith . . . because the Daughters of Zion are haughty therefore he will discover their Nakedness . . .* [as] when the *Indians* have taken so many and stripped them naked as in the day that they were born. *And instead of a sweet smell there shall be a Stink.* Is not this verified when poor Creatures are carried away Captive into the Indians filthy and stinking *Wigwams?*"[8]

Ministers often found a hanging to be a particularly good opportunity to stress the public shame and early death that might await disobedient children. Although the Massachusetts law prescribing death for disobedience to parents was never enforced, ministers never let the children forget God's

---

[7] Michael Wigglesworth, *The Day of Doom*, ed. Kenneth B. Murdock (New York: The Spiral Press, 1929), p. 23.

[8] Increase Mather, *Earnest Exhortation*, p. 7.

punishment: "So when children shall rebel against their Parents, wickedness is excessively great. And such Children do usually die before their time." The biblical story of Absalom carried a fitting message for willful children: "Absalom, he was a rebellious child, and what became of him? Was he not hanged at last: And three darts thrust through his heart while he was yet alive. . . . Thus shall be done to the son that rebels against his Father, Thus shall be done to the child that riseth up against Parents. . . . The eye mocketh his Father and despiseth to obey his Master, the raven of the valley shall pick it out and the young eagles eat it."[9] Even long after he was an adult, Edward Taylor remembered how he trembled when his mother told him of the ravens and young eagles.[10]

Increase Mather was not the only minister who chastized the children, but he must have recognized that he had a particular talent for choosing images that aroused fear in young hearts. On one occasion, he warned: "If death find a young man in his sins . . . woe to him that he was ever born: His naked soul must appear before God his Creator, and receive a Sentence of eternal Damnation."[11] Mather's imagery was designed to evoke from children not only fears of shame and death but also the terror of separation from their godly parents. He imagined that on Judgment Day the parents of disobedient children would join with God in condemning them to eternal damnation: "What a dismal thing will it be when a Child shall see his Father at the right Hand of Christ in the day of Judgment, but himself at His left Hand: And when his Father shall join with Christ in passing a Sentence of Eternal Death upon him, saying, *Amen O Lord, thou art Righteous in thus Judging*: And when after the Judgment, Children shall see their

9 Increase Mather, *Wicked Man's Portion*, pp. 9 and 18.

10 See Shea, *Spiritual Autobiography*, p. 97.

11 Increase Mather, *A Call from Heaven to the Present and Succeeding Generation* (Boston, 1679), p. 103.

Father going with Christ to Heaven, but themselves going away into Everlasting Punishment."[12]

For a New England child who had been raised to be unusually dependent upon his parents and for whom abandonment by the parents was frequently threatened as a punishment for disobedience, such a description must have had special poignancy. After studying a collection of such sermons preached to New England children, the Mather bibliographer, Thomas J. Holmes, concluded: "The work reveals some of the terrors of religious teaching which the children of that day endured. . . . The heart of the child was not then understood, scarcely even discovered. Pestalozzi or Frobel was not born."[13]

In their use of images of death and shame to suppress young wills, ministers were only following some of the best advice on child-rearing available in their day. In his thoughts on children Calvin had concluded with impeccable logic: "Those who violate the parental authority by contempt or rebellion are not men but monsters. Therefore, the Lord commands all those who are disobedient to be put to death."[14] His teaching informed such works as John Robinson's "Of Children and Their Education," which advised that "children's wills and willfulness [should] be restrained and repressed" since, as children of Adam, the children are "children of wrath" deserving of hell's fire

[12] Increase Mather, *Earnest Exhortation*, pp. 35-36. See a similar passage in *A Call from Heaven*, p. 28.

[13] Thomas James Holmes, *Cotton Mather: A Bibliography of His Works* (Cambridge: Harvard University Press, 1940), I, 197. See also D'Alté A. Welch, "A Bibliography of American Children's Books Printed Prior to 1821," *Pro. of the AAS*, 73 (1963), pp. 121-324. Welch discovered that "the majority of the books for children in New England were sermons pointing out the depravity of youth" (p. 135), and he notes that harrowing accounts such as those in Fox's *Book of Martyrs* were popular (p. 135).

[14] John Calvin, *Institutes of the Christian Religion*, trans. Ford L. Battles (Philadelphia: Westminster Press, 1960), I, 344. See also pp. 360, 364-367.

at birth for their corruption.[15] And Anne Bradstreet echoed such convictions in her famous lines: "Stained from birth with Adam's sinful fact,/ Thence I began to sin as soon as act."[16]

There was an insistent emphasis upon the shaming of children as an effective technique of child-rearing. Thomas Cobbett believed: "A young person of a pious mind will realize the eye of God upon him and behave as having his very Heart Naked and Open before him."[17] The methods of community and church discipline, with their accent upon public exposure and shaming as punishments, reinforced the child-rearing practices.[18] For an adult excommunication from the church and expulsion from the community were among the severest penalties just as separation from the parents had been during childhood. The administrative procedures which required that legal complaints and petitions for church membership be made orally in public declarations acted as yet another control upon the unassertive younger people. For parents who desired to maintain parental authority over their children well into the children's adult years, advice on child-rearing designed to exact unquestioned obedience surely must have seemed to make practical sense.

EARLY PIETY

Although most children responded to these tactics of fear and shaming by developing the expected obedience and

[15] John Robinson, "Of Children and Their Education," in *The Works of John Robinson*, ed. Robert Ashton (London, 1851), I, 246-247.

[16] *The Works of Anne Bradstreet*, ed. Jeannine Hensley (Cambridge: Harvard University Press, 1967), p. 54.

[17] Cobbett, *Useful Discourse*, p. 93.

[18] For the public nature of New England law, see Emil Oberholzer, Jr., *Delinquent Saints: Disciplinary Action in the Early Congregational Churches of Massachusetts* (New York: Columbia University Press, 1956), in particular his section on public confession, pp. 36-37.

dutifulness, others experienced severe psychological distress that took the form of early religious experiences and demonstrations of early piety. For the precocious child religion provided an opportunity for gaining a sense of superiority over friends and parents through a distorted form of self-assertion.[19] Such children learned their lessons in religion well and studied the steps of conversion so that they could manifest the signs of saving grace to their ministers and parents. When the churches instituted the Half-Way Covenant that bestowed baptism upon the children and provided the opportunity for them to become full communicants, the ministers began to encourage and praise demonstrations of early piety in children even more. Pious children were held up as examples to their peers and adults as well. One of the most popular books in New England in the last quarter of the seventeenth century was a collection of fourteen narratives about early conversion and death, James Janeway's *A Token for Children*.[20]

Janeway's stories, and others like them in sermons, present striking evidence of the effects of the extreme emotional pressure that children of the period endured. Each narrative follows the same pattern: a conversion experience occurs in the child's early years, followed in puberty by a serious physical and psychological crisis during which the child becomes convinced of his inner corruption, falls ill, and dies; immediately preceding his death, assurance of salvation is restored. These stories clearly demonstrate some of the adverse effects of the kind of psychological environ-

[19] For a discussion of the harm of this practice, see Seybolt, *Apprenticeship*, passim; also Fleming, *Children and Puritanism*, particularly p. 122.

[20] James Janeway, *A Token for Children* (Boston, 1700). Although this work was originally published in London in 1672, it enjoyed wide popularity in America and appeared in several American editions, including the one used for the present study. Similar narratives appeared frequently in sermons, and Cotton Mather collected five such stories in his *Magnalia*, Volume II. For discussion of the history of Janeway's work, see Thomas Holmes, *Bibliography*, III, 385.

ment in which the second and third generations of New
England children were reared.

The narrative of Sarah Howley who was "highly awakened" when she was eight years old is representative of the
collection. On the day that Sarah experienced conversion:
"She wept bitterly to think what a case she was in; and went
home, and got by herself in a Chamber, and upon her knees
she wept and cried to the Lord. . . . She got her little
Brother and Sister into a Chamber with her, and told them
of their condition by Nature, and wept over them. . . . She
spent a great part of the night in weeping and praying and
could scarce take any rest day or night for some time together, desiring . . . to escape from everlasting flames" (p. 2).

After her experience Sarah became a model child: "She
was exceedingly dutiful to her Parents, very loth to grieve
them in the least; and if she had at any time (which was
very rare) offended them, she would weep bitterly" (pp. 3-4).
For the next five years Sarah spent all her leisure hours
reading the Bible and other religious works, but: "When
she was about fourteen years old she broke a Vein in her
Lungs. . . . She was in great distress of Soul. . . . She said
O mother, pray, pray, pray for me for Satan is so busy . . .
I feel I am undone. . . . O I am undone unto all Eternity.
. . . Her Mother asked her what Sin it was that was so
burdensome to her Spirit: O Mother, said she . . . the sin
of my Nature. One time when she fell into a fit, she cried
out, *O I am a going, I am a going: But what shall I do to
be Saved?*" (pp. 4-6).

When "her Father bid her be of good cheer," Sarah only
"fell into a great passion, and said . . . I am a poor sinner"
(p. 6). When friends and relatives came to visit her, "she
would look with so much eagerness upon them, as if she
desired nothing in the world so much as that they would
pity her. . . . O the piteous moan that she would make! O
the agonies that her Soul was in" (p. 7). Soon Sarah grew
very weak and was silent for several days, but then "to the
astonishment of her Friends she broke forth thus with a

71

very Audible Voice and Cheerful Countenance." With a renewed conviction of salvation she would "run on repeating many of these things a hundred times over: '*O so sweet! O so glorious is Jesus! O I have the sweet and glorious Jesus; he is sweet, he is sweet, he is sweet! O the admirable love of God in sending Christ!*'" (p. 9). Now that she was certain to enter heaven, "she was exceeding desirous to die" (p. 12). Thus she implored: "*Come Lord Jesus, come quickly, conduct me to thy Tabernacle. . . . How long sweet Jesus? Finish thy work sweet Jesus, Come away sweet dear Lord Jesus, come quickly sweet Lord help, come away, now, now, dear Jesus come quickly*" (pp. 12-13). She died on the following day.

ANXIETIES OF ADOLESCENCE

The pattern of development in the Janeway stories suggests that many Puritan children suffered traumatic episodes in puberty and adolescence. The fact that the town records reveal little open rebellion of adolescents suggests that the young people struggled privately and often silently during their periods of crisis. Documents like the Janeway narratives and the diaries of Michael Wigglesworth and Cotton Mather expose the effects that the Puritan stress upon corruption and shame could have upon young minds. Because the society repressed the young, it thereby prolonged and heightened the agony of adolescence.

Because trouble over sexuality and confusion over a calling usually occurred during the same years, the young often endured a twofold torment. For example, Wigglesworth became convinced that his sexual temptations were the cause of his difficulty in deciding upon his proper calling. Fearing that God had abandoned him because of his lusts, young Michael searched for something to read on the subject of sexual temptation: "*I find such irresistable torments of carnal lusts or provocation unto the ejection of seed that I find my self unable to read any thing to inform me about my distemper.*"[21] He found that he could not confidently consider his vocation so long as he labored under these afflictions: "Now that I am to go into the world I am afraid. . . . Lord thou art the guide of my youth; into thy hands I commit my spirit [but] ah Lord I am vile" (p. 4). Because the Puritan doctrine of the calling created such an intimate relationship between the state of one's spiritual life and practical life, Wigglesworth was convinced that his sinfulness had caused his lack of a clear call: "*The last night a filthy dream and so pollution escaped me in my sleep for which I desire to hang down my head with shame and beseech the Lord not to make me possess the sin of my youth and give me into the hands of my abomination. . . .* I despair of ever pleasing god by my endeavours in the world" (p. 5). A week later he cried out for some assurance about the state of his affairs: "*Some filthiness escaped me in a filthy dream. . . .* [Give] me an effectual call, a personal call, a clear call taking away all my objections, and bringing my spirit to gospel terms" (pp. 6-7). He sadly concluded: "I am laden with a body of death" (p. 8).

Cotton Mather experienced similar anguish in adolescence, but he fought against the flesh more violently than did Wigglesworth; whenever temptation overwhelmed him, he would fast until physical weakness removed his sinful desires: "I found Satan buffeting of me with *unclean Temptations* and used *Fasting and Prayer.* . . . That I may pluck out my *right Eye*, and cut off my *right Hand*, these are MY PURPOSES. . . . If my Sin do still rage, I will spend a Day in *Fasting* and *Prayer.*"[22] Then he would rejoice in his physical weakness, assured that God had given him the grace to prevail. But when his health was restored and temptation returned, he would be more tormented than ever, convinced that presumption and pride had led him to deceive himself about God's grace. Apparently this pattern

21 *Diary of Michael Wigglesworth*, p. 4.

22 *Diary of Cotton Mather* (New York: Frederick Ungar Publishing Co., 1957), I, 78-79.

was not unique to Cotton Mather. In his study of the Puritan autobiographies, Daniel Shea observed that many Puritan adolescents followed these methods: "Puritan autobiographers . . . suffered chronically from an adolescent disease that masqueraded as true conviction until it disappeared and left good health and a heart more depraved than ever."[23] The great majority of Puritan youths were quite alone when they underwent the anguish of adolescence, for most spent their teenage years away from their own homes.

APPRENTICESHIP

The absence of open rebellion against parents during this difficult period of the child's life was certainly insured by the English practice that the settlers retained in New England: when children had reached the age of twelve or thirteen, they were placed for seven years with another family in a state that amounted virtually to servitude. Even in seventeenth-century England this practice appeared to a visitor from Italy to cause undue hardship for children: "The want of affection in the English is strongly manifested toward their children, for having kept them at home till they arrive at the age of seven or nine years, they put them out, both males and females to hard service in the homes of other people. . . . For every one, however rich he may be, sends away his children into the homes of others."[24]

In England the apprenticeship system served the practical purpose of training skilled laborers. But in America children could have learned as well from their parents the skills of farming and housekeeping they were forced to learn from strangers. Modern historians have been puzzled by the continuation of forced apprenticeship in New England, and Edmund Morgan in his study of the Puritan family found the practice "psychologically wrongheaded": "The

[23] Shea, *Spiritual Autobiography*, p. 106.
[24] Quoted in Calhoun, *American Family*, I, 36.

removal of a child from his parents when he was only four-teen years old or less seems a little strange, in view of the importance which the puritans attached to family relations. The mere force of custom must have been partly respon-sible. . . . Yet something more than custom must have been behind the practice for Puritan children were frequently brought up in other families than their own even when there was no apparent educational advantage involved."[25]

Indeed, for people who used parental rejection as a form of punishment of the child in his early years, the practice of seeming to expel the child from his home in puberty must have had serious psychological repercussions. Children who were sent out of their homes at the very time in their lives when they were experiencing renewed doubts about the state of their souls would have been inclined to make an unconscious connection, at least, between their sinful-ness and the actions of their parents. Michael Wiggles-worth's biographer has demonstrated that for much of his life Wigglesworth compounded his sense of guilt over sex-ual temptation with guilt feelings caused by his lack of affection for his parents.[26] By the time his father died, he confessed: "I am afraid of my senselessness of my father's death."[27] When Samuel Sewall took his daughter Hanna to live with a family in Rowley, a long twenty-five miles from her Boston home, she was only thirteen years old. He re-cords in his *Diary* that he had "much ado to pacify my dear daughter, she weeping and pleading to go with me."[28]

[25] Morgan, *Puritan Family*, p. 75-76. There is some confusion over the ages at which children left the home; Calhoun believes that chil-dren left at the age of about nine or ten while Morgan's evidence puts the age at about thirteen or fourteen: see Calhoun, *American Family*, I, 36, and Morgan, *Puritan Family*, p. 68.

[26] Richard Crowder, *No Featherbed to Heaven: A Biography of Michael Wigglesworth, 1631-1705* (East Lansing, Mich.: Michigan State University Press, 1962), pp. 51, 53-55, 61, 64-65, 74.

[27] *Diary of Michael Wigglesworth*, p. 60.

[28] *The Diary of Samuel Sewall, 1674-1729, Coll. of the MHS*, v (1878), p. 385. For comment on the hardship of separation, see Morgan, *Puri-tan Family*, pp. 37-38.

75

Yet it did not occur to Sewall that there was little real point in leaving her.

In spite of the hardship that the apprenticeship system created for the children, New England parents continued their practice of sending the children out of the home. In the view of the patriarchs the practice of apprenticeship served New England parents well by forestalling the open conflicts normal in adolescence. The system removed their children during their periods of greatest emotional difficulties and placed them under the control of a master who would continue to exact obedience and submission. When the children returned home after seven years, they would appear to be past the worst of their inner struggles and would be ready for another six or seven years of employment at the father's home before marriage.

The Development of the Puritan Unconscious

While historians have always been convinced that the nature of child-rearing and religious education employed in early New England was somehow "psychologically wrong-headed," there had been no attempts until quite recently to understand just how the personality development of the children of the second and third generations may have been affected by their religious and social environment.[29] With-

29 Cf. Demos, *Little Commonwealth,* in particular pp. 120-148. For comment on the confusion over identity resulting from cultural changes, see Miller, *From Colony to Province,* pp. 1-39, and *Errand into the Wilderness* (New York: Harper & Row, 1956), in particular his opening essay, pp. 1-15. For the assumptions about the psychological difficulties caused in a period of cultural transition, see Margaret Mead, "The Implication of Culture Change for Personality Development," *American Journal of Orthopsychiatry,* 17 (1947), 633-646, and *Childhood in Contemporary Cultures,* ed. Margaret Mead and Martha Wolfstein (Chicago, 1955), in particular the commentary on child-rearing literature, pp. 145ff; and Kirkpatrick, *Family as Process,* pp. 90-95. The language Erik H. Erikson uses in his essay on the stages of early child development in *Childhood and Society* (New York, W. W.

out question such a study can be undertaken only with an awareness that its conclusions will be highly conjectural at best. However, an examination of the pattern of early New England child-rearing yields some interesting suggestions about the emotional lives of the second and third generations that are of significant value for discerning the symbolic meaning of their literature. Therefore, with this awareness and purpose, we may attempt to explore the depths of the Puritan unconscious mind.

Psychologists have now shown us that it is necessary for parents to assist the child in the first and second years to develop a basic trust in himself and in his surroundings. Such trust "forms the basis in the child for a sense of identity which will later combine a sense of being 'all right,' of being oneself, and of becoming what other people trust one will become" (CS, p. 249). During the first stage of a child's development, parents must help him develop this trust by a system of prohibition and permission, and especially by demonstrating to the child, through their own example and through their response to his personality, that his actions have meaning in the wider context of society—that there is continuity between his childhood experiences and what he will find to be the experiences of adult life. However, even when the parents do provide a sense of the continuity between childhood and adulthood, this period still introduces into the child's unconscious emotional life "a sense of inner division and universal nostalgia for a paradise forfeited . . . a sense of . . . having been abandoned" (CS, p. 250). For many children, religion plays an important role in helping them cope with these unconscious forces of separation and division because religion provides a means of trying "to make up for vague deeds against a maternal

Norton and Co., 1963), 2nd ed., pp. 247-274, is so appropriate for describing the situation in Puritan New England that I have employed his terminology in these pages. Quotations from *Childhood and Society* will be cited as *CS* in the text.

matrix" by allowing one "to restore faith in the goodness of one's strivings and in the kindness of the powers of the universe" (*CS*, p. 251).

A consideration of the Puritan discouragement of self-trust in children suggests that Puritan children were likely to suffer from an acute lack of self-trust that evidenced itself in expressions of "inner division and universal nostalgia." For the Puritans self-trust was heresy. For anyone to forget that he was totally dependent upon God's grace was a sin of presumption. To slight one's dependence on his earthly father constituted a violation of the social order. In order to destroy the self-trust of Puritan children, parents and ministers constantly reminded children of their depravity and demanded obedience to God's word and to the authority of His earthly representatives. The introspection and doubt of Puritan diaries and autobiographies testify to the success of these efforts. In addition, Puritanism as it developed in New England was not designed to assuage guilt and to provide opportunity for atonement, one of the great emotional benefits of religion. The religious message of the 1650's through the 1670's told the young that they were a corrupt generation divided from God—perhaps even abandoned by Him forever—and that there was nothing they could do themselves to "make up for" the "the vague deeds" that had brought their ruin.

An important aspect of the cultivation of self-trust is the demonstration to the child that there is continuity between his present childhood experiences and his future adult role. Parents must set the direction toward realizable goals of adult life. But the first-generation Puritan parents presented a baffling contradiction to their children in respect to what they expected their children to be as adults. As young Englishmen the founders had been pioneering and adventurous themselves. They had been outspoken and daring non-conformists, revolutionaries, and virile planters of a new society in a virgin land. But they did not want their children to imitate these qualities. They told their children

that in New England they should be conformists and submissive laborers in the new society and leave leadership to
the elders. The first fathers could not raise their children
to re-enact their own liberating rebellion, and perhaps by
suppressing the young they were attempting to expiate their
guilt for their own revolt against authority. Thus in their
tales of their flight from persecution and the founding of
the colony, the fathers presented to their children an image
of vigorous independence, but in their directions to the
young they preached submissiveness and obedience.

In this perplexing situation, children were unlikely to
achieve that "sense of being 'all right,' of being oneself, and
of becoming what other people trust one will become" that
is essential for genuine self-trust. Some young men like
Increase Mather and Urian Oakes even went to England in
order to imitate their fathers. During the renewed persecutions of the Restoration they played the role of non-
conformists; Mather's *Diary* reveals him psychologically
healthier upon his return.[30] But few could afford the luxury
of such costly therapy. As evidenced by Janeway's *A Token
for Children* and by many autobiographies, one of the ways
that children defended against the confusion and frustration of a lack of self-trust was to project their own sense of
inner corruption onto external evils. They came to see various external forces as the source of corruption against which
they had to protect themselves. Cotton Mather, a third-
generation son, helped his congregation toward a personal
self-assurance when he encouraged them to make the devil
their scapegoat,[31] but his device had unexpected and vio-

[30] See Kenneth B. Murdock, *Increase Mather: The Foremost American Puritan* (Cambridge: Harvard University Press, 1925), pp. 56-85.

[31] See discussion of Cotton Mather's use of the figure of Satan in
Chapter v. For evidence of Mather's use of Satan in this way, see his
The Wonders of the Invisible World (Boston, 1692; reprinted, London:
J. R. Smith, 1862), pp. 12-27. For commentary on the psychological
forces operating in the witchcraft delusion, see Marion L. Starkey,
*The Devil in Massachusetts: A Modern Inquiry Into the Salem Witch

lent results as the witchcraft episode suggests. Some children introjected external qualities of piety and moral superiority that they found in their ministers and parents, and thus gained assurances otherwise denied them. They discovered that if they would assume an attitude of the certainty of salvation, their parents and ministers would give them reinforcement and praise. Through such means a few children were able to achieve a measure of self-trust that could sustain them until they reached adolescence. When the crisis of identity came at adolescence, however, this artificial form of self-trust collapsed because in reality there was no continuity between childhood piety and the morally complex adult roles ahead.

During the second stage of a child's early emotional development, it is necessary that the parent protect the child against arbitrary experiences of shame and early doubt if the self-trust already acquired is to mature. If the child is one day to integrate into society without irrational suspicion and fear of himself, his environment, and his fellow men, he must be allowed to develop self-esteem. Parents must be firm enough with the child to protect him against his own untrained will, but they need also to encourage him to experience new things and express himself freely. Otherwise, from undue shaming and "foreign overcontrol comes a lasting propensity for doubt and shame" (CS, p. 254).

Erik Erikson's comments on what usually occurs in a child who is denied protection from doubt and who is exposed to excessive instances of shaming are highly relevant to the study of the emotional lives of the Puritans: "If denied the gradual and well-guided experience of the autonomy of free choice (or if, indeed, weakened by an ini-

Trials (Garden City, N.Y.: Doubleday, 1961), in particular, p. 32, Kai T. Erikson, Wayward Puritans (New York: Wiley and Co., 1966), pp. 65-159, and Chadwick Hansen, Witchcraft at Salem (New York: George Braziller, 1969), passim.

tial loss of trust), the child will turn against himself all his urge to discriminate and to manipulate. He will over-manipulate himself, he will develop a precocious con-science. Instead of taking possession of things in order to test them by purposeful repetition, he will become obsessed by his own repetitiveness. . . . [This stage] is also the infan-tile source of later attempts in adult life to govern by the letter, rather than by the spirit" (*CS*, p. 252).

Development of a precocious conscience, overmanipula-tion of self and others, governing by the letter—these phrases have, of course, been frequently used to describe the Puritans. These traits were considered ideals the chil-dren were taught to emulate. Parents of the first generation were not alarmed when their children turned naturally to overmanipulation of themselves and others in their efforts to gain temporary self-control and power in order to com-pensate for the absence of genuine autonomy. The Puritan parents praised any evidence of a precocious conscience as long as the child remained obedient. But, again, such chil-dren gained only a hollow and temporary victory over emo-tional problems. In adolescence, when they experienced doubt and shame anew, these children would require a more solid and enduring sense of self-esteem.

In the third and last crucial stage of the child's early development before the relatively calm period of latency, he enters a conflict between genital initiative and the sense of guilt. He learns that the objects of his initiative are "wrong"—forbidden by social taboo and by his own physi-cal limitations. A child who learns self-control but who is prevented from overcontrolling himself during this stage will emerge with a foundation for the development of a mature moral sense. The task of the parents during this period is to protect the child from his own sense of guilt, which, if allowed to develop without guidance and direc-tion, will often prove overpowering: "For the superego of the child can be primitive, cruel, and uncompromising, as may be observed in instances where children overcontrol

81

and overconstrict themselves to a point of self-obliteration; where they develop an overobedience more literal than the one the parent has wished to exact" (*CS*, p. 257).

Children who are allowed to become overstrict with themselves and to develop an inordinate sense of guilt at this stage may later "plunge into psychosomatic disease . . . as if the culture had made a man overadvertise himself and so identify with his own advertisement that only disease can offer him escape" (*CS*, p. 257). As Erikson defines it, guilt is "a sense of badness to be had all by oneself when nobody watches and when everything is quiet—except the voice of the superego" (*CS*, p. 253).

Again Erikson's language seems remarkably applicable to the Puritans. Puritan ministers urged children to hide themselves in closets and to pray secretly to God for their sins. Parents praised children who were overobedient and overstrict with themselves and discouraged initiative of any kind, while ministers argued that initiative was the mother of heresy. The Janeway stories, Cotton Mather's diary, and Wigglesworth's life with its long illness suggest that psychosomatic disease may have provided Puritan adolescents with a form of escape.

The only period of emotional relief for Puritan children came between the three early stages of emotional development and the adolescent period. Puritan children enjoyed a pleasant latency period working at home with their parents. As long as he was industrious and obedient, the child was treated with respect and could take pride in being a productive member of his family. Indeed, the turning of the second generation to industry and capitalism and the initial alliance between the merchants and the younger generation may have been the result of an attempt by the second generation to recapture the pleasure and the lost security and intimacy of this period of emotional development. It is clear, at least, that during the latency period the drive for personal autonomy that had been frustrated during the early stages of childhood was submerged until puberty, when "adolescents have to refight many of the same battles of earlier years" (*CS*, p. 261). For Puritan youths puberty was unusually critical because they had to refight the battles that had apparently been won before through obedience or piety.

In puberty children are most concerned with their own identity, and they search for continuity and sameness. If their parents have been careful to stress the continuity of childhood and adult experiences through all of the early stages, the search will be fruitful. In a culture in which the adult social roles available have a fairly clear relation to the image of self that the child has been encouraged to develop during childhood, the danger of role confusion will be lessened. But for cultures in which this continuity is missing there is a greater likelihood of episodes of delinquent and psychotic behavior.

As we have seen, the problem of role definition and continuity for the second-generation New England child was acute. As far as the parents were concerned, they had provided continuity—obedience in childhood would make a submissive adult and a dutiful son to his aging parents. Yet this parental desire to prolong childhood did not provide genuine continuity or role identification. While the young person recognized that it was only by continued submissiveness and obedience that freedom would ever come, he was also bewildered by the recognition that he could not satisfy his changing and compelling physical and emotional needs through prolonged dependence. In addition, there was genuine doubt about the nature of the adult role the young people were expected to play in New England. The question of a worldly calling and a heavenly calling became intertwined, and for young Puritans doubt over one's adult role took the form of doubt over the state of the soul.

During his youth Increase Mather suffered such confusion over his calling. He later remembered his adolescence as a time when "the Lord broke in upon my conscience with very terrible convictions and awakenings. . . . I was in extremity of anguish and horror in my soul. . . . Yea I thought I die for it."[32] In an attempt to find a suitable role for himself in life, Mather first sought examples in Old Testament prototypes. Failing there, he resorted to a daring confrontation with God the Father that he recorded in his autobiography. He reminded God that if others should happen to read his autobiography and discover that his plea for a calling had not been answered, He might lose some believers:

"I that day begged of God, that He would give me leave to plead with Him, (and with Tears and meltings of heart I did plead with Him,) that if He should not answer me graciously, others after my decease, that should see the papers which I had written which I had kept as remembrances of my walking before God, would be discouraged. For they would see and say 'Here was one that prayed for bodily and spiritual Healing, yea and believed for it also, and yet he perished in his affliction without that Healing.' "[33]

Interestingly enough, after he had received a clear call to the ministry, Increase had a serious confrontation with his own father over church membership when Richard wanted to liberalize the church policies.[34]

Perhaps one of the most striking examples of the trials of Puritan adolescence is presented in Cotton Mather's biography of his brother, Nathaniel, who died at the age of nineteen. Cotton recalled that during his childhood Nathaniel showed "the common effect of such a pious education as the family in which he lived afforded unto him" so that "secret prayer became very betimes one of his infant exercises."[35] However, after his death Cotton examined his

[32] "The Autobiography of Increase Mather," ed. M. G. Hall, *Pro. of the MHS*, 71 (1961), p. 294.

[33] *Ibid.*, p. 298; for commentary on this tendency in Increase Mather, see Shea, *Spiritual Autobiography*, pp. 155-163.

[34] For discussion of the conflict between Increase and Richard, see Murdock, *Increase Mather*, pp. 71-85.

[35] Cotton Mather, *Magnalia Christi Americana* (Hartford: Silas Andrus and Sons, 1853), II, 159.

brother's diary to discover that Nathaniel had undergone a serious emotional crisis at the beginning of adolescence: "When he was twelve (or more) years old. . . . Now it was that he allowed his pen to write these, among other expressions of his trouble about his estate: 'Feb. 19, 1682.— What shall I do? What shall I do to be sav'd? Without a Christ I am undone, undone, undone for evermore! O Lord, let me have Christ, tho' I lye in the mire for ever! O for a Christ! O for a Christ: a Christ! Lord, give me a Christ or I die!' " (p. 159).

Cotton told how his brother tried to overcome these fears, anxieties, and melancholy by burying himself in study; Nathaniel was "not without such very afflictive touches of melancholy, too, as made him sometimes to write himself *deodatus melancholicus*. This was his way of—*living*, shall I say, or of *dying*? . . . While he thus *devoured books*, it came to pass that *books devoured* him. . . . It may be truly written on his grave, 'Study kill'd him' " (pp. 157-158).

While we can assume that most young people did not go to such extremes in their efforts to sublimate their emerging sexual energies and to repress their feelings of guilt and shame, there is sufficient evidence that anxiety of the kind expressed by Nathaniel Mather was widespread. The degree of anxiety suffered by Puritan adolescents was surely to be intensified by the awareness that the state of their souls had an immediate bearing upon their total identities and upon their successful integration into adult society. When faced with the requirement that they must publicly declare themselves "saints" in order to join the church and be in the accepted social order, large numbers of the young people of the second and third generations found themselves spiritually impotent and socially restricted.[36] Young people

[36] For the controversy over the reason that the second generation found it difficult to present themselves for full membership, see Edmund S. Morgan, "New England Puritanism: Another Approach," *WMQ*, 3rd ser., 18 (1961), 236-242, where he argues that the non-members were prevented by their own scruples because they felt un-

could not declare themselves elected when they had daily evidence of their inner "corruption." Such confusion over their proper roles in society and a general malaise of the spirit that accompanied this confusion were baffling to the ministers who wanted new church members. In an effort to correct this situation, the ministers in the 1650's and 1660's increased the number of sermons on the corruption of the rising generation. They declared a need for greater strictness in the home during the period of early childhood, with the aim that the young adults would be more docile and cooperative. But, of course, such methods would only serve to make the adolescent crisis more severe.

The young people of the second generation responded to their frustration as we might expect. Some suffered from extremes of melancholy, physical and psychological illness that bordered upon the suicidal. Most gave evidence of restlessness, or of lethargy, and a sense of nostalgia, while others seemed to have found relief in alcohol.[37] A few in whom repressed drives took the form of shamelessness found emotional outlet in parading naked into church in a band of so-called "Quakers," a term ministers often used to define and to account for any form of public scandalous actions. The witchcraft episode and the Janeway narratives reveal some of the serious and sometimes fatal consequences of this organized, if often unconscious, repression of the young.

As the ministers attacked the rising generation in their sermons, the tensions merely increased, to be eased only with the passing of the first generation from the New Eng-

worthy of membership; and Darrett Rutman, "God's Bridge Falling Down: Another Approach to New England Puritanism Assayed," *WMQ*, 3rd ser., 19 (1962), 408-421, in which he argues that the rigidity of the churches in refusing to accommodate the younger generation was the cause. In either instance younger people were effectively excluded.

[37] On intemperance in New England, see "The Diary of Reverend Increase Mather, 1674-87" in *The Pro. of the MHS*, 2nd ser., 13 (1899-1900), pp. 358-359.

land scene when the people of the second generation, then in their forties and fifties, had an opportunity to assert their independence and establish their own identities. The fact that they seemed to have been able to assert themselves at all in the face of Indian Wars and the threat of foreign oppression and control is a credit to the strength of the human will and the talent and sensitivity of the ministers who preached the sermons of the 1680's and 1690's. At a time when things seemed darkest for New England, men like Samuel Willard, Joshua Moodey, and later Cotton Mather were able to accommodate the message of New England theology and the metaphors of the Puritan sermon to the second generation's need for assurance and emotional stability.[38]

[38] See Clifford K. Shipton, "The New England Clergy of the 'Glacial Age,'" *Pub. of the Col. Soc. of Mass., Transactions,* 32 (1933), pp. 24-54. Shipton places the development of the sermon much later than I do, and he is more concerned with the changing role of the authority of the church than with the developments in the language of the sermons.

THREE

STORMS OF GOD'S WRATH
The Message of Doom and Decay

This is true of all symbols, and this is the reason nobody can invent them. They always are results of a creative encounter with reality. They are born out of such an encounter; they die if this encounter ceases.
Paul J. Tillich, "Theology
and Symbolism"

THE MINISTERS who dominated the presses and pulpits of New England from about 1665 to 1679 devoted much of their creative energy and literary art to creating a myth about their society. In spite of full churches and growing prosperity they envisioned the society as one in decay: a society that was losing the strength and zeal of the founders, was rapidly being passed to a weak and degenerate generation, was threatened on all sides by the forces of evil and from above by the hand of an angry God, and was therefore doomed to likely destruction. To give these themes a compelling imaginative power, the ministers searched the Scriptures for striking imagery and for typological parallels between the Old Testament Hebrews and the Puritans. For symbols of loss, sickness, and insecurity they drew upon the language of everyday life in order to give their message variety and vividness.

The appeal of the myth of the decline for the remaining members of the first generation is clear enough: this theme reinforced their own conviction that the great errand had failed and that the new generation was an ineffectual, ungodly lot. However, the wide popularity of these sermons throughout the 1670's indicates that the message of decay and doom had a remarkable appeal for the younger people themselves, sometimes even arousing in them what Michael Wigglesworth called "tears [which] flow with pleasure."[1]

The most noteworthy preacher of the myth of decline and doom was Increase Mather. The language of Mather's sermons is so rich and diverse and the development of his controlling metaphors so complex and interesting that I have devoted the second part of this chapter to a full discussion of several of his writings. Mather was not alone, however, in exploring the possible ways of capturing the imaginations of the New England congregations and readers; the writings of ministers like Thomas Walley, Samuel Torrey, Samuel Arnold, and Eleazar Mather deserve closer study than they have received. In the first part of this chapter I have taken up the predominant imagery and metaphors of the sermons in the first phase of the quest of the rising generation as revealed in the works of these other Puritan spokesmen.

THE MYTH OF THE DECLINE

When the men of the first-generation patriarchy were no longer able to dominate and control their sons in life, the ministers gave these patriarchs heroic stature in the sermons of the 1660's and 1670's in order to arouse the guilt and shame of their thankless children. The younger generation was compared to the fathers in every aspect of life, practical as well as spiritual. For example, in his artillery election sermon of June 3, 1678, *Abraham in Arms*, Samuel Nowell (1634-1688) recounted the bravery and physical prowess of the founders as soldiers and leaders and then turned to the younger men, whom he found to be "effeminate and wanton," "men not so bold," and therefore, "not disposed to breed up soldiers."[2] Similarly, Increase Mather frequently

[1] Michael Wigglesworth, "The Praise of Eloquence," *The Puritans*, eds. Miller and Johnson, p. 675.

[2] Samuel Nowell, *Abraham in Arms* (Boston, 1678), p. 15.

used the pulpit to attack another weakness of the younger men, their intemperance, which he contrasted to the sobriety of their fathers: "Our Fathers were *Patterns of Sobriety*, they would not drink a cup of wine nor strong drink more than should suffice nature . . . [but] men of latter time could transact no business, nor hardly engage in any discourses, but it must be over a pint of wine or a pot of beer, yea so as that Drunkenness in the sight of man is become a common Sin."[3] Though Mather reported in his diary that he had a disagreement with Governor Randolph over this issue when the Governor remembered "that there was more drunkenness in New England many years ago than there is now, yea at the beginning of this Colony,"[4] Mather still found intemperance to be a capital sin only of the rising generation: there could be no blemish upon the glorious record of the fathers.

Most of the attacks upon the younger generation concerned the issue of religious apostasy. The ministers argued that the failure of so many young adults to demonstrate the workings of God's grace in their hearts by becoming full church members was proof of their corruption and sinfulness; compared with their fathers the present generation was "a poor perishing, . . . unconverted, and . . . undone generation."[5] The ministers joined with Thomas Shepard, Jr. (1635-1677), son of the illustrious pastor of the church at Cambridge, in recalling the founders' "many Prayers and Tears, hazards and labors, and watching and studies, night and day, [expended] to lay a sound and sure, and happy Foundation of prosperity for this people."[6] And they shared John Wilson's (1588-1667) view of the present as he observed it in his last sermon: "I have known New England about thirty-six years, and I never knew such a

---

[3] Increase Mather, *Earnest Exhortation*, p. 7.

[4] "Diary of Reverend Increase Mather," p. 358.

[5] Increase Mather, *Pray for the Rising Generation* (Boston, 1679), p. 17.

[6] Shepard, Jr., *Eye-Salve*, p. 18.

STORMS OF GOD'S WRATH

time as this is that we live in."[7] It is worth noting, as Cotton
Mather did, that Wilson altered his preaching style in his
later years from the *"methodical* way" to a more spirited
manner consisting "chiefly in exhortations and admonitions"; but that even though in his preaching he became a
"Son of Thunder," he remained a man who was "full of
affection" and possessed a special regard for children.[8] It
was Increase Mather who could expound the theme most
eloquently:

"In the last age, in the days of our Fathers . . . scarce a
sermon was preached but some evidently converted; yea
sometimes a hundred in a sermon. Which of us can say we
have seen the like? . . . Alas! they are not the same men
that they were thirty or forty years ago. . . . Again that
which is spoken in Jer. 2.21 may in too sad degree be
applied to New England: 'I planted thee a noble vine,
wholly a right seed, how then art thou turned into the
degenerate Plant of a strange vine unto me?' If the body
of the present generation be compared with what was here
forty years ago, What a sad Degeneracy is evident in the
view of every man."[9]

For the ministers who preached of the apostasy, the
imagery of plants and trees provided apt metaphors for
describing the inadequacies of the young people. William
Stoughton (1631-1701), who later became the chief justice
and prosecutor of the witch trials, asked his congregation
in 1670: *"Shall our vine be of the vine of Sodom and of
the fields of Gomorrah?"*[10] Other ministers used the image
of a hardy and flourishing tree as a symbol of the first generation's fertility but saw the present society in "a barren

[7] John Wilson, *A Seasonable Watch-Word unto Christians against
the Dreams & Dreamers of This Generation* (Cambridge, 1677), p. 8.
Wilson's sermon was preached in 1665, recorded in notes by his listeners, and published in 1677.

[8] Cotton Mather, *Magnalia*, I, 311-313.

[9] Increase Mather, *Pray for the Rising Generation*, p. 17.

[10] William Stoughton, *New-Englands True Interest* (Cambridge,
1670), p. 27.

91

Tree" or "a Withered Twig" or a tree with "a worm at the root and vitals" ready to be "chopt down or fall."[11]

"A Mortal Contagion"

One of the most popular metaphors for describing the failure of the younger generation was the description of New England as a sickly society, suffering with chills, fever, drowsiness, and lethargy and auguring a certain and early death. For the reader whose family had been touched by the plagues that swept New England in the late 1660's and 1670's, such metaphors must have been particularly effective. For the younger generation the metaphor of physical dissolution was fitting to express a sense of inferiority and psychological paralysis that is not uncommon in adolescents or troubled young adults. The imagery of sickness reveals much about the nature of the society and the perceptions and temperaments of the individual ministers because such language allowed the ministers to describe the particular symptoms of New England's illness and to prescribe the cures.

For example, John Norton (1635-1665) made early use of this imagery when in 1660 he defined the apostasy of the rising generation as a cancerous disease and imagined God as the physician who proposed a remedy his patients seemed reluctant to accept: "God proposeth to us Remedy or Calamity; we have our option . . . if you do not accept it, you may look at it as the beginning of sorrow. That we are Out-casts, this doth speak us sick; but our not accepting of the remedy speaks our sickness incurable."[12] Norton, who remained childless through two marriages, also noted an "infection of lethargy" in the younger people, and, citing their tolerance of the Quakers in New England, concluded

[11] *Diary of Cotton Mather*, p. 57; *The Poems of Edward Taylor*, ed. Sanford, p. 47; Oakes, *New England Pleaded With*, p. 33.

[12] John Norton, *Three Choice and Profitable Sermons* (Cambridge, 1664), p. 7.

that a people so obviously weakened were likely to succumb to their sickness (p. 20).

Thomas Walley (1618?-1679) made extensive use of the imagery of sickness in his sermon of 1669, *Balm in Gilead . . . or a treatise wherein There is a Clear Discovery of the Most Prevailing sickness of New England*. Walley, who had assumed the ministerial post at Barnstable when that church was "miserably broken with divisions,"[13] began by assuming that the people of New England were indeed sick, but he was troubled that New England continued to remain ill when God and his ministers held a ready cure. His text from Jeremiah 8:22 professed his puzzlement: *"Is there no Balm in Gilead? is there no Physician there? Why then is not the health of the daughters of my people recovered?"*[14] Walley feigned naivete in explicating his text and appeared shocked that the people of Israel persisted in their illness even though "the Prophet shows them what will be the fruit of their folly in trusting to false Prophets, and relying upon their Predictions" (p. 3). Assuming that his New England congregation would apply the biblical type of Israel to its own situation, Walley recounted the story of the Hebrews, who possessed good health, had the prophets and sacred ordinances, and were guided by God's favor when they went into the wilderness only to arrive at Canaan diseased and languishing in corruption. Worst of all, the Hebrews were unable to find a cure for their sickness: *"Sometimes a People may be sick, and though they have the most proper and suitable Means of Health, yet no Means may be effectual for their Recovery"* (p. 5). Walley further demonstrated that the Hebrews did not seek a cure because, like the people of New England, they were not even aware of their sickness. The process of spiritual decline is so imperceptible that sometimes even the minister, the prophet-physician, cannot discover the secret cancer that devours the people from within: "Because oft times the Diseases of Kingdoms,

---

[13] *Magnalia*, I, 600.   [14] Walley, *Balm in Gilead*, p. 3.

Countries, and Churches are so occult and hid, that the wisest of Physicians cannot find them out" (p. 6). In such cases, "it comes to pass that a people perish, or continue sick, because they do not find out the reason for their sickness," and before the people are aware of it, "the Disease is old, and deeply rooted, grown Malignant" (p. 6).

Thus, in spite of signs of external health and prosperity, Walley sensed a sickness lying beneath the surface of the Puritan society: "We have cause to fear that our condition is but sad this day, for our case looks like the case of this people that the Prophet speaks of: We have *Gilead's Balm*, and *Gilead's Physicians*, and yet we are a sick people. . . . We continue a wounded and weak people. . . . Surely this day *New England* is sick . . . the Country is full of healthful Bodies, but sick Souls" (p. 8).

Walley first searched within the hearts of the people and discovered a "*Lethargy*, a cold sleepy Disease; there seems to be an insensibleness of sin and danger; *Faith* is dead; and *Love* is cold"; and even though "the *Trumpet* sounds, the *Alarm* is given, yet the most sleep on . . . asleep, in a deep sleep of *Security*" (p. 8). Then he examined the external activities of the society where he found "a *Burning Fever* amongst us, a *Fire of Contention* in Towns and in Churches; Fuel is laid upon the Fire daily" (p. 8), which he was convinced "comes from pride and self love: Proud Nature is discontented with the condition that God hath put man in" (p. 9). Walley recognized that social aspirations had much to do with contentions among the people: "The great reason why many are *Unquiet* is because they do not think they are high enough" (p. 9). But he was convinced that there was something wrong deeper within the society as well. He struggled to find the hidden causes.

Lacking modern scientific terminology, he used the metaphors of his day to explain his findings: "*Many are possessed with an Evil Spirit.* . . . Some, *with a Spirit of Oppression, Cruelty* and *Covetousness*, . . . some, *with a Spirit of Envy* and *Jealousy*; others are filled with *Pride in heart*

94

and manners" (p. 9). In seeking a cause for the spirit of
contention and jealousy, Walley focused upon the conflict
between the generations. He urged moderation by both the
young and the old. For the young people he prescribed
patience and greater obedience and respect toward elders;
for the older generation he urged a deeper awareness of the
problems and needs of the young: "Let not the Kids of the
Flock be forgotten, they are members of the same Body"
(p. 16). As a model for all he held up the image of a
benevolent God the Father: "For your Encouragement,
know that the Lord doth in a special manner care for *Zion*
. . . as a *Father* he cares for the Church" (p. 19). But such
hope on the part of a minister and such gentleness in the
image of God were rare in the sermons of the late 1660's.

Another minister who found the source of New England's
disease in the conflict between the generations was Samuel
Arnold (1622-1693), who recognized that the dissatisfaction
of the younger generation was becoming a serious problem
for the churches. In *David Serving His Generation* (1674)
he used typological parallels to try to instill in the young
people some pride in their role as dutiful sons. Confidently,
Arnold declared that "every Generation hath . . . some special Service to do for God," and he found the contrast between David and Solomon an appropriate metaphor for
the relationship between the founders and their sons:
"Some are to lay the foundation for God and others are to
build thereupon; *David*'s work was to settle the *Ark* in
Zion under the Curtains, and *Solomon*'s was to build a
Temple for it."[15] But while he set out to embolden the
rising generation, the more Arnold explained the role of
second-generation Solomons in New England, the more it
became clear that their labors were distinctly subordinate
to those of the first-generation Davids: "*Our generation is
our Master's Family*, God is the Father and Master of the
great Family in Heaven and Earth," and as for the role of

15 Samuel Arnold, *David Serving His Generation* (Cambridge, 1674),
p. 3.

this generation, "we serve the God of our Generation as a Steward of a *great man* in serving his *Master's Family* according to his will, serves his Master" (p. 4).

In answer to the question of the young, "*Why must Christians in serving their Generation be ruled by the will of God and not by the will of their Generation nor by their own will?*" (p. 5), he showed how inadequacy and perversion made it necessary for the second generation to remain humble and obedient: "Reason 1. Because sometimes our Generation is exceedingly vile, very corrupt and sinful, . . . an evil Generation, *Deut. 32:5, a perverse and crooked Generation*, ver. 20, *a forward and faithless Generation*, Judg. 2:10, *a Generation which know not the Lord*, Psalm 78:8, *a stubborn and rebellious Generation that set not their Hearts aright*, Psalm. 95:10, . . . *a Generation of Vipers*, Mark 8:38, *an Adulterous and Sinful Generation*, Act. 2:40, *an untoward Generation*. Reason 2. . . . [They are] a divided generation. . . . Reason 3. Because our Generation is changeable, they may say *Hosanna* today and Crucify Christ soon after . . . they admire his gracious words, Luke 4:28, 29, they are filled with wrath and would kill him presently" (p. 5).

Thus Arnold's words to the young vacillate between building confidence and destroying it, and his stipulation of how the younger generation should conduct itself wavers between a call to action and an insistence upon a defensive passivity: "Endeavor with all your might after godliness and holiness, and . . . Labor to improve your Piety in fervent Supplications for the good of your generation, be prayer-ful for your generation. . . . Be peaceable. . . . Observe order. True Gospel Peace is the calmness of order. . . . Keep your Ranks and Files that the Enemy break not in. . . . It is certain the work of our generation is to carry on Temple-work, our Fathers have laid the foundation, and left the carrying on of the *Super-structure* to us" (pp. 7-8). For the young people of New England Arnold's advice repeated what they had learned from their fathers: the heroic days

STORMS OF GOD'S WRATH

were over and now they must maintain their fathers' estate
and submit to the orders of the patriarchy and of God the
Father.

Another minister who found the metaphor of the sickness
of the society a useful one was Samuel Torrey (1632-1707).
As two of his sermons preached nearly ten years apart
reveal, Torrey labored throughout his years in the ministry
to discover the underlying causes of New England's disease
and to find a cure. In *An Exhortation Unto Reformation*
(1674) he recognized that New England suffered under a
"heavy aggravation" that had sapped the "internal, spiritual
power and purity" of the people, and he feared that "if we
do not speedily recover . . . we shall let go and lose all, pull
down all, and bury ourselves in our own ruins."[16] To add
drama to his presentation, Torrey imagined God the Father
as a physician addressing His fallen New England: "Thou
art fallen . . . thou hast left thy first life, . . . thou art not
what thou hast been, thou art fallen into a state, frame,
and way of backsliding and Apostasy" (pp. 2-3). Torrey
himself counselled his sick people to "remember therefore
from whence thou art fallen and labour to recover thyself
speedily from thy declension and defection" (p. 3).

Like Norton and Walley before him, Torrey found the
disease of the people to be characterized by a languor that
left them vulnerable to the invasion of other infections. He
feared that the people's unmindfulness of their disease
would expose them to a contamination of the purity of their
worship since "ill-worship doth ordinarily creep into Re-
formed Church[es] while they are asleep, gradually, secretly,
and insensibly, and grow up into a considerable and formidable height and strength before it appears, before
Churches are aware" (p. 19). Because he believed that "the
sins of Youth (which are many of them some of the most
flagitious sins of the Times) are become the sins of the
Churches," he sought to cure the disease at its source by

16 Torrey, *An Exhortation*, pp. 19 and 24.

97

chastising the young people of the congregation (p. 24). But, at this stage in his career, Torrey held little hope that the younger generation would recover, and he feared that certain destruction was near: "Remember that the *Children of the Kingdom* may be *cast out,* and that will cause weeping, wailing and gnashing of teeth. . . . We may fear, (and that justly) that God will depart from us: . . . And Alas! upon you is likely to fall all the Calamity and Misery of this Apostasy which is begun, you will see and feel the sad and lamentable Effects of it" (pp. 14 and 37).

In answer to the question of the cure for this sickness, Torrey could only advise the young to reform by becoming more submissive and humble; he desired that the younger generation help itself, but he was uncertain about precisely what it should do. He counselled only "that Youth and Young persons could lay this Consideration unto their hearts . . . before it be too late. . . . O that all thus concerned would *Up and be doing!*" (p. 37). As with so many ministers who preached the sermons of decay and doom, Torrey was restrained from offering assurance by the doctrine of the Covenant of Grace, which seemed to hold that men could do nothing to help themselves, and he was much confounded, as were the young people themselves, by a cultural situation that left undefined the role of the second generation in the church and the society.

Throughout the next decade Torrey continued to search for a more precise answer for the young people. In his *A Plea for the Life of Dying Religion* (1683) he prescribed his cure for the *"vital decay, a decay upon the very Vitals* of Religion" that had caused an angry God to "smitten us with a deadly destruction: The killing sword, a moral Contagion."[17] He reasserted his conviction that the "carelessness, slothfulness, unfaithfulness" of the younger generations had allowed the religion of their fathers to "decay, languish, and die away" (p. 36). But the only remedy he

[17] Samuel Torrey, *A Plea for the Life of Dying Religion* (Boston, 1683), pp. 11 and A2.

98

could propose was for the young people to recognize the *"confounding shame and scandal unto this Generation of New-England Christians* before the World" (p. 36) and arouse in their own hearts a self-loathing and a desperate fear of the wrath of God. He urged weeping and mourning to purge corruption and restore health to New England:

"Charge, judge, condemn, loath, and abhor ourselves for all that Sin and Apostasy. . . . *Do and perform all with Mourning and deep Humiliation*: Mourning for and over ourselves, mourning for and over sinners, mourning over our Families, mourning over our Churches, mourning over the rising Generations, and over this whole People; mourning under the sense of our own Sins, and the Sins of others. . . . Mourn alone in secret places . . . and always without ceasing, without intermission. . . . If we will not mourn, we shall perish in our Apostasy" (pp. 17-26).

But by the time Torrey published this sermon in the early 1680's, public demonstrations of self-loathing were becoming less popular as the people looked for a message of assurance and a redefinition of their role in the church. Perhaps it was a sense of this impending change that contributed to the decisions of both Torrey and Increase Mather to decline the offer of the presidency of Harvard when it was offered to each of them in 1682.[18]

"THE DEPARTURE OF GOD"

In addition to imagery of sickness and weakness, the ministers used symbolism of deprivation and loss to describe the condition of New England in the 1670's. With the purpose of arousing their readers and listeners to reform, the ministers lamented the loss of the spirit of the founders and predicted ultimate loss of all of God's favor and protection. For a generation of sons who had waited long to inherit the lands of their fathers and who had been taught that

18 Morison, *Harvard College*, II, 440-441.

they lacked the ability, strength, and character needed to make these lands bear fruit, the imagery depicting the loss of their crops to the elements, the loss of their lives and property to their enemies, and the inevitable loss of their heavenly inheritance had special conscious significance. These images were also analogues for feelings of frustration and of lost identity appropriate to the psychic conflicts present in the lives of many second-generation sons. The popular image of the loss of the candlestick, a symbol of spiritual and physical power, may serve as an example.

The ministers used the image of the seven-branched candlestick from the Book of Revelation to identify the Church of New England with the seven churches of the early Christians: "The seven candlesticks which thou saw are the seven churches."[19] God threatened the early churches to reform "or else I will come unto thee quickly, and will remove any candlestick out of this place" (Rev. 2:5). For the ministers of New England the biblical image of the candlestick became a symbol of the church's strength and of the presence of God's favor granted to the first generation. As they employed the image in their sermons addressed to the members of the second generation, the ministers tried to awaken their congregations to the fear that God's favor would be lost and the new generation would be rendered spiritually castrated and impotent if the sons did not equal the religious fervor and strength of their fathers: "God threatens to *remove the Candlestick*,"[20] declared William Stoughton, and Samuel Danforth (1626-1674) warned of "the Breaking of the Candlesticks."[21]

Another fear was that the candlesticks would lose their purity and become corrupt: "We may then justly fear that these Golden Candlesticks, will no longer, but become Dross and Tin, and Reprobate Silver, until the Lord's ax has

19 Revelation: 4:11-13, 20; 2:1, 18:23.
20 Stoughton, *True Interest*, p. 11.
21 Samuel Danforth, *A Brief Recognition of New-Englands Errand into the Wilderness* (Cambridge, 1671), p. 19.

rejected them."[22] Even the usually gentle Willard feared that if the second generation did not rekindle the fires of the original zeal, God might not remove their candlesticks, but He would surely subject them to a fiery cleansing: "By it he burns off the dirt that clave to them: Metal when it is first taken out in Ore from the Mineral, hath much of the heterogeneous matter (dirt and filth) cleaving to it, and that the fire burns off. . . . Hypocrites cannot long abide the fiery trial."[23] Funeral sermons for deceased ministers and leaders of the patriarchy were also good opportunities to expound upon the inadequacy of the young, and many preachers mourned the death of one of the first generation with the image: "we are bereaved, the Lights are put out of our Candlesticks."[24] In employing the image of the candlestick the ministers were trying to move the members of their congregations to action by touching the same fears and sense of inadequacy and shame that the parents had used to impose passivity, obedience, and subjection upon the children. The image thus became a symbol of a general sense of powerlessness and the lack of social and religious identity of the second and third generations.

Frequently, ministers made use of the imagery of loss by envisioning the covenant as a family contract between God the Father and his New England sons with inheritance of earthly as well as spiritual reward at stake. In *New-Englands True Interest*, preached in 1668 and printed in 1670, the thirty-nine-year-old William Stoughton tried to show his own generation how to earn the promised inheritance by carrying on the labors of the fathers; he promised "the good sons of the Lord saw their hard work increase and the value of their inheritance and in due time they

---

[22] Increase Mather, *The Day of Trouble Is Near* (Cambridge, 1674), p. 32.

[23] Samuel Willard, *The Fiery Tryal No Strange Thing* (Boston, 1682), p. 8.

[24] Samuel Willard, *Useful Instructions for a Professing People in Times of Great Security and Degeneracy* (Cambridge, 1673), p. 77.

will go to a place of brisk rivers and streams."[25] Certain of the worth of the inheritance to be gained, Stoughton declared: "Surely our Fathers have not *inherited lies or vanity and things* wherein there is no profit"; but he was less certain that his generation would be worthy of inheriting its full due. There was no question that illustrious parentage stood his generation in good stead because "as for Extraction and Descent, if we be considered as a Posterity, O what Parents and Predecessors may we the most of us look back upon . . . choice and picked ones, whom He eminently prepared and trained up and qualified for service" (pp. 17, 30). And, as Stoughton proved from his text (Isa. 63:8), "They are my people, children that will not lie," worthy parents place their children in a special relationship to God the Father: "This is implied in that expression of *Children* in the Text . . . [it] notes not only their Relation unto *God* as a Father, but unto *pious and religious Parents*, the Lord's faithful Convenanting Servants. Righteous Parentage and Descent is of great moment with the Lord; hence he calls and names his people so often in Scripture from their pious Ancestors. . . . They are a *holy Root* unto their Seed and the Lord may well expect that the Branches should be answerable to the Root" (p. 9).

But Stoughton feared that his generation was incapable of carrying forward its family heritage: "But *we*, poor *we*, alas what are we! we want many seasonings which our Fathers had, we are poor raw things. . . . Shall we lose our share in those times of Refreshment which are so near to come?" (p. 30). So different from their fathers have the New England children become that they may indeed be said to "lie"; for by their sins and corruption they have assumed the identity of an alien people and have effectively denied their birthright: "Alas, how is *New-England* in danger this day to be lost even in *New-England*? . . . But we who rise up to tread out the footsteps of them that are gone before

25 Stoughton, *True Interest*, p. 11.

STORMS OF GOD'S WRATH

us, alas! what are we?" (p. 21). Because "a Parent expects more from a *Child* than from any other because of the Relation" (p. 8), Stoughton concluded that his generation would be deeply ashamed on Judgment Day when the family histories of the saints will be read: "Consider and remember always, that . . . the *Books* that shall be opened at the last day will contain *Genealogies* in them. . . . How shall we, many of us, hold up our faces then, when there shall be a solemn rehearsal of our *descent* as well as our *degeneracies*? To have it published whose Child thou art will be cutting unto thy soul, as well as to have the Crimes reckoned up that thou art guilty of" (p. 33). A sermon that began with the promise of a glorious inheritance ended as another expression of loss, confusion, and shame.

The figure most often repeated in the sermons of the 1670's was the departing of the father, usually symbolized by the abandonment of New England by God the Father. In *A Serious Exhortation to the Present and Succeeding Generation*, a sermon composed before 1669 and printed in 1671, Eleazar Mather (1637-1669) demonstrated the social and psychological importance of this image in his careful explication of the meaning of the "*Presence* of God." He explained that the "*Presence* of God"[26] described a feeling of being at peace with oneself and one's fellow men and of having a sense of personal and community security that in turn leads to social accord and prosperity: "There is a *Gracious Presence* of God, and this is the thing here desired, and this contains as much as possibly can be desired; universality, fullness, perpetuity of good is in the Lord's gracious Presence. This in the inchoation of it is the beginning of Heaven, in the perfection of it, tis the compleatment of Heaven" (p. 2). In short, the man who has the feeling of God's presence possesses a bit of heaven on earth. In contrast, Eleazar Mather described the feeling a people have when God abandons them: they undergo a sense of de-

26 Eleazar Mather, *A Serious Exhortation*, p. 2.

rangement as God "casts off" and "sets a people adrift as it were, and lets them go off to sea," where they might "break in pieces" (p. 4). They feel as though the bottom has fallen out of the ground that they have stood upon (p. 6).

After he established the general meaning of his central metaphor, Mather turned to his own endangered generation: "Hence take notice what bottom and foundation it is that we stand on" (p. 6). He warned that the "presence of God" that had brought economic progress and a spirit of unity to New England "in the days of Old" and "hath blessed our fathers" would not necessarily continue: "No verily, he that hath been with them, may leave us. . . . It is not what God hath done heretofore that will make us a happy people at present" (p. 6). As he probed deeper into the full meaning of the "presence of God," Eleazar Mather came the closest of any one of the ministers before Willard to defining the problem of the second generation in the 1670's. He recognized that insecurity had created tensions and disturbances in the society that had led to the feeling that God was abandoning New England; after all, "What father wants to be among his fighting and quarreling children?" When he asked, "Are you to have good days? Are you like to have things go well in your times?" (p. 17), Mather seemed on the verge of suggesting what Willard and Cotton Mather would later understand—that the secret for bringing God back to New England, for restoring inner peace in the society, would be to instill in the people a new confidence that God was indeed still present among them.

But Mather stopped short of this insight, and he concluded that his generation was caught in the hopeless cycle of its own degeneracy: "Secure hearts that have had many Means, many Warnings, many years, and not awakened, if one should rise from the dead to such a one he will do little good" (p. 27). He predicted that for this generation "in this life [there will be] nothing but plagues, woes, miseries" (p. 31), and in eternity there would be the continued sense of having been abandoned by both earthly and heavenly parents: "Your godly Parents will be so far from helping you that they will rejoice and bless God for executing Justice upon you to all Eternity; neither your fathers nor the God of your fathers will own you" (p. 31).

Perhaps Mather was too caught up in the myth of the decline to abandon the rhetoric of doom. On the other hand, it is possible that he viewed his role as that of an articulator of inner feelings and did not believe his people ready yet for the change in religious imagery and theme that would come in the 1680's. In either case Eleazar Mather proved himself an intelligent and sensitive social critic whose early death in 1669 at the age of thirty-two may well have delayed his generation's quest toward self-definition.

"A Breach, an In-let to Sorrow"

The image of the abandonment of New England by God had special meaning during the Indian Wars, when the ministers followed the biblical tradition of imagining God as the supreme military commander protecting his chosen from the powers of destruction so long as his people maintained his favor. The high number of casualties in the King Phillip's War (1674-1675) became more evidence for the belief that God was indeed abandoning New England. As the writer of the Preface for Jonathan Mitchell's (1624-1668) *Nehemiah on the Wall in Troublesom Times* declared, "*The still out-stretched hand of God's powerful wrath over this poor Country, in smiting down our Pillars, plucking up our Stakes, and taking from us the breath of our Nostrils, is a matter so doleful and solemnly awful and tremendous, that we may well sigh out our sorrows, in the words of the lamenting Church*: Lam. 5:16, 17. The crown is fallen from our head; woe unto us that we have sinned. For this is our heart faint, for these things our eyes are dim.

105

. . . Let those dreadful Thunder-claps, which of late have broken over our heads, awaken and call us up from the bed of Sloth."[27]

During this period the "presence of God" was expressed in imagery of the wall protecting the garden of the chosen from the howling wilderness; God had provided his wall of defense for the founders, but if provoked he was ready to remove it and expose the sons to the enemy. The ministers imagined the death of each one of God's first-generation saints as weakening New England's defenses by leaving another gap in the wall, a gap that could hardly be filled by those of the weak rising generation. The wars gave the ministers one of their best opportunities for linking external events to human corruption. By interpreting every defeat as another sign of the sins of the rising generation that had caused God to unleash his wrath and punishment, the ministers made the image of the wall and the garden into one of the most vivid symbols of the intimacy between inner corruption and exterior events.

For example, in the vulnerable wilderness community of Hartford in 1674 James Fitch (1622-1702) preached *A Holy Connextion, or a True Agreement between Jehovah's Being a Wall of Fire to his People, and the Glory in the Midst thereof.* In answer to the people's protest that the Father's wrath was unwarranted, Fitch declared that the people could not perceive the evil within themselves and their community because "the gradual withdrawing of the Lord's Glory from a professing People are imperceptible things, and also not discerned unless it be by those who have the eye-salve of the Spirit and are held under special awakenings."[28] Fitch possessed the "eye-salve," and he found "withdrawing of the inward and heavenly, that hearty and most real communion with God and one another in the

[27] Jonathan Mitchell, *Nehemiah on the Wall in Troublesom Times* (Cambridge, 1671), p. A2.

[28] James Fitch, *A Holy Connextion* (Cambridge, 1674), p. 13.

ways of God, that which while enjoyed makes a Christian society a Heaven upon Earth" (p. 13). Thus Fitch concluded, with God's glory absent in Hartford, the people could expect that Jehovah's *"Wall of Fire"* would be removed.

Certainly there must have been many ministers like Fitch in outpost communities who attempted to terrify the people with the threat of destruction from the actual Indian attacks, but for most ministers, particularly those in the relatively secure city of Boston, the Indian was only one of a number of enemies, including Satan, witches, and the European anti-christ, who lurked outside the imagined walls around New England and threatened God's people. For the imagery of the wilderness, of the wall, and of the garden not only served to express a general sense of insecurity and loss, but it also allowed the people to project the evils that they had been taught to find within themselves outward upon an external enemy. Cotton Mather would make the fullest use of this process of projection and purgation in his repeated use of the Devil and demons as scapegoats for the feelings of guilt he found in his people.

In his sermon of 1673, *Eye Salve, or a Watch-Word . . . to take Heed of Apostasy*, Thomas Shepard, Jr. demonstrated some of the richness and complexity of this imagery. Like Fitch, Shepard insisted that the people lacked the sensitivity necessary for detecting the devious workings of their apostasy: "A revolt from God is usually graduated, having its more imperceptible beginnings."[29] The wall of protection against "the leaven, infection, poison, of anything tending to debauch" God's people had been the people's Covenant with God (p. 43): Because of the Covenant, "God himself hath been a Wall of fire to us . . . The Lord hath enclosed us, set a hedge about his people . . . from the noise and tumults, and disturbance of the World" (p. 14). But now the protection of the Covenant had been so

[29] Shepard, Jr., *Eye-Salve*, p. 31.

weakened by the people's apostasy that even the little children were vulnerable to mortal danger: "The tender ones will be exposed to those little foxes (heretics and quakers) who have tried to get into the garden to eat the buds of the new grapes off the vines." In the wake of the invasion of the evil forces, Shepard envisioned the garden of New England turned into a wilderness in which the new generation would languish in darkness among "fiery serpents" (p. 4).

In explicating the scriptural passage, "Have I been a wilderness unto Israel? a land of Darkness? (Jer. 2:31), Shepard revealed the wilderness to be a symbol of all the primitive impulses manifest in the uncivilized condition. He explained that "The words are metaphorical," so that when God says *Have I been a Wilderness to Israel?*" what he means is "Have I been that to my People which a Wilderness is unto men that are made to [be] wilder therein, where they meet with nothing but wants, and terror, and woe" (p. 3). Specifically, Shepard offered these five meanings of the metaphor of the wilderness to the people of the second generation.

"There are these five things which we may consider of in a Wilderness: 1. A Wilderness notes a desolate, solitary place without Inhabitant and where there is nothing but confusion and disorder. 2. A Wilderness speaks a place uncultivated, a condition destitute of many necessary comforts, as aforesaid, there's suffering, hunger, and thirst. 3. In a Wilderness there is not a beaten path; whence it is that men there are in danger to be lost and are made to wander about for want of a way before them. . . . 4. There is a danger as to many positive evils which such are exposed unto . . . pits and fiery serpents . . . [it is] a place of temptation. 5. *A wilderness is not hedged in nor fenced about*; what is in the wilderness hath no defense but lies open to the injury of those that will break in to Bark the Trees thereof and root up the same. . . . [It is] *a land of Darkness*—darkness betokens the privation of light; it is diverse times in

108

Scripture taken for trouble, ignorance, sorrow, and (in a word) *all woeful evil"* (pp. 3-5).

The sermon became a mosaic of the imagery of the decline as Shepard lamented the contrast between the heroism of the first generation, which provided protection for their children against the darkness and terrors of the wilderness, and the folly of the young people, who have dared to risk all by tolerating new religious ideas (pp. 11-18). Shepard felt that the enemies of the people had already invaded the garden, and he cried out: "O let no hand therefore be suffered to lay the Axe of destruction to the root of that Tree, by an direct or indirect means" (p. 11). Shepard's own son, Thomas Shepard, III (1658-1685) may have been deeply affected by his father's message of doom, for he always feared that he would die early. Thomas, III, did die young at the age of twenty-six.[30]

In *Righteousness Rained from Heaven* (1677), Samuel Hooker (1635-1697), minister of Framington, Connecticut, employed the imagery of the wilderness as a metaphor both of external troubles in the society and of the sense of emptiness and dissatisfaction within the individual. With an actual period of drought as the occasion for his sermon, he imagined all of New England as drying up not only from the lack of actual rain but from the lack of the rain of righteousness, the absence of God's grace in the souls of his people. For the first seven pages he described the trees and crops of New England withering away as the land returned to a "wilderness condition," resulting in destruction of all life: "There is no living thing without [rain]. . . . No wonder though Blasting and Mildew, sickness and Sword come upon us."[31]

[30] William B. Sprague, *Annals of the American Pulpit* (New York: Robert Carter and Brothers, 1857), p. 67. See a "Letter from the Reverend Mr. Thomas Shepard to His Son at His Admission into the College" (Massachusetts, 1672) in *Remarkable Providences: 1600-1760*, ed. John Demos (New York: George Braziller, 1972), pp. 130-135.

[31] Samuel Hooker, *Righteousness Rained from Heaven* (Cambridge, 1677), p. 7.

But then in one of the most encouraging statements of the 1670's, Hooker proceeded to describe the wonderful recovery that can come to the land if the people chose to make themselves righteous before God: rain will return to make their land rich fields, and they will "inherit prosperity" and have "peace at home, inward contentment and quietness, this is another fruit of righteousness" (p. 11). Convinced that "the Vine brought from far and planted here may still retain its ancient Nobility" in spite of the fact that "the older generation [is] almost gone" (p. 15), Hooker assured his listeners that if they but humble themselves before God, "the Lord will satisfy thy soul in drought, and make fat thy dry bones and [thou] shalt be like a watered garden." But unwilling yet to abandon the language of fear and guilt, he shifted the meaning of his metaphor in a parting word to those who refuse to humble themselves: "If God rain not righteousness on you it may be expected that he will rain something else: Seek this gentle rain that the storm of his wrath [will] fall not upon you" (p. 18).

There were two occasions when the audience could always be certain that the preacher would employ the imagery of the wall and the wilderness—addresses to military companies and funeral sermons. The early works of the Reverend Samuel Willard provide interesting examples of the use of this imagery in each of these sermon forms. Even as early as the writing of his artillery sermon, *The Heart Garrisoned* in 1676, Willard was introducing moderation in theme and modifications in the use of the standard imagery. Instead of imagining a wall around the entire community, Willard tried to appeal to the individual soldier by identifying the property to be defended with the heart of the soldier himself and describing everything outside the soldier's body as a moral wilderness to be confronted and subdued. Unlike those ministers who found the real cause of war to be the corrupt hearts of the people themselves, Willard assumed the heart of the man to be pure and therefore most deserving of vigorous defense against the forces of evil outside. Willard also broadened the meaning of the images of the "watchmen" and "gap-men" of New England; previously these were symbols reserved only for the leaders of the first generation and for the ministers, but Willard saw that every ordinary Christian is a "gap-man." Thus he tried to instill pride and dignity in the average soldier. His tone throughout is forceful and encouraging: "Hence it comes to pass that Religion lies a bleeding, and many strong men fall before the *Force* and *Fraud* of their Enemies; this deserves a Reproof; Is not the Heart undervalued? . . . Remember you carry your *Life, Honour, Glory,* and *Liberty* in your right hand, which must either manfully be defended, or basely lost."[32] Willard recognized that if New England were to be protected against its enemies, the wall surrounding it would have to be built with the pride and confidence of the rising generation.

Nowhere is this feature of Willard's attitude more conspicuous than in his use of the wall in his funeral sermon on the death of Governor John Leveret. His beginning was traditional enough: Leveret's death was a sign of "God sitting as a Judge upon an apostatized and guilty people,"[33] and his text expressed the usual fear that the death of the leader may be but the beginning of a storm of wrath from an angry God (p. 1). Yet in his explication of the metaphor of the wall around New England, Willard showed that the strength of the wall of protection depended upon the self-confidence of the people themselves: when a people are secure and at peace with one another, they display a more unified and formidable image to possible enemies. Insecurity and unhealthy fears only render a people defenseless and entice their enemies to attack: "When he [God] takes away the Spirits and Courage from his People and fills them

---

[32] Samuel Willard, *The Heart Garrisoned* (Cambridge, 1676), pp. 8-9. For a fuller discussion of Willard, see Chapter iv.

[33] Samuel Willard, *A Sermon . . . Occasioned by the Death of the Much Honoured John Leveret* (Boston, 1679), p. 1.

with panic fears: when their heart faints, and Spirit dies in them, when they are made to be afraid of a shadow, to start at a fancy, and flee when none pursues, these are miseries menaced against a backsliding people. . . . Magnanimity and resolution in a people is a defense, it renders them formidable; but when once their Courage is gone, there is a breach, an in-let to sorrows, it renders a people a scorn and reproach to their Neighbors, and every one will have a snap at them" (p. 4).

It is the jealousy and prejudice that result from a lack of mutual trust that leave people vulnerable because "divisions are rents" and expose them as "easy prey to any devourers while they are busy devouring one another" (p. 5). Combining the imagery of sickness with that of the hedge, Willard closed by emphasizing that the "thornes and thistles" within the garden must be rooted out before the rebuilding of the wall of defense can be undertaken: "We are a sick People, the Symptoms are visible and manifest. . . . Heal the wounds. . . . Our fence is tottering and in many places open. . . . Whole Cataracts of misery will soon break in upon us; there are enough waiting to make a prey of us; the mouths of devouring Beasts are open upon us" (p. 13). Willard found the imagery of sickness, planting, and the wall befitting his purposes, but he had begun to give these symbols new meaning.

The sermons on the themes of degeneracy and decline appear to have served as a kind of primitive group psychotherapy that objectified the doubts and fears of the young people and allowed them to confront the threatening primal forces that seemed ready to punish disobedience with destruction. Through their chastisement and lamentation, the ministers inadvertently acted as group spokesmen who provided the opportunity for the release of irrational and antagonistic emotions and allowed for the eventual purgation of fears and doubts. Thus the ministers who expounded these themes actually helped the second generation through an important phase of their quest, the separation from the fathers, and prepared the young adults for the subsequent search for cultural identity.

THE REVEREND INCREASE MATHER (1639-1723)

Increase Mather's sermons of the 1670's deserve special attention, for not only was Mather the most prolific and powerful spokesman of the bitterness of the patriarchs in his repetition of the theme of "the degeneracy of the Rising Generation," but in his own way Mather exposed, mollified, and managed the anxieties of his generation during the critical decade of their social maturation. In the 1670's his writing served as a ritualistic incantation of troubled minds; and in the 1680's, when his generation no longer needed such expressions, Mather was able to adjust his language and themes to accommodate the changing needs of his people. The purpose of the present discussion is to examine Mather's management of the metaphors of the decline in his early works and to trace the development of his thought and religious language. For clarity I have divided the sermons from 1670 to 1686 into three groups: those which focus upon the theme of impending disaster, those on the corruption of the younger generation, and those which reveal a change in Mather's thought and imagery. While there is considerable overlap within these groups, such an organization serves best to highlight the most significant features of Mather's writing.[34]

"Cataracts of his Wrath"

Mather's most practiced and perhaps most effective technique for attempting to arouse at once both the fear and the guilt of his listeners and readers was to show that disasters like storms, droughts, or social and political disorders

[34] For a recent study of the intellectual development of Increase Mather, see Robert Middlekauff, *The Mathers: Three Generations of Puritan Intellectuals, 1596-1728* (New York: Oxford University Press, 1971).

were only the external signs of the secret internal sinfulness of the people. Since every unfavorable external event was a sign from God of His anger, every crisis became an occasion for lamenting present inner corruption and anticipating future calamity. By interpreting external events in the light of typological readings of Scripture, Mather managed to bring the whole weight of current events and biblical history to bear upon the hearts of the guilty.

In *The Day of Trouble Is Near* (1674, preached 1673) he first employed these techniques to show "the *Signs of a Day of Trouble being near and particularly what reason there is for New-England to expect a Day of Trouble.*"[35] Mather began with an account of the religious decline of the second-generation Israelites and the resulting wrath of God, and then he showed that the *"inward spiritual troubles,* Soul troubles"* (p. 5) in New England indicated the approach of apocalyptic destruction: "There is a day of trouble coming upon all the world and such trouble too, as the like hath not been, for I am persuaded that the Scripture is yet to be fulfilled" (p. 10). But at the same time that he aroused the people's fear, he used that fear itself as proof of the impending disaster: "Secret dismal fears upon the spirits of men are sometimes a sign that a day of trouble is near" (p. 9). Even the fact that he had been moved to speak of such disaster was evidence that God was removing His protection from His people: "Also when God begins to depart, he stirs up the trumpet of his messengers" (p. 10).

Besides the traditional imagery of storms and floods, the ruin of the walls, and the outpouring of the vials of wrath, Mather added a peculiarly American touch to his vision of inevitable calamity by using reports of present troubles in Europe as a sure sign of future unrest in America: "What do we hear of at this day, but Wars and Rumors of Wars? and Nation rising up against Nation, and Kingdom against Kingdom? Now if these are the beginnings of sorrows, what, and where, and when will the end be? There's an over-

[35] *Day of Trouble,* title page.

flowing scourge breaking in upon the world . . . that will
not keep within ordinary banks or bounds. . . . And how
far will it go? Where will the Tail of this Storm fall at last
do we think? How if it should fall upon *America*? Will not
some drops at least light upon *New England*? . . . It is then
high time for us to awake out of sleep" (p. 21).

Mather foresaw this "black cloud" (p. 27) moving over
New England and bringing loss of lives and property. Such
losses had been prefigured in the recent deaths of so many
of the first ministers and leaders: "Ah! *poor New England,
thy Chariots and thy Horsemen are gone from thee, and
now thine Enemies are coming against thee*" (p. 21). These
horsemen cannot be replaced, for the rising generation that
had been counted upon to man the chariots had failed; the
"good seed" planted in God's garden had proved "a strange
vine" (p. 27). Thus, inner corruption both caused the disaster and rendered the people incapable of defense; and
since men can really do nothing to help themselves, Mather
could only lament the fortune of the young: "If thou hast
but one Tear in thy eyes, if thou hast but one Prayer in
thy heart spend it now" (p. 31).

Mather treated this theme of the powerlessness of man
at greater length in a sermon published the following year,
The Times of Man are in the Hands of God, in which he
again used the external events of the day to arouse fear and
to urge his listeners to search within. Mather's subtitle described the tragic event in detail: "*that awful Providence
which happened in Boston in New England . . . (when part
of a Vessel was blown up in the Harbour, and nine men
hurt, and three mortally wounded) wherein is shown how
we should sanctify the dreadful Name of God under such
awful Dispensations.*" From the Preface it is clear that
Mather had had some difficulty before he preached the
sermon in convincing the relatives and friends of the victims that God's ways are just. The people protested that
God seems to punish good men while letting the wicked
live long and apparently comfortable lives, but Mather

115

found such questions to be only more proof of man's stubbornness and presumption. He declared that God's "judgments are great and deep," and "it is foolish to say that tomorrow you will do such and such. You cannot know." And he warned that "this especially applies to young men who think they can repent in their later years."[36] Only God's ministers can predict the future because they know how to interpret the natural and scriptural signs God has provided them.

After declaring himself such a prophet, Mather shifted the tone of the sermon: the minor tragedy in Boston harbor became just one more foreshadowing of the total "fiery destruction": "Woe to us if we will not see when the Lord's hand is lifted up in such an awful manner, what can we then expect but utter Confusion? We may then expect that the Lord . . . will take away others that are useful . . . that there shall be a Calamity and *Lamentation generally.* It is mentioned as a dreadful Presage of general Calamity coming upon the Children of Israel . . . by sudden and fiery destruction, Amos 4:11. And Christ doth intimate to the Jews [that] that sudden and awful destruction which came upon a few of them, did (without repentance) forerun and foretell a day of general Calamity coming upon them" (p. 17).

Faced with such awesome prospects, Mather's audience asked him for a plan of action: "What shall we do . . . under this awful hand of his upon us?" (p. 17). Mather could only advise them to be patient, obedient, and submissive before the hand of the Father: "Follow these *Directions:* 1. *Take notice of the hand of God in this that is come to pass.* . . . 2. *Lay it to heart.* . . . 3. *Let us adore the hand of God.* . . . 4. *Let us labor to understand the Lord's mind and meaning in this awful Providence.* . . . 5. *Let us Repent of past and present Iniquities.* . . . Lastly, *Be prepared for [a] change of Times.* Now you are in Prosperity, but prepare for a day of Adversity; who knoweth how soon the Iniquity of

36 *Times of Men* (Boston, 1675), p. 14.

thy heels will overtake thee, and the days of evil come upon thee?" (pp. 17-20).

In the early 1670's Mather's conception of the relationship between man and God did not yet include the possibility of man's actively struggling to overcome evil and win the favor of his Father. The notion that Christ has atoned for man's sins and acts as his mediator with the Father was not a consideration in Mather's early works. For Mather impotence and weakness, evidenced most clearly in his own generation, were the characteristics of man, and this theme made Mather's sermons the most popular of the decade.

As the people began in the late 1670's to long for a sign that their period of trials might be ending, Mather at first resisted their changing mood. Evidence of this resistance is ample in his post-war sermon of 1676. In the face of the people's rejoicing over the end of the King Phillip's War, Mather preached *An Earnest Exhortation to the Inhabitants of New England to Hearken to the Voice of God in his late and present dispensations As ever they desire to escape another judgment seven times greater than any thing which as yet hath been.* In this sermon Mather tried to counter those who had taken solace in the end of the war as a sign of the return of God's favor to New England; he warned them to "*Take we heed how we embrace [false] notions . . .* e.g. that imagination which some have that all this is come upon us, only for trial, and not for Correction on the account of sins, without doubt it is for both." And he asked, "Why should we suppose that God is not offended with us when his displeasure is written in such visible and bloody character?"[37] Mather strained his imagery and employed his best rhetoric to show the deaths of so many young men of the colony to be only more evidence of the wastage of New England at the hand of God. Just as God said to Jerusalem, "Be instructed lest my Soul depart from thee and thou become desolate, a Land not inhabited," He has used the

37 *An Earnest Exhortation*, p. 3.

117

recent losses of war to speak to New England: "Be thou instructed that I depart from thee, and thou become desolate" (p. 1). For other examples of the subsequent ordeals that awaited the people, Mather turned to Scripture: the Book of Revelations warns *"Famine and Pestilence* are not far off. We have seen the Lord come riding among us upon his *Red horse"* (p. 2); the Book of Kings scorns young soldiers who celebrate victory: "let the young men now arise and play before us, it may be it will be bitterness in the latter end" (p. 11); because "the haughty *Daughters of Zion"* wear their "whorish Fashions," God is "fulfilling the third chapter of Isaiah" (p. 7). The young people of the second generation had waited for some sign of God's favor and had tried to view their victory in the King Phillip's War as such a sign. But Mather was still convinced of their apostasy, and in response to their rejoicing he launched one of his shrillest statements of impending doom.

Mather also found evidence of approaching doom in the movement of the heavens. In *Heaven's Alarm to the World, or . . . that fearful Sights and Signs in Heaven are the Presages of great Calamities at hand* (1681) he explained God's use of the stars and comets as warnings to his people of coming disasters and defined the role of the minister as an interpreter of the signs of the heavens, in contrast to the scientist, who is a mere observer and recorder: "Concerning those admirable and amazing works of God. . . . The scope of the ensuing discourse is only (that being most proper for one under my circumstances) to make a *Theological* Improvement thereof."[38] In answer to the "many that have published their Sentiments" and have used the recent heavenly signs to predict better times for New England, Mather offered a counterstatement: his studies revealed that events like a recent comet usually preceded war, persecution, and death: "I see little reason to conclude that it is an Omen of happy days to the world . . . Especially considering that

[38] *Heaven's Alarm to the World* (Boston, 1681, reprinted, 1682), p. A2.

we are fallen into the dregs of time, wherein the days must and shall be perilous. It was long since conjectured that in the Ages more immediately preceding the day of Judgment, *Comets* and other *fearful sights* should be more frequent than formerly" (p. A3). To support his prophecy Mather chose his text from Luke 21:11: "Fearful Sights and great Signs shall there be from Heaven."

As he shifted his focus back and forth from New England to biblical history, Mather found certain signs of the end of the world written in recent events: the anti-christ had appeared in the restoration of the English monarch; famines and plagues had ravaged both America and Europe; and symbolic earthquakes had occurred in the "statequakes" of political turmoil (pp. 1-3). While his more optimistic brethren were "sleeping and dreaming . . . nothing but worldly Prosperity at such times as this," Mather declared, "O take heed" because the signs of heaven foretell the coming of "miserable Dearths and Scarcity," of "War among nations," and of "Lamentable Deaths and destruction" (pp. 8-9).

For more support for his reading of the heavens, Mather found close connection between the nature of comets and the sins of youth. Just as comets are heavenly signs, the long hair of the young men and the fashionable attire of the young women are earthly signs of present corruption. Giving unusual variation upon the traditional Puritan imagery of cutting and loss, he warned the young men: "[Do not be as the Emperor who] when there was a long hairy *Comet* seen he did but deride at it, and make a Joke of it, saying, that it concerned the *Parthians* that wore long hair, and not him who was bald. . . . [For the comet prefigures] God's sharp Razors on mankind whereby he doth Poll; his Scythe whereby he doth shear down multitudes of sinful creatures . . . that Generation of hairy Scalps, who go on still in their trespasses" (p. 12).

Mather found significance in the comet for young women as well: "Will not the haughty daughters of Sion reform their Pride in apparel? Will they have *the attire of an har-*

119

lot? Will they lay out their hair and wear their false locks, their borders, and towers like *Comets* about their heads? Will they do so until God send his arrows from heaven to smite them down into the Grave where their days of darkness shall be many" (p. 16).

Although Mather was still "persuaded that God is about to open the windows of heaven and to pour down the Cataracts of his wrath, ere this Generation is passed away" (p. 12), he did indicate at the end of this sermon that he had begun to reshape his image of God the Father. With the slightest suggestion of hope that his people may yet be spared, he imagined God the Father offering comfort to his chosen: " 'O *New England, New England!* dost thou not know that the birds of prey are designing to devour thee? But my wings are broad enough to secure and shelter thee, when the black and stormy tempest shall break upon the world' " (p. 18). He was still certain that a disaster was inevitable but expressed a hope that "if we be found a praying, an humble, a reforming People, we need not doubt but that *under the shadow of his wings, we shall make our refuge, until the calamity be overpast*" (p. 18).

"Pray for the Rising Generation"

No analysis of Mather's early period is complete without a look at a few of his most vitriolic attacks upon the young in those sermons of the 1670's devoted entirely to the theme of the apostasy of the rising generation. For his first extended attack upon the rising generation Mather used the occasion of an execution of two men accused of murdering their master. In *The Wicked Mans Portion* (preached, 1674) he asserted that it was rebellion against their master that made the crime of the two murders most odious since *"rebellion* is a crime which they that are guilty of are *wicked overmuch."*[39] Thus Mather was able to make the central theme of this execution sermon the disobedience of

[39] *Wicked Mans Portion*, p. 8.

120

children *"especially such as are of* the Rising Generation" (p. A2). With the condemned men on the scaffold behind him, Mather told the children and young people of his audience that the sin of disobedience constituted a crime as serious as murder and as worthy of capital punishment: "So when children shall rebel against their Parents, their wickedness is excessively great. And such Children do usually die *before their Time"* (p. 9). As proof, Mather presented the confession of one of the murderers who had admitted that his life of sin began with his disobedience to his parents. Mather thereby reasoned that such has been the case with many criminals: "It is greatly to be observed that most of those that die upon the Gallows do confess that they have been guilty of disobedience to Parents" (p. 19).

Turning to the Scriptures, Mather recalled the stories of Absalom, who was destroyed for his rebellion against his father, and of the Sons of Eli, who were slain by God for failing to follow the counsel of their Father. These scriptural episodes of "those proud and profane young men . . . [who] died before their Time" should serve as reminders to those ambitious young men of the second generation who are so bold as to ignore the advice of their fathers: "Doth thy Father give thee good counsel? But Wilt thou not harken to him? This is a sign, that *the Lord will slay thee.* . . . This cometh of not hearkening to the voice of a Father" (p. 11). And Mather concluded that those who have not learned from scriptural example should heed God's most recent warning against the increasing discontent and impatience of the young men of New England: "Therefore, no marvel that such an awful Providence doth come to rebuke and humble us, that servants have conspired together to Kill their Master. . . . If ever *New England* be destroyed, this very sin of disobedience . . . will be the ruin of this Land" (p. 17).

Mather's bitterest attacks on the young appeared in three of his most popular writings: *Renewal of Covenant the Great Duty Incumbent on Decaying or Distressed Churches*

121

(1677), *Pray for the Rising Generation* (1678, reprinted in 1679), and *A Call from Heaven to the Present and Succeeding Generations* (1679), which included the title sermon and two others on the same theme, "A Discourse Concerning the Danger of Apostasy" and an untitled sermon on the doctrine: "that as it is the duty of all, so more especially of young men, to remember God their creator."[40] These sermons tell of God's "everlasting rejection" of the rising generation, of the flames of hell—flames made hotter by the tears of their weeping parents in heaven—and of their worldwide shame: "the Lord is wont to leave marks of his wrath upon such sinners. He brands them that all the world may be afraid of that iniquity" (p. 54). So striking are the statements on degeneracy in these sermons that I have already found occasions to quote passages at length in earlier sections of the present study. Two of these works, however, are also important because they provide evidence that Mather's message was beginning to meet resistance in the late 1670's and because they give early indications of the direction that Mather's preaching would begin to take in the 1680's.

Renewal of Covenant the Great Duty Incumbent on Decaying or Distressed Churches (1677) concerns Mather's most ambitious project of the 1670's, the institution of a colony-wide day of fast and covenant renewal. It was a sign of the changing times that it took Mather and his fellow ministers five years to convince the General Court to authorize such a fast in 1679. In this sermon Mather set out to present a rational and deliberate defense of the idea of covenant renewal against those critics who opposed all covenants on the grounds that Christians live under the New Dispensation, not under the laws of the Old Testament: "There are . . . [those] who have opposed the Doc-

---

[40] *A Call from Heaven*, title page. The reprinting of this sermon in 1684 indicates the continued popularity of Mather's theme of doom well into the new phase of assurance.

trine of the *Church-covenant,* not only as to *Renewals* thereof, but they strike at the thing itself, denying it to be an Ordinance of Christ. . . . Others have objected that we find nothing in the New Testament concerning a *Church Covenant.*"[41]

At the heart of the argument was a disagreement over typological interpretation of Scripture. While Mather had to admit slim scriptural evidence, he insisted that the denial of the covenant was based upon narrow literalism and upon a limited understanding of the purpose and values of the ritual of covenant renewal. He believed that the covenant had an important underlying social benefit because it reminded people of their subjection and submission before God. Mather used a metaphor of household subordination to describe the ritual's effect. He showed that *"this making* [of] *a Covenant doth imply a professed subjection to the revealed will of God"* just as when there is "a Covenant between Master and Servant, the Servant is bound to obey the Master, and to fulfill his will" (p. 4). The humbling involved in a day of general fast, Mather explained, could help not only to revive religion and reestablish God's favor, but to create a spirit of submission in the people and make them more willing to subject themselves to the covenant of their fathers.

Although Mather maintained this tone of calm deliberation for several pages, he would not rely on reasoning alone to carry his message to the hearts of the people. About midway through his sermon he shifted his strategy to present a more emotionally charged argument. He declared that, had the people not been so proud and stubborn, "that doleful Judgment and misery [the Indian Wars] which hath filled the Land would have been prevented" and "possibly we had not seen so many candlesticks . . . removed out of their places" (p. 12). He warned that unless the people now "subject themselves to the Government of Christ amongst his

[41] *Renewal of Covenant,* pp. A2-A3.

people," they continue to commit "a Sin that is wont to be attended with heavy Desolation" (p. 12). And what began as a rational defense ends with another incantation of the "lamentable decay" that makes "this Generation . . . far short of the former" and with prediction of impending wrath: "We have cause to fear another Storm of wrath, seven times greater than the last, is yet impending and not far off" (p. 16). In 1677 Mather had begun to recognize the need to defend his message, but he was not prepared to abandon it.

Two years later in *A Call from Heaven*, there was another indication that Mather was beginning to modify his theme. He opened by acknowledging the complaints of some clever young men who had turned the Scriptures against him in order to take issue with his assertions that the former age was better than the present and the future. They had argued that biblical history reveals the past age to be the "iron age" while the promised golden age of the millennium still lies ahead. Mather admitted the validity of this interpretation and even cited the words of the preacher in Ecclesiastes who declared it is "folly" to complain that *"the former days were better than these,"*[42] but he still scorned these rebellious "Professors of this Age [who] have more of Light and Notion, but less of Love and Zeal and Power than did appear in the Martyrs and blessed *Puritans"* (p. A2).

After this opening sarcasm, however, Mather's tone toward the younger generation was noticeably milder. For the first time he admitted that there had been many fine young men in the second generation, and he regretted the loss of so many of them in the recent Indian Wars. He expressed concern that the wars had left New England with a deep sense of frustration that he compared to "the desire and affections of a thirsty man carried out after water in a thirsty Land where no water is" (p. 4). Like Willard he also described the sons with images that had been previ-

---

[42] *A Call from Heaven*, p. A2.

ously reserved for eulogies of the founders: "God hath been removing the Pillars of this Generation, even those that have stood in the Gap and would have done much towards keeping out a Deluge of overflowing Judgments" (p. A3).

Mather also altered his image of God the Father significantly in order to appeal to the changing mood. He encouraged those who had lost earthly fathers to look upon God as a family friend who could act as a substitute parent to them. Just as after the death of a father one of the father's friends provides for the unfortunate children, so God the Father will provide if His aid is sought (pp. 25-26). To be sure, this sermon still had its share of images like that of "death climbing in at windows and carrying away young men apace" (p. 30), but it marked a change in Mather's central themes and the beginning of an adjustment of his metaphors and imagery to the changing times.

"The Seeds of Grace"

In the years between 1680 and 1685 Increase Mather struggled to redefine his position in relation to some of the important issues of his time, especially the question of full church membership for those who had not presented evidence of a conversion experience. Mather has been accused of opportunism in shifting his position on such issues during this period because some of his writings in 1685-1686 present a striking contrast to his works of the 1670's. However, three sermons published in the early 1680's—two in 1680 and one in 1684—show that the change in Mather's vision of the nature of God's church in New England and the character of man's relationship to God was difficult and gradual.

In *The Divine Right of Infant Baptism* (1680) Mather assumed the *persona* of a lawyer who used Scripture and precedents from antiquity to prove the case that the children of baptized members of the church had the right to be baptized as well. Originally an enemy of such liberal policies regarding baptism, Mather now attacked those staunch church members who feared that admission of the children of the second generation "half-way" members would defile the purity of the church. Mather opened with a preface by the Reverend Oakes accusing the members of the opposition of "barbarous and unnatural Persecution in their injurious and cruel usage of poor Children,"[43] and Mather redefined his own position: "It is an Act both of Charity and Justice to appear as an Advocate for those that being wronged are not able to speak for themselves. . . . And such is the case of the children of God's Servants when there are designs on foot to turn them out of the Lords and their Inheritance . . . [to] be cashiered and deprived of all the privileges thereof" (p. 1). In answer to the argument that infants are by their very natural states damned and wicked from birth, Mather used evidence from Janeway's *Token's for Children* to support his case that "many of the Elect of God have had the seeds of grace wrought in their Souls, whilst in their Childhood"; besides Janeway's stories Mather had found that "daily experience confirms the Truth of this" (p. 8). This sermon indicates Mather's changing attitude toward the young that he would develop and refine in subsequent writings in the 1680's.

More evidence of Mather's changing temper is contained in another sermon of 1680, *Returning Unto God the Great Concernment of a Covenant People.* In the beginning of this work Mather preached a new theme: the importance of the mission of the second and third generations and their special abilities for carrying on the work of their fathers. He reviewed the glorious history of the establishment of his own Second Church of Boston and then declared that the work of the new generation in the church was every bit as important as the mission of their fathers: "The greatest work is yet to do, viz. *sincere endeavors to keep Covenant.*"[44] Picturing the people as the moral leaders of the world,

[43] *The Divine Right of Infant Baptism* (Boston, 1680), p. 2 of preface.
[44] *Returning Unto God* (Boston, 1680), p. 2 of preface.

Mather tried to instill a sense of pride in his congregation. He stressed that New Englanders were still known and respected throughout Europe for their purity: "Let us remember . . . that the Eyes of the World are now upon us more than ever; Men will be inquiring what fruit is there of such a solemn Transaction?" (p. 2 of preface). And he emphasized the responsibility that New England had to Christians throughout the world; for if the American Puritans failed, "others will be discouraged from following the Example that hath been set before them, and they that bear ill will to Zion will reproach Religion and the holy ways of Christ" (p. 2 of preface).

There is also a difference, in this sermon, in the way Mather handles typological parallels. Although he still went to the Old Testament for types of the situation in New England (p. 2), he no longer pressed an obvious relationship between these types and the second generation. In *Returning unto God* he presented these figures only as scriptural examples, as "lessons," not prophecies, for New England. He said that the calamities that fell upon the Hebrews need not fall upon the colonists, if they would show their willingness to return to God. Still, Mather wavered in this sermon between his desire to charge the new generation with confidence and his own pessimism about the younger generation. Therefore, he returned to his standard cry that "a sad Degeneracy is evident to the view of every man that hath his heart exercised in discerning things of this nature" (p. 9) and that "there seems to be an hour of Temptation coming upon *all the World*, i.e. upon all the *Churches* of Christ *dispersed throughout the World*" (p. 15).

In the early 1680's many dedicated Puritans were beginning to take note of the fact that recent immigrants like Samuel Shrimpton, an Anglican and the richest man in New England, had reaped a great harvest in the markets of Boston and continued to live in pleasure and affluence, while many faithful and godly Puritan merchants seemed to go unrewarded by God. The people asked their ministers, "Does a just God reward the wicked and punish the good? If such situations are Providences of God, i.e. signs of his favor and anger, what is their meaning?" In a collection of sermons, *The Doctrine of Divine Providence Opened and Applied* (1684), Increase Mather labored with real sympathy to explain these puzzling actions of God: *"Sometimes there is a seeming contradiction in divine providence. . . .* The providences of God seem to Interfere with one another sometimes, One providence seems to look this way another providence seems to look that way, quite contrary to one another. . . . The works of God sometimes seem to run counter with his word so that there is dark and amazing intricacy in the ways of providence. This is a wheel within a wheel. Not only wise but good men have sometimes been put to a non-plus here."[45]

In an obvious attempt to mollify the open dissatisfaction of his people, Mather asserted that even though these rich Anglicans and impious merchants might appear to be comfortable and happy, "wicked men do not always go unpunished in this world, [for] wicked men notwithstanding their Prosperity are miserable" (p. 28). Instead of using the signs of providence as indications of God's anger, Mather now urged his audience to "call to mind the former times" (p. 58) and to look upon the whole history of New England as a sign of God's favor. In the second sermon in the collection, "The Works of Divine Providence are great and wonderful," Mather cited specific events in the record of the colony that had proved that ultimately the Puritans would remain God's saints, for "the Lord may afflict us . . . but he will not destroy us" (p. 58). Such a millenarian interpretation of New England's history would be the controlling metaphor of Cotton Mather's great history, the *Magnalia Christi Americana*.

The most striking demonstrations of the changes in Mather's message and language appeared in two works pub-

[45] *Doctrine of Divine Providence* (Boston, 1684), p. 43.

128

lished in 1686. Both revealed his endorsement of the return to the use of Old Testament types in order to focus upon the events in the New Testament rather than upon New England history, and they indicated his acceptance of the figure of Christ as the image of the deity that would dominate New England Puritanism for the next decade. The title alone, *The Greatest Sinner Exhorted and Encouraged to Come to Christ and that Now without Delaying*, disclosed Mather's new openness toward sinners; he left no question about his new position: "The Law *must be preached, inasmuch as thereby is the* Knowledge of Sin *without which men will never be duly sensible of their need of* Christ. *But it is the* Gospel (*and not the Law*) *which is* the WORD of Faith. *Sinners will never come to Christ except they be persuaded of His Ability and Willingness to save.*"[46]

Instead of choosing his text from Isaiah or Jeremiah, Mather found his meaning in Christ's words in John 6:37: "And him that come to me, I will in no wise cast him out." And instead of a patriarchal God the Father to be feared, Mather presented Christ as a lover to be embraced: "When God brings a man home to Christ, He lets him see that surpassing Excellency in his Person as to cause the soul to fall in love with Him, and to choose Christ rather than any other person. Cant. 5.9.10.16. '*What is thy beloved more than another's beloved? My beloved is the chiefst among ten thousand, yea he is altogether lovely.*' This is the Language of the real comer to Christ. The believing soul seeth Christ to be a lovely Christ indeed, and therefore cometh *to* Him as being enamoured *with* Him" (p. 5). For those who had feared that the mere desire to be saved was a selfish motive and not enough to be saved, Mather offered encouragement: "It is a very needless scruple which some have concerning their Coming to Christ, as if it were not right, *because Desire of Salvation puts them upon it*" (p. 6).

[46] *The Greatest Sinner* (Boston, 1686), p. 1 of preface.

129

Indeed, such a desire for redemption is the first sign of election.

One of the most intriguing developments in Mather's imagery is his revision of the image of the Last Judgment. Previously he had always regarded some segments of his congregation—such as the children or young people—as the group undergoing the wrathful judgments of God, but in this sermon he stressed the pleasanter aspects of Judgment Day for God's faithful, when Christ will reveal "the good Designs and gracious purposes which have been in the hearts of holy men" and will "speak of them to their praise before all the World" (p. 72). Mather explained that there has been some controversy over the exact nature of the Judgment Day: "Believers shall at the Day of Judgment be publically absolved and acquitted from the guilt of all their sins. A sentence of *Absolution* will be passed upon them. . . . It is Controverted among Divines whether the secret sins of Believers will be at all spoken of at the Day of Judgment: Some think they shall *not* because that would tend to their Reproach and shame. But there is much to be said for the Affirmative that they shall *some* of them be spoken of: For some of the Elect of God did commit their sins with such as are Reprobate" (p. 77).

Having considered the alternatives, Mather believed that the sins of the faithful would be acknowledged but they would not be enumerated, for Christ will say to his faithful, "Though thou wast guilty of many and great sins, yet because I died for thee, and thou didst believe in me, thy sins are all forgiven, and therefore do thou rejoice forever" (p. 78). For the believers the last day will be joyous as they join with Christ on the throne of heaven and assist him in passing judgment upon the sins of the reprobate: "Believers shall at the last judgment be as so many Kings with Crowns on their heads. . . . They shall reign on the earth then. . . . Though Christ only shall pass the Sentence of death upon the reprobate world, yet the Saints shall sit with Him upon Thrones of judgment as Assessors and Approbators of that judgment" (pp. 78-79). Since one only needs to believe in Christ to be saved, Mather assumed that there were probably few present that would be included with the reprobate.

Another of Mather's new themes is the equal opportunity that the ministers and the ordinary people have to merit God's rewards. In answering the criticism that ministers do little for average men because they hold themselves too far above the common people, Mather portrayed the ministers as husbandmen who labor by the sweat of their brows to bear fruit in God's vineyard and thereby harvest souls and reap God's favor for the entire community. The minister and average Christian are fellow workers in God's garden and equally capable of attaining rewards commensurate with their labors. And though he tried to stay clear of the heresy that one can merit God's favor through good works, he came very near indeed to this tenet: "So God does therefore love some Christians above others because they are more fruitful, and He has more glory to his Name by them than he has by others" (p. 107). Mather insisted that "God's love or *Good-will* does [not] at all depend upon the works or goodness of men." Yet, protest as he might, his imagery suggested the connection between good works and God's favor: "Men, if they have Vines or Trees in their Orchards which are very fruitful, they take a peculiar delight in them. So does the Lord do" (p. 107). Mather also echoed the early Puritan idea of the calling with his insistence that even those whose worldly vocations are lowly may take pride in their spiritual calling: "I will suppose a poor man, or a poor woman, that is little taken notice of by the world, but is much in prayer, and is upon all occasions getting others together and inciting them to Prayer and provoking them to love and to good works; I say the whole Town and Land fareth the better for that poor man, for that poor godly woman" (p. 114).

Mather tried to restore community pride by reasserting the early Puritan declaration: God "hath planted us in a very fruitful soil. What Liberties do we enjoy! Mention, if

131

you can, a People in the world so privileged as we are!"
(p. 115). There is no reference to the degenerate and strange
plant that Mather had found rising up in that vineyard a
few years before; instead of using the Old Testament
imagery of the corrupt vine, Mather now found his meaning in the New Testament imagery of Christ: "*I am the vine
and ye are the branches*," and in the words of Saint Paul:
"*We must be married to Him that was raised from the
dead that so we might bring forth fruit unto God*" (p. 116).

In 1686 Mather published a collection of sermons on the
nature of Christ, *The Mystery of Christ Opened and Applied,* a work frequently compared with Edward Taylor's
Christographia. After a preface in which he reprimanded
the preachers of New England for leaving the people in
ignorance and confusion about the meaning of the New
Dispensation and Christ's life, Mather attempted to rectify
some misunderstandings about Christ in his opening sermon with its reassuring title, "There is a Covenant of
Redemption." Mather followed Samuel Willard by defining the role of Christ through a metaphor that had special
meaning for the second-generation audience; he portrayed
Christ as an obedient son who adhered to the terms of the
family contract and performed the duties his Father demanded in order to reap a glorious inheritance for his
believers: "God and Christ . . . hold each other to the agreement which has been between them: the Father holds Christ
to the Terms of the covenant," and Christ did not "ever
desire to *have* any abatement thereof, which would be de-
rogatory from the Glory of God."[47] Mather explained that
even in the heavenly family there was some dickering over
the terms of the contract. At first the Father would only
grant the salvation of the Hebrews as reward for His Son's
sacrifice: "Those that make bargains begin low at first, so
God bids Christ *low,* comparatively at first" (p. 9). But
Christ bargained for the souls of all his believers through-

[47] *The Mystery of Christ* (Boston, 1686), p. 14.

132

out the world: "saith Christ 'I must have more than that; My blood is of greater value than to be given for them only' " (p. 9). Once they arrived at their pact, the relationship between the Father and Son was an ideal one: *"God and Christ do confide in one another.* They do, as it were, take one another's word. The Father trusts Christ" (p. 15). Such is the exemplary family bond that is a "consolation *to those that are concerned in this Covenant"* (p. 17).

In the rest of this sermon and in the remaining works of the collection, Mather labored to assure those who believe in Christ of the advantages of their faith on earth as well as in heaven. Most important is the sense of security and inner peace that the faithful derive from knowing that because Christ has atoned for their sins their belief in Him assures their salvation. For emphasis Mather described the uncertainty which non-believers must endure: "A poor Christless Creature, when he lies down at night, he knows not but that he may be in *Hell* before morning; when Morning comes he knows not but that he may be in *Hell* before Night, how sad is that! For a man to have the life of his Body hang in doubt is very uncomfortable, but the man is a Thousand times more miserable, the life of whose immortal soul is uncertain" (p. 144). And he cried out to the poor unbeliever to save himself from the feelings of guilt and shame, torments from which those who trust in Christ are free: "O Christless Sinner, look about thee and see where thou art! Thy soul is hanging over the mouth of hell by the rotten thread of a frail life: if *that* break, the devouring Gulf will swallow thee up for ever. . . . Awake thou that sleepest and rise from the Dead, and *Christ shall give thee Light. . . . Here is a matter of glorious Consolation, and Encouragement unto those that come to Jesus Christ.* There is admirable Sweetness and Consolation in these two or three words, JESUS THE MEDIATOR" (pp. 145-148).

As he had done throughout the 1680's, Mather again defined the important difference between the Old and the New Testament times. The words of the wrathful Father

133

and the Laws of the Old Testament do not apply to Christians in the same way that they applied to the Hebrews: "Jesus is better than *Moses*. The *New* Testament than the *Old*. . . . It is better being a Christian than a Jew" (p. 117). While the Old Testament Law still "cryeth and says, This is a poor guilty sinner, let him be *condemned* for ever," Mather assured that "the blood of Christ cries *louder* and says, 'All his sins are satisfied for, and therefore let him be *pardoned*, and his soul live for ever' " (p. 151). Under the New Dispensation the mediation of Christ has become the believer's protection against the anger of the Father so that when the Christian arrives in heaven he will be greeted and defended by his mediator and redeemer: "By him we have *Access unto the Father*. Jesus the *Son* of God does as it were take the believing soul by the hand, and leadeth him into the *Presence*-Chamber. He opens the door for him, and presents him before the *Father of Glory*, and says "Behold O Father, Here is a soul that I died for, this soul is washed in my blood, and therefore do thou look upon him with a favorable eye for my sake" (p. 151).

In a striking departure from the rhetoric of doom and decay, Mather raised his voice in 1686 in exaltation of the message of redemption and assurance: *"Are you the Seed of Christ?* Are you become His Children in respect of a Spiritual Regeneration? *If any man be in Christ, he is a new creature*, 2 Cor. 5:17 Hast thou a new *heart*, a new *head*, a new *tongue*, a new *life*, and all? . . . It is a comfortable consideration to think on the Ancient Love of God. If thou are concerned in this Covenant, God loves *thou*. . . . Thy Name was written in the Lamb's *Book of Life* before the foundation of the world, even from all Eternity . . . Hence thy Salvation is *certain*" (pp. 18-19). With Christ as the father of the New World and the members of the churches of New England assured of their salvation in Christ: "By [being] reconciled to God by the *death* of his Son, we are saved by his life. . . . Christ as Mediator is Father of the *new world*" (pp. 139-140). Increase Mather was now convinced that the sacrifice of the Son of God had reconciled the sons of the rising generation with the Father: "God the Father has received full satisfaction in the Obedience of His Son, Jesus Christ" (p. 157).

Because the change in Mather's thought at first appears strikingly rapid and complete, it has raised questions about Mather's intellectual integrity. However, the process of development of Mather's religious message that became obvious about 1678 and culminated in 1685 and 1686 must be viewed in the larger context of the general shift in the meaning of Puritan theology that had begun to receive expression in the works of some ministers as early as the 1660's. For nearly a decade Mather strongly resisted the trend of the new theology before he began to recognize the necessity for striking new chords in the hearts of the people. Even in 1686 he had by no means totally abandoned his rhetoric of wrath, as he demonstrated in an execution sermon of that year that echoes his *Wicked Mans Portion* of 1675. Furthermore, the period in which Mather was reshaping his vision of man's relationship to God was an important and even crucial time in his own life: by 1679 he was forty years old, he had been acknowledged at home and abroad as one of the two or three most prominent ministers in New England, and he had an intelligent and sensitive son, Cotton, nearing the age of twenty-two, who in a few years would begin to preach a message of assurance far more radical than his father's. The 1680's were the years in Increase Mather's life when he was most open to the forces of change.

CLOGGING MISTS AND
OBSCURING CLOUDS

The Search for New Meaning

*Any human language represents a special kind of order
superimposed upon existence. Generations live in it as a
habitat in which they are born and die. . . . Thus the poets
or seers who purify the language of the tribe are truly
world-makers, and the "unacknowledged legislators of the
world."*

Amos N. Wilder, *The Language
of the Gospel*

IT TOOK Increase Mather until the mid-1680's to accommodate his message and imagery to the changing needs of the
people, but other ministers like Samuel Willard and Urian
Oakes had been searching throughout the 1670's for ways
of revitalizing the meaning of Puritanism for a new generation. The writings of these ministers vacillated between the
images of God as a wrathful Father and as a benevolent
deity and between the themes of imminent damnation and
assurance of salvation. In intricate ways the imagery and
themes of those concerned men touched the ambivalent
feelings of the second generation and guided them through
their quest for a cultural identity of their own in the American wilderness. Thus their works reflected the period of
psychological adjustment of the new generation to the religion and society it had inherited.

Of all the ministers preaching in the 1670's, Samuel Willard was the most acutely aware of the needs of the younger
generation. Painstakingly, he sought to recapture the Pauline spirit of the early Puritan fathers that had been the
source of the profound spiritual confidence of the founders.
The evolution of Willard's thought and language deserves

the detailed examination it receives in the second part of this chapter. In addition to Willard there were several other ministers who sought throughout the 1670's to redefine the relationship of the rising generation to God and the church. Men like Urian Oakes, John Oxenbridge, Thomas Thatcher, and William Hubbard found unsatisfactory the vision of the younger generation as totally degenerate and doomed. But they were not prepared to follow Solomon Stoddard in his readiness to cast aside stormy issues of doctrine and church polity in order to welcome the new generation into immediate full church membership.[1] Caught between the iconoclasm of Stoddard and the resistance of Increase Mather, these ministers attempted to retain the doctrinal purity of their religion while revivifying its language and meaning for a new generation of Puritans.

"A GENERATION OF GREAT HOPES AND GREAT FEARS"

The earliest challenge to the theme of the declension of the rising generation was made by the youthful spokesman for the second generation, Eleazar Mather (1637-1669). Eleazar was the fifth of the patriarch Richard Mather's six sons, four of whom became eminent ministers of the Gospel: Samuel, the eldest (1626-1671), and Nathaniel, the third child (1630-1697), were born in England, to which they returned after graduating from Harvard. Born in 1637 and 1639 respectively, Eleazar and Increase were the only two of Richard's six children born in America. Increase, who was clearly the favorite of his parents, far outshone his older brother Eleazar in early piety and in intellectual precocity. Increase surpassed Eleazar in school and the only reason they happened to graduate together from Harvard in the class of 1656 is that Increase's ill health interrupted his studies for a year. While Eleazar waited for two years after graduation to be called to a ministerial post, Increase

[1] See Miller on Solomon Stoddard in *From Colony to Province*, pp. 227-231, 256-261, 277-280.

achieved renown at Trinity College, Dublin, where he was chosen a Fellow of the College and was awarded an M.A. degree. Although Increase was always inclined to return to England permanently after his five-year stay there, Eleazar was content to serve as the pastor of the church at the outpost of Northampton (1658-1669), where he was the immediate predecessor of Solomon Stoddard. Eleazar's rather unconventional view of the authority of the fathers may have prepared the people at Northampton for the radical changes Stoddard would propose in reinterpreting the rules for admission to full church membership.[2]

In his sermon, *A Serious Exhortation to the Present and Succeeding Generation in New England,* preached before his untimely death in 1669 and published in 1671 and 1678, Eleazar Mather took the elders to task for their irresponsibility regarding the young. He argued that any deficiencies the fathers found in the sons reflected upon the errors of the fathers themselves. Mather was diplomatic enough to admit that his generation had many shortcomings, but he tried in this sermon to put the elder generation on the defensive: "Men, Brethren, and Fathers, you had once another Spirit, had you not? *A right New-England Spirit.* Oh! should I knock at your breast? . . . Are you the same men you were? Are you not strangely changed? Have you as much of God as you had? Hath not the World got something? Wife and Children something? Trials and Temptations of a *New Place* or hard beginnings got something?"[3]

Mather used the early rhetoric of the first generation to remind the fathers that "it was not for your sake only, but for the sake of your Children that God made himself known unto you" (p. 14). He appealed to the pride of the elders: *"To you is committed a special opportunity. . . .* They are a generation of your betrustments, a Generation committed to your care and charge to bring up for the Lord" (pp. 15-

---

[2] *American Pulpit*, pp. 151-160; and *Magnalia*, I, 457-458.

[3] Eleazar Mather, *A Serious Exhortation*, p. 21. Perhaps it is a sign that the times were changing that this sermon was reprinted in 1678.

16); and he appealed to their self-interest: *"What comfort will this be* . . . [for there is] no greater joy than [to know] that you have had a care of Posterity. . . . This glads the hearts of godly Parents" (p. 18). Finally, he resorted to pleading: "I charge thee. . . . Oh what love, what affections, what bowels towards your Children? Have you none?" (p. 16) and to exhortation: *"Get a sympathizing Spirit with the gasping, groaning, bleeding, and dying condition of that Generation.* . . . Oh! look upon them with an eye of pity" (p. 25).

In response to the elders' assertion that the young people had not demonstrated enough religious fervor, Mather presented his justification. He declared that lack of external evidence of zeal does not prove the absence of religious commitment, for the situation in New England had not afforded the second generation the opportunity to display its zeal. Therefore, the young should not be scorned for failing to undergo the conversion experience because they had been "freed from such Persecutions, Afflictions, etc." which the founders had experienced in England and, as a result, "have not had such opportunities their fathers had to know and see what was in their hearts" (p. 17). However, Mather insisted that the elders should not believe that these circumstances had reduced the stature of the new generation or the importance of its work: "In respect to the weightiness of the work, the work of one Generation is no less than of another. . . . Oh, how weighty and difficult is their work that are now called out" (pp. 7, 30). Indeed, the new generation "call for the utmost care and help" because it is "a poor needy Generation hard bestead, it may be more than their fathers in some respects" (pp. 16-17).

To the young, Mather offered his sympathy: "You are a Generation of great hopes and great fears" (p. 28). The elders he rebuked for frustrating the efforts of their children: "That which concerns their Interest is made the Butt of Contention" (p. 26). From the Scriptures, which had so often been used to confirm the corruption of the rising generation, Mather drew a new interpretation: "The second Generation seldom or ever prove total Apostates, but the First are deep, secret Heart-revolters" (p. 21).

A minister for whom the problems of the younger generation presented a serious dilemma was John Oxenbridge (1609-1674). Successor of John Davenport, who had led the First Church of Boston in its strenuous opposition to the "Half-Way Covenant," Oxenbridge was quite different in background and temperament from his predecessor. Davenport, who was known for his gravity of countenance, had come to New England in 1638 and was nearly seventy when he was installed as pastor in 1668. Oxenbridge, who was ten years younger than Davenport, had come to America in 1669 and was immediately noted for his elegant writing, eloquent preaching, and habitual conversation. When he was unanimously elected to serve as co-pastor with the young James Allen (1632-1710), Oxenbridge must have been somewhat perplexed by the contrast between the great vitality of the people and their drive for more open admission and the rigidity of the membership rules as they had evolved in New England.[4] Forced by the elders to take a strict stand on the admission of young people into the church, he nevertheless recognized that the survival of the church depended upon an increase in the number of younger members. He was accordingly torn between his own desire to encourage the rising generation and the insistence of the elders that the church maintain its purity. One of his sermons published in 1670 demonstrates his ambivalence.

Even the title of Oxenbridge's sermon of 1670 suggests a balance of chastisement and comfort: *A Quickening Word for Hastening a Sluggish Soul to a Seasonable Answer to the Divine Call, Published by a poor Sinner that found it such to him.* Unlike those ministers who preached that the people must await God's call, Oxenbridge suggested that man may "seek the Lord with desire, design, and hope

---

[4] *American Pulpit*, pp. 170-171, 93-98; and *Magnalia*, I, 321-331, 597-599.

of finding."[5] And in order to lead the unregenerate to seek the Lord, Oxenbridge modified the fearful image of God the Father with the gentle image of Christ the Redeemer. He began by warning that "God's hand hath been lifted up on one or other of you" and has threatened to destroy New England with "Drought," "Storm," and "Sickness" (p. 14). Next, in a striking new metaphor he compared New England to the adulteress in the Book of Revelation of whom the Lord has spoken: " *'I gave her space to repent of her fornication and she repented not: Behold, I will cast her into a bed, and them that commit Adultery with her into great Tribulation, except they repent their deeds'*: If she leave not the bed of Security, she shall know the Bed of Anxiety. . . . [Thus] God will lay you fast upon a Bed of Destruction" (pp. 13-14).

Then, with a masterful twist of his imagery, Oxenbridge retained the metaphor of the lover but shifted from the image of the adulteress to the image of Christ as lover, "knocking and calling till the dews of the evening fall upon him" (p. 16) and waiting to embrace the poor sinner who will answer his entreaty: "Hadst thou any love and desire kindled in thy Souls to Christ, thou wouldst not be at rest . . . Oh think how dearly Jesus Christ hath engaged you to love him" (p. 16). In this sermon Oxenbridge also presented Christ as a kinsman who has come to help the young men redeem their rightful inheritance: "Christ thy Kinsman came to Redeem thee" (p. 17).

But as encouraging as Oxenbridge appeared to be in this imagery, the ambivalence of his position remained apparent throughout his career. In *A Quickening Word* the answer to a hypothetical sinner who cried out, *"Oh Sir, how gladly would I embrace this Exhortation: but I fear my time is past . . . he (Christ) will now not be found, and then, in vain is all my seeking,"* was only that "there is a sin unto death, and a sin that is not unto death" (p. 18). The ambi-

[5] John Oxenbridge, *A Quickening Word* (Cambridge, 1670), p. 4.

141

guity of this answer testifies to the hesitancy of Oxenbridge to offer any answers; the members of his congregation were free to interpret this oracle as optimistically or pessimistically as their temperaments would allow. Oxenbridge was not prepared to offer real assurance of God's forgiveness. Again in his *New-England Freemen Warned and Warmed* in 1673 he acknowledged the grave spiritual difficulties of the young people who did not have outward signs like circumcision to prove that they were among the elect. But after sympathizing with their plight, he gave the standard exhortation: "Your backsliding will not only be vanity, but vexation [and] for this you will lose the good ye have had."[6] Although Oxenbridge was deeply aware of the problem of the younger generation, it would remain for other ministers to provide the keys for change. One such minister was residing at Harvard College in Cambridge.

"NEW ENGLAND PLEADED WITH"

Urian Oakes (1631-1681), a tutor at Harvard from 1671, President *pro tempore* from 1675, and President from 1680 until his death in 1681, was a most dedicated spokesman of the second generation. After a seventeen-year visit to England from 1654 to 1671, Oakes returned to the colony as the minister of the Cambridge Church. Son of Edward Oakes (d. 1689), a prominent citizen who served as a selectman for twenty-nine years and representative to the General Court for seventeen years and who outlived his son, Urian was noted for his good nature, his rich sense of humor, and his diminutive stature.[7] Cotton Mather reports that observers said of Oakes, "If good nature could ever carry one to heaven, this youth hath enough to carry him thither."[8] Oakes' commencement addresses during his years as president of Harvard were rich in wit and grace as he sought to

6 Oxenbridge, *Freemen Warned*, p. 19.
7 *American Pulpit*, pp. 140-143; *Magnalia*, II, 114-118.
8 *Magnalia*, II, 114.

guide the college through the darkest days of its history. Always a defender of the young, Oakes pleaded with the fathers of the college in his first commencement oration in 1675: "We beg you, O nursing fathers of the University, assume toward your children the disposition and feeling of parents, pardon those humbly seeking refuge; it is not fair for old men, not prone to those things that youth do, to censure boys."[9] Perhaps his extended absence from New England and the close contact with the young men at Cambridge gave him a special objectivity and a particular awareness of the problems of youth, for in his sermons of the 1670's Oakes sought to ameliorate the generational struggle and to seek new ways of adapting the word of God to the younger people. "His English," wrote the literary historian Moses Coit Tyler, "furnishes the most brilliant examples of originality, breadth, and force of thought, set aglow by flame of passion, by flame of imagination, to be met with in our sermon-literature from the settlement of the country down to the Revolution."[10] Three of his sermons published in the 1670's reveal his efforts at reshaping the religious language and imagery to address the new generation.

Though religious decline was the major theme of his election sermon of 1673, *New-England Pleaded with*, Oakes clearly offered a counter-theme to the notion that continued decay and doom were inevitable. Oakes was dedicated to the principle that men could use their intelligence and reason to try to understand God's ways and to regain God's favor. Thus, he chose for his text Deut. 32:29, "Oh that they were wise, that they understood this, that they would consider their latter end."[11] To a congregation torn by con-

[9] As quoted in Morison, *Harvard College*, II, 421. For excerpts from Oakes' commencement addresses and commentary on his style and humor, see pp. 396-398 and 430-435.

[10] Moses Coit Tyler, *A History of American Literature, 1607-1765* (New York: G. P. Putnam's Sons, 1878; reissued, Ithaca, N.Y.: Cornell University Press, 1949), p. 269; see also pp. 402-405.

[11] Oakes, *New-England Pleaded with*, p. 1.

fusion and doubt, Oakes presented a sophisticated analysis of the relationship between man and God and of the parallels between the Old Testament Hebrews and New England.

In order to modify the inordinately one-sided image of God as a wrathful and jealous father, Oakes explained that the image of God presented in the Scriptures and by the preachers is never a totally accurate representation of God's nature. In the Scriptures God has sought to make Himself comprehensible to men through metaphor: God uses "expression borrowed from the manner of men" (p. 6), but the ministers may choose to emphasize certain passages of Scripture and thus limit the people's understanding of God. As an example, Oakes pointed out that "the Lord doth not really and properly carry himself as a Father that stands wringing his hands over a prodigal Son, and [who] says 'O that thou wouldst be wise . . . and consider what will be the issue of these lewd ways and courses' " (p. 6). Such had been the popular image of God in New England. Oakes argued that God, who has the power to alter human lives instantly, need not lament over his people as an earthly father. In order to broaden his congregation's understanding of the various images of God, Oakes opened his sermon with quotations from two complementary passages of Scripture: in Deut. 28:58-59 the people may fear the wrathful voice of God as He threatens *"Plagues wonderful, and the Plagues of thy seed even great Plagues, and of long continuance, and sore sicknesses"* (title page), but in Mic. 2:3-4 they may hear the milder tones of a sorrowful God: *"O my People what have I done unto thee, and wherein have I wearied thee? . . . I brought thee up out of the Land of Egypt, and redeemed thee out of the house of servants"* (title page).

In this sermon Oakes also addressed himself to the subject of the minister's role as interpreter of God's meaning and the prophetic use the preacher may make of biblical history. As an example of the ideal preacher, Oakes presented the figure of Moses, whose last sermon to the Israelites contained all that his people needed to know in order to endure the trials God would send them: "*Moses* by the spirit of Prophesy" gave his people "as in a true Glass, the feature of that People as it looked in after times" (p. 1). He predicted the people's apostasy and the "dreadful and almost unparalleled judgments and calamities" God would send, but he also assured that in the end God would "glorify himself in their deliverance. He would certainly preserve alive *an Holy Seed* . . . and show himself faithful and bountiful even to an undeserving people" (p. 3). Had the Hebrews only heeded the teaching of Moses, just as New England might yet heed the words of its ministers, they could have understood the trials of God and thus avoided many of their afflictions. For it was true for the Israelites, as it is true of all peoples, that "the ground and occasion of that Misery and Ruine . . . [was] namely their want of Counsel and Understanding" (p. 4). Oakes believed that disaster could be avoided if men would increase in wisdom: "The Cure, the Help, the only Remedy or rather that which would have saved them and secured their Nation with all the concernments of it from those Ruins, and prevented such a sad issue and calamitous event, namely Wisdom" (p. 4). For Oakes a repetition of the events of biblical history was not inevitable in New England; indeed, the Bible could teach a wise people how they might escape ruin.

After he had painstakingly established his principles for understanding God through His sacred Scriptures, Oakes took up what he considered to be New England's most critical problem—the lack of unity among the people and the resulting atmosphere of tension and anxiety within the society. Upon his return to the colony in 1671 after his seventeen-year stay in England, he found "that the Contentions which are among us are not merely sudden . . . of anger and passion . . . but that there seems to be a Forward and perverse spirit mingled among us" (p. 36). His search for the underlying cause of this perverse spirit led him to examine the conflict between the generations. But unlike so many of his peers, who laid full blame upon the rising

generation, Oakes found both generations to be at fault.
He knew how to mock the pretensions of youth:

"All thy ways of sin will end in Judgment or a dreadful
sentence of wrath, and everlasting separation from God.
Thou are now pleasing thy self in the ways of thy own heart.
. . . Now the Gospel is foolishness, Religion is foolishness,
Praying in secret, walking humbly, and mournfully with
God is foolishness in thy deluded apprehension: and the
people of God that deny themselves . . . are a company of
weak and foolish men in thy valuation; but who dost thou
think will be the fool at last. Oh think over and over what
will be the end of Impenitency" (p. 15).

However, he soundly chastised the elders as well for their
"private selfish spirit," which had caused them to "neglect
the Rising Generation among us" (p. 32): "Alas! *What good
do we do them?* Our Children are little beholden to us. We
own them so far as to baptize them: But then Fare ye well
Children, we have nothing more to do with you. This is
(as a wise Man said ingeniously) *just as you are wont to
Brand your Cattle, and then turn them into the woods*"
(p. 58).

In spite of this serious division in the people, Oakes still
possessed an abiding faith in the ability of men to understand and rectify their problems. In the conclusion of this
sermon of 1673 Oakes expressed his belief that the generations could overcome their differences so that *"verily, the
Latter End of such men and women shall be Unspeakable
peace and Happiness"* (p. 64).

A year later Oakes continued to voice the theme of assurance that would become central to the Puritan sermon
in the 1680's. The title of his artillery election day sermon of 1674 expressed his faith: *The Unconquerable, All-
Conquering, & More-Than-Conquering Souldier or the Successful War which a Believer Wageth with the Enemies of
his Soul: As also the Absolute and Unparalleled VICTORY
that he attains finally over them through the love of God
in Jesus Christ.* St. Paul provided the text of assurance of

146

Oakes' sermon: *"In all these Things we are more than Conquerers, through him that loved us."*[12] In this sermon Oakes presented images that would dominate many of the sermons of the last two decades of the century. He imagined God's people enclosed in a garden of God's love with "Satan and an evil world [trying to] do their worst against Believers that are thus entrenched in and walled about with the Love of God" (p. 2). Besides shifting the burden of guilt for New England's trials from the rising generation to an external enemy, he also developed the new image of Christ the Savior as he tried to charge his young listeners with confidence: *"Every true Believer is a Soldier, and engaged in a Warfare"* (p. 4). And every Christian soldier could rely upon Christ as an invincible ally in the field: "He [Christ] represents to us the Christian as a person that may be opposed, combated, and contended withal, but never routed, run down, totally defeated or overthrown in any Engagement" (p. 2). It is certain, Oakes concluded, that "his called and Faithful, and Chosen shall certainly *more than overcome* at last" (p. 22).

As Oakes neared the end of his years, he failed to remain so hopeful about New England. In one of his last writings, *A Seasonable Discourse* (1682), published only a few months after his death in 1681, Oakes presented an attack upon the members of the rising generation. Perhaps his anger had been aroused by his trying years at Harvard College, which had been torn by financial problems, political factionalism, and student unrest, for now Oakes bitterly scorned the younger generation for their "deceit and errors" and their "hypocrisy and sloth."[13] In their relationship to their parents he found the young to be "weary of family government" and longing "to be at liberty . . . to live at their own hand, that they may not be troubled with commands, counsels, corrections of their pious Parents," a generation "that

[12] Urian Oakes, *The Unconquerable . . . Souldier* (Cambridge, 1674), p. 1.

[13] Urian Oakes, *A Seasonable Discourse* (Cambridge, 1682), p. 20.

cannot bear reproofs, admonitions, the rod of discipline" (p. 22).

Even more disturbed by the younger generation's continued unwillingness to embrace wholeheartedly the church of their fathers, Oakes charged that on the "Road of Duty" the young "jog on in a formal, heartless manner," uttering *"cold, dead, sleepy Prayers"* and offering *"dull and drowsy work"* (p. 8). Because of their weaknesses and irresponsibility, they have treated God's covenant capriciously:

"[They] are sorry [that] they are so far engaged in Church-covenant and fellowship, that they are under such strict solemn ties, and obligations to service and obedience. It troubles them that they are tied up so short, so chained, so bound with the bonds of the Covenant, that their hands are so manacled that they cannot act as they would, feet so fettered that they cannot walk as they please. They cannot endure these shackles, could wish they were handsomely quit of their Covenant-engagements which hold them in, abridge and infringe their liberty to live as they list. They are impatient of being staked down to so short a tether, that they cannot range as they please" (pp. 19-20).

Although Oakes himself had been a leader in offering hope and confidence to the new generation, he was now determined to resist the tendency toward a new religious message of assurance. He declared that the younger people desired "smooth things, not right things prophesied unto them" because "they cannot endure sound Doctrine" (p. 20); they are a generation that "love[s] dawbing with untempered Morter, to be stroked, and flattered and strengthened in a way of looseness, and to have Pillows sewed under their Elbows" (p. 20). Sadly, Oakes joined those who foresaw New England's destiny prophesied in the apostasy of the Old Testament Hebrews: "I need not tell you that *Israel* here is the same with *Jacob* there: Children descended from that holy, powerful Patriarch, whose Names were *Jacob* and *Israel*, inheriting their Father's Name, even when they had little of His Piety" (pp. 12-13).

148

In 1671 Oakes had set out to redefine God's relationship to New England and to restore the people's spiritual confidence, but the new generation, still confused and unsettled, was not yet prepared to respond to that message. *A Seasonable Discourse* reflected Oakes' frustration and dismay. Yet even at the end of this work he still had hope that "doubtless, the Lord remembers the kindness of our youth . . . when we came after Him into this Wilderness" (p. 24). He recalled nostalgically "those Worthies that laid the Foundation of this Plantation" and concluded "He hath many among us at this day of the same spirit" (p. 24).

"WORDS IN SEASON"

One minister whose eighty-three years permitted him to witness the maturity of three generations of New England Puritans was William Hubbard (1621-1704). Hubbard was never quite certain that there had actually been a decline of religion in New England in the 1670's, and he tended to distrust the mythologizing of New England history and the prophecies of doom, particularly those of Increase Mather. Hubbard's opposition to Increase Mather is well-known. As preacher at Ipswich Hubbard occupied one of the most enviable positions for a minister in New England, for Ipswich possessed a larger degree of talent and intelligence than almost any other town.[14] In 1676 he published his own *History of the Indian Wars,* an account of events in the wars to balance the spiritualized rendering in Increase Mather's *Brief History of the War with the Indians.* Hubbard's later *General History of New England,* commissioned by the General Court and completed in 1682, was never published because of Mather's opposition.[15] Hubbard was a shrewd man who nevertheless brought to the pulpit of the 1670's a rational voice and an intellectual skepticism

[14] *American Pulpit,* pp. 148-150.

[15] See Perry Miller on Hubbard in *From Colony to Province,* pp. 135-136 and 140-141.

unmatched by his peers. Accordingly, his departures from conventional preaching and from traditional doctrine were subtle enough to avoid the condemnation of his fellow ministers. Thus, even in those sermons that at first appear to be standard jeremiads, there are important differences in his rhetoric that seem to have been designed to counter the myth of decline and doom.

In *The Happiness of a People* (1676) he began traditionally with an eloquent description of the planting and growth of the New England settlement: "The time was not long since, that we in New England might have said with Job, 'The eye that saw us, whether of friends or foes, was ready to bless us, or envy our prosperity.' . . . When God first brought this vine out of another land where it might be much over-shadowed, he cast out the heathen, and planted it; he caused it to take deep root, and it was ready to fill the land, the hills began to be covered with the shadow of it, its boughs began to look like goodly cedars: it might have been said in some sense that we sent our boughs to the Seas and our branches to the rivers."[16] But later in the sermon Hubbard expressed his bewilderment that a people who had had such an auspicious beginning now complained that the best days of the colony had passed: "But now we may take up the Lamentation following: 'Why are our hedges broken down, and the wild boar out of the wood doth waste it, and the wild beast out of the field doth devour it?' " (p. 49). Although Hubbard did admit that it seemed that "God hath a controversy with New-England" and that "the rod of affliction hath not only budded and blossomed but brought forth its fruit" (p. 54), he was not ready to conclude that a decay of religion had already occurred or that the rising generation was the cause of God's displeasure. Indeed, he was convinced that "there are many hopeful buds [that] spring up among the Rising Generation" (p. 55). Surely, there "is something [which] lies

[16] William Hubbard, *The Happiness of a People* (Boston, 1676), p. 49.

as a worm at the root and vitals of Religion, threatening and endangering a great decay" and which may "bring a Consumption upon the very vitals and power of Religion" (p. 55), but Hubbard believed this almost imperceptible infection could be found only deep within the people themselves—"some secret heart evil . . . that neither civil nor ecclesiastical censures can reach" (p. 55). Thus Hubbard shunned the rhetoric of decay and doom, and during the next six years he sought ways to use the power of language to expose and cure the people's "secret heart evil."

By the time Hubbard published his *The Benefit of a Well-Ordered Conversation* in 1684, his efforts to provide new metaphors for new religious problems had been recognized. In their preface to the sermon John Allin and Joshua Moodey praised Hubbard as a preacher who could compose "Words in season [which] are as Apples of Gold in Pictures of Silver" and whose *"fitness of words (well tuning them) is the grace of them, and puts wheels to the Chariots to carry them to the mind."*[17] Perhaps Hubbard's choice of the text revealed his own awareness of the importance of language as the key to man's life: Psa. 51:27: *"And to him that ordereth his Conversation aright will I shew the salvation of God"* (p. 1). At the risk of being accused of Arminianism, Hubbard made the central theme of this sermon man's ability to conduct his affairs and order his life with the aim of meriting God's favor and grace. Rather than state this theme explicitly, however, Hubbard used metaphor to carry his meaning. He established that the word "conversation" in the Psalms did not simply refer to spoken conversation but served as a metaphor of all of the activities of a man's life because "according to the Original word (conversation), nothing is intended therein but the way or course of a man's life" (p. 3). Thus, a man can conclude that "to him that ordereth" his life aright God will show his salvation.

[17] William Hubbard, *The Benefit of a Well-Ordered Conversation* (Boston, 1684), p. A3.

151

To those who had scruples about occasional disruptions in the order of their lives that resulted from human failings, Hubbard offered consolation. "According to the Metaphor usual in the Scriptures" (p. 3) life is a journey along a path, and men should not be surprised to find the way to be less than straight. Indeed, Christians must be flexible and re-silient: they should anticipate delays and join "the wisdom of the Serpent with the innocence of the Dove" (p. 5) to overcome adversity: "As Horse-men in a Battle, that turn this way and that way as occasion serves; yet still aims to carry on the main design . . . so must every Christian, in a sense shape his course according as the Wind and Current; . . . or as the Seaman's Phrase is when they pass through difficult and dangerous passages on either hand, aloof for one and bear up for another, yet still keeping on in the direct way that leads to the Haven of rest and happiness" (pp. 4-5).

Hubbard also used metaphors from the practical life of the skillful seaman or shrewd merchant in order to stress his point that for every Christian "there is a need of a great deal of skill and artifice, as well as care and industry in the ordering the frame of our lives" (p. 5). His suggestion that the saint might do well to possess the wisdom of the serpent represented a departure from the traditional use of the serpent as a symbol for repulsive evil, but Hubbard recognized that he was addressing a new generation in a new phase of New England's history and his "apples of Gold" must "fit the season."

In this sermon Hubbard also tried to lift the spirits of his people by clarifying how the New Dispensation of Christ had modified the meaning of the Old Testament for New England and how Christ's redemptive act had affected the lives of every Christian. While Hubbard warned against the misuse of Old Testament types for making false, overly spe-cific prophecies about New England, he argued that the most important lesson to be learned from biblical history is that men tend to bring their own troubles upon themselves by their failure to use their God-given reason: "If we cast an eye upon all the following Histories of the Church in succeeding Ages, we shall find that much of those sufferings which have fallen upon the Generation of the just, might either have been prevented or much abated if they had governed their affairs by a suitable measure of Wisdom in their concerns with themselves or others" (p. 47).

Because Christ has given his believers every reason to look forward joyfully to eternal happiness rather than backward to the wrath and damnation threatened under the Old Covenant, Christians need not repeat the errors of the Hebrews. When the Puritans must compare themselves with the Hebrews, Hubbard encouraged them to keep in mind the possibilities for contrasts between the two peoples as well as parallels: "It was a joyful time with *Israel* when they encamped in the *Wilderness* at *Elim*, where [there] were . . . twelve wells of water," but Hubbard emphasized that with Christ "there are wells of Salvation now under the Gospel in every station" (p. 80). To those who have feared that evil invaders would break down New England's wall of protection, Hubbard assured: *"We have a strong City, Salvation will God appoint for Walls and Bulwarks*: mountains of Brass and Gates of Iron are not so strong as the promise of God" (pp. 86-87). Against the menacing storms of political struggle with England, Hubbard was also certain that New England would be protected: "The storm may be sharp, yet it will be but short. If Christ be in the Ship, all that are embarked shall be saved" (p. 91). With certainty Hubbard declared, "The Ship of Christ's Church may be tossed, yet it shall be preserved" (p. 91) and "The Church may sing her triumphant Song in all her troubles" (p. 86).

Hubbard's confidence in the power of human reason and understanding applied to the subject of child-rearing and the religious education of children as well. Because he recognized that the use of coercion in exacting religious devotion from children was harmful, he spoke out in opposition to such practices, which he felt were detrimental to mature spiritual development. The eldest of three sons and a father of three children himself, Hubbard had discovered that in New England "none are found more vicious in their lives than such as have had the best advantage for piety by their education" (p. 13) and that "none ever proved worse Children than those who have had the best of men for their Parents" (p. 13). Therefore, he warned parents: "Though you may by force imprint another motion for the present, yet it will not hold long" (p. 15). In the place of force Hubbard recommended patience, for eventually the children "shall bring forth their fruit in the season of it" (p. 17).

Finally, Hubbard turned to the members of the rising generation themselves, who he believed were willing but "they know not [yet] how to perform" (p. 110). In another remarkable departure from convention he encouraged the young to seek their own individual and personal relationships with God in whatever form that seemed best for them, and he urged them not to worry if their spiritual strivings did not conform to some pattern designed by the society. A man who at the age of seventy-three married his second wife much to the displeasure of his parish, Hubbard stressed sincerity before God rather than conformity before men: "Let every one say for himself in his own particular . . . '*I and my Family will serve the Lord*,' and then we may with comfort conclude in the Words of the Psalmist, '*That whatever troubles befall us in the way that yet at the end we shall be made to see the Salvation of God*'" (pp. 110-111). A genuine radical among the ministers, with his appeal for assurance, individualism, and less coercive child-rearing, Hubbard would eventually be followed by many of the younger ministers as they began to accommodate the message of Puritanism to the new generation.

Hubbard, Oakes, Oxenbridge, and Eleazar Mather were not the only ministers who tried to ameliorate the generational conflict and draw the new generation into the church with a renewed religious message. Others like James Allen

154

and Thomas Thatcher also searched for new religious language and themes.

"Light in Darkness"

In 1668 when James Allen (1632-1710) was ordained to serve as co-pastor with John Davenport in the First Church of Boston, he was a staunch resister of the Half-Way Covenant. However, over the next eleven years as Allen became a father to three sons, James, John, and Jeremiah born between 1670 and 1673, he came to modify his position on church membership. In his election sermon of 1679, *New Englands Choicest Blessing*, James Allen made a cautious but deliberate attempt to adjust his language to the changing social atmosphere. Very delicately, Allen tried to placate the elders while at the same time offering encouragement to the young. Early in the sermon he mildly chastized the new generation in the traditional terms. As he pointed to the elders present, he declared to their sons: "These are your gap-men who prevent God's going away, and ruine coming . . . the old and faithful ones, that have seen the works of the Lord."[18] And surely the elders nodded in approval as Allen disdainfully asked the young people: "But do you not think them [the elders] the troublers of Israel? Are you not weary of them, and fain would be rid of them . . . that you might have more elbow room?" (p. 5). Thus Allen's beginning seemed to be a prelude for another formulaic attack upon the rising generation.

But there was a subtle modification of tone and meaning in Allen's subsequent address. He warned those who ceaselessly lament the decay of the present times: "The Wise man reproves the saying so that former days were better . . . nor should we complain that our Lot is cast in such a day" (pp. 5-6). Certainly, Allen admitted, "The Lord hath removed many choice and precious ones from the Bench and the Pulpits" (pp. 5-6), but instead of concentrating upon such

[18] James Allen, *New Englands Choicest Blessing* (Boston, 1679), p. 5.

losses, "we ought to take notice with thankfulness of the precious ones there whom he hath left" (p. 6). Too many both of the young and the old had begun to despair that economic difficulties in "trades and estates" and the "outward evils" in the society were caused by the "evil times" they linked to the rise of the new generation. "That [view] is folly," Allen declared. The way for New England to regain God's favor was for both generations to join together and study "the History of the glorious works of God for this people in former times. . . . Fathers should tell it to their Children" (p. 13). Such an enterprise would gladden the hearts of both teachers and students because "the full story of this people to this day would be one of the best of human Histories" (p. 13). And from the study of this history the young could learn how to regain God's favor and rescue the people from the present sense of desperation. Allen urged the newly elected public officials, "You are our public Fathers, tell it then to your Children" (p. 13). As an encouragement to the elders to cooperate in the spirit of his constructive plan, Allen assured that both generations would reap mutual rewards: "Your Children shall be taught of God and great shall be their peace . . . [and] when you shall lay your heads in the dust . . . the succeeding Generation will bless God for you and call you Blessed" (p. 14). Although his emphasis was upon "New England's Choicest Blessings," Allen certainly stopped short of offering assurance to the younger generation that they were as worthy as their fathers and would equally enjoy God's favor. But in this sermon his moderate tone toward the young, his insistence that things do not need to be worse in the present age, and his suggestion that the new generation can yet merit God's grace demonstrated Allen's readiness to adjust his language in the Puritan sermon to the changing needs of his congregation.

By virtue of the moderate nature of the members of his congregation, Thomas Thatcher (1620-1678) had considerably more freedom than did Allen when in 1674 he preached his *A Fast of Gods Choosing*, which is unfortunately the only one of Thatcher's sermons to be preserved in print. A father of four children, two of whom became distinguished ministers, Thatcher was known for his special attentiveness to children and young people.[19] The controversial Third Church had been from its beginning amenable toward the young, and as its pastor Thatcher offered a message of hope to the merchants and young people who filled his church. In the *Fast of Gods Choosing* Thatcher used imagery of light and darkness, sickness and healing, and drought followed by rain. The richness and vividness of his imagery are rare in the Puritan sermons of the 1670's.

Instead of threats and warnings, Thatcher employed highly sensuous imagery to entice his people to seek the emotionally refreshing release that can follow a day of fast and prayer. Thus Thatcher described the process of renewal: "First," the sinner will see "Light in darkness," the knowledge that comes "when you see darkness hath covered your Soul [so] that you have not known your . . . state or condition."[20] Then, once the sinner has acknowledged his unworthiness, there would come "Light after darkness": "Now God causes Light to spring after darkness, some glimpses of hope, some raisings up of your Spirits and expectations of good days" (p. 12). Gradually God will begin to reveal his beauty like the appearance of the sun at dawn: "This light that is promised is gradual like the Light of the morning that *shines more and more unto the perfect day.* You must not say there is no Light because it is not noon at first, if it be but the dawning of the day, or the Light of the morning star, you have cause to acknowledge it as an Answer [to your] Prayers" (p. 12).

For those who have feared that the spark of their spiritual inclinations seemed too faint to testify to the presence of

[19] *American Pulpit*, pp. 126-129; and *Magnalia*, I, 488-496.
[20] Thomas Thatcher, *A Fast of Gods Choosing* (Boston, 1678), p. 12. Although this sermon was not published until 1678, it was preached in Boston in 1674.

God's saving grace, Thatcher promised that though "it [is] as a springing Light . . . [which] may be weak at first and obscure through the clouds of darkness and temptation," even so dim a light "foreshadow[s] the beginning of your return from spiritual Captivity, or outward calamity" and "shall be victorious and overcoming at the last" (p. 12). The light of God's grace will finally prevail because "this light is from the *rising of the Sun of Righteousness* . . . Light from the face of Jesus Christ" (p. 12), and will be accompanied by the restoration of health to the individual and to the whole of New England. "Thy health shall spring forth speedily," Thatcher predicted, and there will be a "healing of your Souls, of your Families, of your Churches, of your commonwealths, healing to your affairs—inward and outward, spiritual and worldly" (p. 12). Finally, Thatcher employed the traditional Puritan imagery of the garden as a symbol of both the inner spiritual life of the individual and the sacred sanctuary of the New England community as he promised fertility and vitality to those who are showered with Christ's saving grace: "He will make your soul as a watered garden, and as a spring of water whose waters fail not: *As a watered Garden*, that is, you shall be enclosed, and secured from them that might spoil your roots or your fruits, . . . and you shall not be barren or unprofitable in the knowledge of our Lord and Savior Jesus Christ. . . . There shall be a blessing to your posterity as well as to your selves" (pp. 14-15). Thatcher's message of comfort and assurance would be carried on and refined by his successor in the Third Church, the Reverend Samuel Willard.

THE REVEREND SAMUEL WILLARD

Of the writings of those ministers who sought to reshape the meaning of New England Puritanism, the works of Samuel Willard (1640-1707) best demonstrate the message of assurance and hope that emerged from the conflicts and tension of the critical transition years. Willard strongly

158

desired to inspire in his people a new confidence and spiritual vitality, but he was also unwilling to sacrifice the doctrinal principles of Puritanism, which he believed "will forever remain the same through all the successive Changes of Philosophy . . . till cloudy transient Time give place to bright and permanent Eternity."[21] Willard found a solution to his dilemma. As a scholar, he returned to the writings of the early Puritan theologians and rediscovered the original Pauline message of assurance that had been altered and obscured in America. Willard saw that in New England the Puritans had placed undue stress upon the Old Testament Law and had become overly exclusive in their church polity. In his preaching and writings he sought to find new symbolic expression that would touch the hearts of the troubled members of the new generation. As Ebenezer Pemberton said of Willard, "He applied himself to *Wounded Consciences* with great Skill, Faithfulness, and Tenderness" and was "a *Son of Consolation* to the Contrite and Broken in Spirit."[22] Thus, while Willard remained dedicated to the doctrines of Puritanism, his language was often daring and innovative as he sought to entice the new generation to embrace the faith of their fathers.[23]

A Compleat Body of Divinity was Willard's most ambitious and important work. It consists of two-hundred and fifty lectures on "the Assembly's Shorter Catechism," which Willard delivered monthly on Tuesday afternoons from

[21] This summary of Willard's conviction was rendered by Reverends Prince and Sewall in their preface to *A Compleat Body of Divinity*, pp. iii-iv.

[22] From the eulogy of Ebenezer Pemberton for Willard printed after the preface in *A Compleat Body*.

[23] For discussions of Willard, see Miller, *From Colony to Province*, in particular pp. 434-435. Also see George Dollar, "The Life and Works of the Reverend Samuel Willard, 1640-1707," unpublished dissertation in modern history, Boston University Graduate School, 1960; *Annals of the American Pulpit*, pp. 164-167; and Seymour Van Dyken, *Samuel Willard, 1640-1707: Preacher of Orthodoxy in an Era of Change* (Grand Rapids, Mich.: William B. Eerdmans Publishing Co., 1972).

January 31, 1687 until his death in 1707. He recognized that important changes in Western thought were in process, and in these lectures he attempted to preserve the core of Puritan doctrines in order that they may "remain alive and flourish . . . throughout all the successive Changes of external Forms and Languages . . . as long as the Sun and Stars shall shine."[24] The central theme of the *Compleat Body* is the meaning of the "Covenant of Redemption" and the place of Christ in Puritan doctrine.

In the first lecture Willard established his fundamental principles: the aim of life is happiness, the way for a person to be happy on earth is for him to "get with God," and the only way to God is through Christ (p. 12). Regarding the relationship between the Old Testament Covenant and the New, Willard declared that "the New Covenant hath taken off the Curse of disobedience from the Believer, and laid it upon Christ" so that Christ's believers are "not now, as before, under a sentence of Death for the least defect in this Duty" (p. 35). Although Willard believed that some form of duty was still demanded of believers, he insisted that God did not demand perfection from men; those who have lived since Christ's sacrifice "may find acceptance with God" through sincere "though imperfect Obedience" (p. 35).

To a generation that had been told that it was a "corrupt and degenerate vine," Willard offered new assurance and cause for rejoicing. He told the young people, "You are not of that company whom God hath forever forsaken, never to have mercy upon them," and he assured them that they were *"freed from those fears and horrors which arise from the . . .* [Old Testament] *Curse"* and *"delivered from the tyranny of Sin, Satan, and World"* (pp. 275-280). Through the salvation of Christ all Christians are *"brought from a state of misery to a state of happiness"* (p. 281). Because he was convinced that the way to bring the people closer to God was to stress the reward and joy of the faith-

[24] Prince and Sewall in *Compleat Body*, p. iv. On pagination of *A Compleat Body*, see my Chapter I, fn. 104.

ful rather than the punishment of the wicked, Willard encouraged his congregation to "beware of doing anything that may disturb our own Consciences . . . let the Peace of God be a continual Feast to us" (p. 511). And he urged them to let outward joy reflect their inner faith and serve as a mark of their religion:

"If any in the World have reason to rejoice, you are they. It is a shame to see . . . a Child of God disconsolate. You hinder yourselves of that Comfort which else you might enjoy . . . if you do not thus rejoice. And you do not a little dishonor God, and prejudice others against the Lord Jesus Christ, by frightening them from such a Religion. . . . Joy will be your everlasting Employment hereafter, begin it then now, and so anticipate the Felicities of the Eternal Kingdom" (p. 515).

As a father himself of six children and son of the eminent legislator and military officer, Major Simon Willard, called the "sage patriot of Israel" by Pemberton, Willard also understood the intimate connection in New England between religion and the family, and he devoted large segments of the lectures to discussion of the relationship between parents and children. He pleaded for parents to be moderate in the instruction and rearing of children and for children to be more understanding of their parents' ways: "Children are not to think that their Parents hate them because they Correct them for their faults, but ascribe it to their tender love . . . and the Parents ought . . . to leave sufficient Conviction of this love" (p. 607). He also instructed parents to observe the stages in the mental maturity of their children and to gauge their instruction and corrections by the child's own development: parents *"ought to attemper their Government according to the Age and Capacity of their Children, . . .* as therefore they grow up to a Capacity, they ought to be treated more with reason" (pp. 603-604). He counselled that correction must not "be administered in a Passion, but with a Meek and Sedate Spirit that they [children] may be made to read Love in it"

161

(p. 604). He felt the problem of child abuse serious enough to warn parents that *"the Authority of Parents over their Children is Limited"* by the government which "allows unto Children a relief against the Unreasonable Treatments of Unnatural Parents" (p. 605).

Willard had some remarks on the treatment of young adults in New England as well. In a direct assault upon the unwritten laws of the patriarchy, he asserted that children who reach maturity "have a liberty to use their own Prudence in ordering their Affairs" and *"when they are Married . . . they are more at their own dispose"* (p. 606). He stressed that in a joyful Christian community there must exist equality between the generations: "There are in all Places some that are *Aged,* and others that are *Young . . .* there is not a special Relation between these so as to give the one a right of Jurisdiction over the other . . . there is a Civil Respect due from the one to the other" (p. 617). And Willard left no question about which generation was inheriting the power in New England when he warned the elders of his congregation that: *"Ancient Persons* ought to carry it towards them that are Younger so as to adorn their Age. Their whole Conversation ought to be such as may Commend them *to* their *Juniors. . . .* Tho' Age itself hath a respect due to it yet if it is not becomingly managed it may be unhappily exposed to Contempt" (p. 617).

Willard did not come suddenly to the convictions he expounded in the lectures of the *Compleat Body*; like Oakes and Hubbard before him, he had searched for a decade for ways of refurbishing the language and meaning of Puritanism. Some of the sermons he preached during the seven years before he undertook the *Compleat Body* lectures demonstrate the gradual emergence of the themes and imagery of assurance in Willard's thought and writings. *A Compleat Body of Divinity* was a remarkable revitalization of Puritan doctrine, and in many ways it was also the declaration of independence of Willard's own risen generation.

162

It was common in Puritan New England for ministers to preach occasionally in the church of a fellow minister. Accordingly, in 1680 Willard preached *The Duty of a People* in Increase Mather's Second Church of Boston. Because Willard had disapproved the colony-wide day of fast and covenant renewal of 1679 that Mather had personally instituted,[25] Mather's invitation to Willard to preach on the nature of the Covenant after the formal renewal ceremonies of the Second Church may have been more of a challenge than a friendly gesture. Willard's discussion of the covenant in this sermon was precise and noticeably cautious, but still the contrast between his approach to the relationship between God and men and that of Increase Mather is apparent. Mather had argued for the practice of covenant renewal on the ground that the grave apostasy of the people required relentless lamentation and humiliation lest calamity follow, but Willard did not believe renewal of church covenants to be necessary. However, Willard was a shrewd and generous-minded man, and he was not one to discourage the religious expressions of Puritan congregations other than his own.

Willard must have taken Mather off guard when he opened by congratulating the members of the church on their act of covenant renewal and proceeded in a warm and heartening tone to try to build their confidence in the strength of their own faith and in God's love for them. Willard explained that the calling of a day of fast and renewal did not necessarily mean that the people were degenerate or needed to repent, for "there are other occasions of Renewing of Covenant besides Apostasy: it may be done for keeping out as well as thrusting out Sin."[26] A covenant renewal might also serve as a people's act of thanksgiving, as "a grateful acknowledgment of God's faithfulness" (p. 2).

[25] See discussion and note in Chapter 1, pp. 53-54 and n. 101.
[26] *The Duty of a People That Have Renewed Their Covenant* (Boston, 1680), pp. 1-2.

Then, perhaps as a defense of his own message of assurance, Willard declared his admiration for Joshua's encouragement of his people back to God. Joshua stressed the benevolent aspects of God's dealings with men because he recognized that "there is nothing fitter to win upon an ingenious spirit than the remembrance of great and long continued kindnesses" (p. 2). And when Joshua found his people practicing a form of worship with which he was not in full agreement, "Joshua's scope . . . was not in any wise to discourage them in what they were doing, but only to render them the more solemn and serious in what they did" (p. 2). Therefore, following the example of Joshua, Willard declared, "As it is a good and commendable, so it is a great and weighty work you have been about . . . you have tasted and seen that God is good, yea the best good" (pp. 4-5).

What Willard found "useful to the occasion" was more assurance. He declared that the people may feel safe because a "gracious and merciful God" had provided them with "an excellent enclosure . . . [so that] you cannot possibly go astray, except you do break over or through the hedge of the Covenant" (pp. 8-10). If, however, "through frailty or Temptation you should . . . fail in the due performance of your duty," Willard was certain that God "will receive and Pardon you" (p. 8). After listening to nearly a decade of Increase Mather's sermons, some of the members of the Second Church must have been startled to hear Willard assert that in men "weakness and frailties must be expected, while we are laboring under the exercise and oppression of a body of death" and that in the end all those present may *"be partakers of the Inheritance of the Saints in Light"* (pp. 12-13). There is no record that Mather ever invited Willard to preach in the Second Church again.

Perhaps more clearly than any other minister of his time, Willard recognized the important interaction in New England between Puritan theology and the emotions of the people. He saw that if he could arouse a spirit of confidence and expectancy in his people, their faith in God's promise for themselves and for His chosen American colony would be restored. Willard was unwilling to sacrifice the doctrines of Puritanism to that end, but with remarkable intelligence and learning he labored to make doctrines amenable to the changing needs of the people. In his *Covenant Keeping, the Way to Blessedness* (1682), Willard took up the thorny question of doctrine that had plagued New England ministers since the time of the Ann Hutchinson affair in 1636—the relationship between the Covenant of Works and the Covenant of Grace. This was an issue Increase Mather believed to be "at the heart of all the contentions in the New England Churches."[27]

Willard knew that the continued growth of religion in New England demanded that the new generation feel it could actually do something to please God and win His favor. Over-emphasis upon the Covenant of Grace—man's dependence upon the predestined designation of God's grace to particular persons—tended to cause pessimism, passivity, and despair, especially among the young. However, there were also aspects to the Covenant of Works that Willard was determined to avoid: the extraordinary fear of God's wrath and impending doom had developed from a concentration upon punishment wreaked in the Old Testament upon those whose works displeased God and violated His law. Willard was faced with the question of how to encourage good works with the hope of meriting God's reward without continuing the inordinate fear of God's wrath.

Willard solved the problem with an ingenious shift of focus to the positive aspects of the Covenant of Works:

[27] *Covenant-Keeping the Way to Blessedness* (Boston, 1682), preface by Increase Mather. Also in 1682 Willard published *The Fiery Tryal No Strange Thing* (preached 1681) in which he employed rhetoric of decay and doom. Although Willard used the preface of the printed version to try to justify his divergence from his usual tone, this sermon demonstrates that Willard could indeed be a "Son of Thunder," as well as a "Son of Consolation." It is a unique work in the Willard canon, however.

"The Covenant of Grace wages no war with the Covenant of Works," he said, for "the Covenant of Works was not destroyed, but accomplished by, the Covenant of Grace [so that] the Covenant of Works was in some sense an everlasting Covenant" (p. 19). By "accomplished" Willard meant that the threatening aspects of the Covenant of Works had been destroyed since the sacrifice of Christ had compensated for the sins of those under the New Dispensation. However, the encouraging aspects of the Old Covenant remained: man's relationship to God is still likened to a business contract—if "the inferior of the Covenant is required to perform a duty to the superior," the superior "is under obligation to the other" by "what is conditioned upon the performance of duty" (pp. 29-30). Willard tried to avoid heresy by failing to state exactly what the terms of God's "obligation" to the dutiful servant might be, but his argument was largely designed to leave the people with the hope that God might pour out his saving grace upon those whose performance merited it.

Although Willard's writings were always judiciously based upon doctrine, not all of them were as heavily doctrinal as these two sermons on the nature of the Covenant. As the 1680's progressed, Willard turned more frequently to metaphor, to imaginative visions of the victory of the saints in heaven, and to the image of a glorious and merciful Christ. The epistles of St. Paul often served as a source of imagery and as a basis for modifications in Puritan doctrine. Both Willard's adherence to Paul and his increasing use of metaphorical language were apparent in his funeral sermon, *The High Esteem Which God Hath of the Death of His Saints* (1683), occasioned by the death of John Hull, one of the founders of the Third Church.

Besides giving consolation to Hull's mourners, Willard's purpose in this sermon was to modify the undue stress upon the seeking of perfection of the church and of the lives of the saints that had become a peculiar feature of Puritanism in New England. St. Paul had described the church and the lives of Christians as plants in the process of constant growth, and in his opening praise of Hull, Willard used Paul's metaphor to show that Hull's near perfect life stood as a sign that God's people "are growing up" and that *"The Righteous shall flourish."*[28] Willard's fear, as had been Paul's, was that scrupulous believers would be discouraged by their own imperfections and would despair of ever being worthy of God's grace, while others more certain of their perfections would become self-righteous.

Therefore, as an encouragement to the humble and a warning to the proud, Willard insisted that the meritorious life of John Hull should not blind others to the equality of all of Christ's believers before God: "There is none on this side [of] the Grave so holy, but to have in him . . . some spots and blemishes" (p. 4). And, in a statement that seems to have been clearly aimed at those who feared that more liberal admission policies would defile the church, Willard made a careful distinction between sainthood before and after death: "There are *Saints* in Heaven, and they are just Men made perfect; and there are *Saints* on the Earth too . . . and these though not at present perfected, are yet perfecting" (p. 4). Recalling the meaning of the spiritual calling as it had been understood by the early Puritans, Willard declared that the spiritual strivings of the most ordinary Christian give his life such significance that, regardless of how lowly his earthly vocation may be, his death will be an event of mourning for the entire community: "A *Saint*, though he be a private Christian, is yet, when he dies, a public loss, and deserves the *tears of Israel.* . . . When a Saint *Dies* there is manifold sound of Mourning; there is then a Pillar plucked out of the Building, a Foundation Stone taken out of the Wall, a Man removed out of the Gap" (p. 14). When believers die, "death comes not armed with a sting against them . . . but as a friendly Messenger to invite them into their Father's presence" (p. 9). Willard imagined that the soul of the saint would

---

[28] *High Esteem*, p. 6.

"ascend like *Frankincense* or *sweet Incense*, in a Cloud of fragrant Smoke" (p. 12). And after death the bodies of believers are carefully preserved: They "are not now rejected as *worthless things*, but are laid up in God's Cabinet, and that with far more tender care than we do the most estimable jewel" (p. 10). To God the body of one of His saints is "more precious than the Gold of *Ophir*" (p. 11). Every true believer will spend eternity "ly[ing] in Christ's Bosom, and be ravished with his dearest love, and most intimate Embraces" (p. 15).

Throughout the years of his ministry Willard was always anxious "to encourage such poor Souls who being under deep conviction do find nothing of advantage in themselves to rely upon, and are here upon ready to say, 'I have nothing to do with the Covenant.' "[29] The publication in 1684 of *Mercy Magnified on the Penitent Prodigal*, a collection of twenty-eight sermons on the parable of the prodigal son, reveals that Willard frequently found the "poor souls" to be those of young people, especially second- and third-generation sons. In the Preface of *Mercy Magnified*, he explained that the story of the prodigal son stands as a type or paradigm for the whole human process of a young man's rebellion and separation from the father, followed by a period of misery and repentance, and concluded in a return home to salvation. In a demonstration of his remarkable awareness of the symbolic function of religious language, Willard first explained the general nature of parables: "Parables are properly Enigmatical or Allegorical comparisons wherein under the representation of other persons, actions, or things, some other like thing is intended and commended to our consideration. . . . They are to wrap up mysterious Truths. . . . They are to explicate and clear up a Truth to our understanding by the help of the senses. They speak of sensible things, such as are obvious to our eyes, ears, etc. and to lead us to a conception of spiritual

---

[29] *Mercy Magnified on a Penitent Prodigal* (Boston, 1684), p. 12.

things. . . . When a Parable is opened it bringeth more light to men's understanding than plain enunciations of Truth and adds to be very useful for the moving of the affections" (pp. 3-4).

He then went on to explain that the "main scope" of the parable of the prodigal son "presents us with the pattern of a grevious sinner . . . what he was before conversion, and how he is converted, and what welcome he finds with God upon his return"; this pattern "is shadowed out to us under the comparison of a Father and his two Sons, and the carriage of each of them" (pp. 5-6). Willard found this parable especially apt for a generation of sons who had rebelled against God their Father, had separated themselves from His church, and now despaired of ever receiving forgiveness; and he composed his sermons on the parable in order to offer such sons comfort and hope: "Though you are a younger Son and a Prodigal too, yet if you go to him in Faith and Repentance, he will own thee for a Son as the Father did such a one" (pp. 12-13). Throughout these sermons, which stressed the "compassion of God" and showed how "God manifests His choice and incomparable love to a sinner," Willard urged his young listeners to "be not then daunted, or beat off with frights and fears, but venture into his presence, he knows how, *Where sin hath abounded, to make Grace more than abound*" (p. 13).

Nowhere is Willard more explicit about his conviction that the people be assured of their salvation and have confidence in the protection of God than in a sermon to which he gave the reassuring title, *A Child's Portion: or the Unseen Glory* (1684), perhaps as a response to Increase Mather's gloomy execution sermon, *A Wicked Mans Portion* (1675). In a blistering attack upon the practice of morbid self-examination that had been recommended by previous ministers, Willard advised his people to "learn we hence not to judge of ourselves or of our own state."[30] "We

30 *A Child's Portion: or the Unseen Glory* (Boston, 1684), p. 70.

live by hope," Willard declared, and only Satan profits from a people's self-inflicted misery: "It is the delight of Satan to be keeping the thoughts of the Children of God looking and poring upon their present sinful and sorrowful condition that they may be held under discouragement by thinking themselves miserable" (p. 70). In spite of the threat of the revocation of the Charter that was viewed by many ministers in 1684 as another sign of God's displeasure, Willard promised his people that they would emerge triumphant from their conflict with England because "God has bestowed on you a Royal Guard of glorious Angels" to protect His people (p. 97). As long as God's people maintain their faith in Christ, "that Rock on which the happiness of the Sons of God is built lies too deep for all the endeavors of their enemies." In the "storms, nay hurricanes" of battle, "no Child of God shall ever be lost" and "no weapon that is formed against them shall ever prosper" (pp. 86-87).

In this spirit of confidence Willard exhorted his people to "let joy dispel the mists of every sorrow and clear up your souls in the midst of all your troubles" (p. 97). Since the present times appeared dark, Willard encouraged his audience to look forward to their final victory in heaven, where "the angels triumphantly wait and joyful look" to their arrival. There God's people will have their final revenge upon their enemies when "they shall be brought forth in their Royalty at the Second Coming of Christ, [and] shall be the wonder and astonishment of Angels, wicked Men and Devils" (p. 97).

At the time of Governor Andros' revocation of the Massachusetts Bay Charter, Willard uttered a declaration of defiance in his *Brief Discourse of Justification* (1686). The sermon bristles with the courageous spirit of independence that marked some of the Puritan writings of the early seventeenth-century England, and it deserves to be quoted at length not only as evidence of Willard's hopefulness but also as proof that Willard's "gentleness" and his willingness to accommodate the changing spiritual needs of his

170

people were in no way signs of any weakness in his character or in his commitment to the basic truths of Puritan
faith:

"*The world can do you no harm.* . . . [your enemies] may
give you a great deal of outward molestation; they may per-
vert Justice, and *condemn* you as wicked persons, they may
rifle your houses, imprison your persons, take away your
lives, and remove you from off the face of the earth, yea
and make you the scorn of men, and expose your names
to slanders and obloquies; but herein lies your comfort in
the midst of all this: when they have done their worst, and
vented *their spleen* with the greatest bitterness, yet they
can never take away your righteousness, but that shall abide
forever . . . nor can they overturn you in your great cause,
or ever *separate you from the love of God which is in Christ
Jesus.*"[31]

Willard labored assiduously during the 1680's to find new
ways of making the original doctrines of Puritanism mean-
ingful in the lives of his second- and third-generation audiences. He was often radically daring in his manipulation
of religious language, as in his sermon of 1686, when he
preached to his merchant class congregation his famous
*Heavenly Merchandize: or the Purchasing of TRUTH
Recommended and the Selling of It Disswaded.* Willard
borrowed his text and central metaphor from the Book of
Proverbs, which teaches: "Buy the Truth, and Sell it not."
He imagined Christ and the word of God to be commodi-
ties on sale in the Boston churches and argued that many
foolishly search for bargains in the market place while the
real bargain is to be found in church. Willard's justification
of such bold use of sacred ideas and figures was that he was
only imitating the literary practice of the Holy Spirit: "The
words are *Metaphorical*; a form of Speech which the Holy
Ghost makes frequent use of in the Holy Scriptures; therein
dressing up of Heavenly Matter in Earthly Language, and
thus accommodating of himself to our capacity: A Meta-

[31] *Brief Discourse*, pp. 162-163.

171

phor being nothing else but a contracted comparison by which he represents the things of God under the resemblance of things here below."[32]

Such understanding of the function and meaning of religious language and symbol made Willard one of the most flexible and imaginative religious writers of his age in New England. While he would find occasion in the 1690's to return briefly to the theme of the threat of impending calamity and doom in his attack on hypocrites in the *Barren Fig Tree's Doom*, the major theme of his writings for thirty years was founded upon the teaching of Isaiah that Willard used as the text of one of his comforting sermons in 1699: "Isa. 35:3, 4. *Strengthen ye the weak hands and confirm the feeble knees. Say to them that are of a fearful heart, be strong, fear not.*"[33] With such words Willard enabled his people to find the courage and strength to endure the burden of their past and surmount many of the problems of their own age.

[32] *Heavenly Merchandize: or the Purchasing of TRUTH Recommended and the Selling of It Disswaded* (Boston, 1686), p. 2.

[33] *Spiritual Desertions Discovered and Remedied* (Boston, 1699), title page.

THE DAWNING OF THAT DAY
The Message of Assurance and Hope

The history of religions has also been the history of great discord. It would seem that nothing can more effectively set people at odds than the demand that they think alike. . . . Though we repeat exactly the same articles of faith, we'd understand them differently. . . . The rich man's prayer is not the poor man's prayer. Youth's God is not the God of the aged.

Kenneth Burke, *The Rhetoric of Religion*

ALTHOUGH most of the original settlers who had come to New England between 1630 and 1650 were gone by 1685, a few of the exceptionally long-lived patriarchs remained, men like John Higginson (1616-1708), John Woodbridge (1613-1696), and Governor Simon Bradstreet (1603-1697). Yet for the most part the positions of leadership and power in the colony during the critical decade between 1685 and 1695 were held by second-generation men, contemporaries of Samuel Willard (1640-1707). Born during the colony's first two decades and now in their middle years, these men had heard throughout their youth that the day they would inherit New England would bring disaster to God's people. With the appointment of Sir Edmund Andros as Royal Governor of Massachusetts in 1686, it appeared that the predicted calamity was at hand.

An appointee of the feared Catholic King James II, the arrogant Andros immediately made a show of power as he revoked the Massachusetts Charter and thus jeopardized the landholdings of all of the colonists. Desperate property owners flocked to the courts of Boston and London to contest their rights. To antagonize the people even more, the

Anglican governor attacked the religious pride of the New Englanders when he insisted that the Old South Church be shared with the Anglicans for services until a suitable meeting place could be constructed. Even those Puritans who had previously manifested little piety were outraged at the insult when the members of Willard's congregation were forced to wait in the street while the Anglicans filled the Old South Church with their popish hymns. For the first time in their lives men like Fitz-John and Wait Still Winthrop encountered the kind of direct threat to their religious freedom that the founders had experienced in England. Such men now felt their hearts warmed by the faith of their fathers and grandfathers. During the late 1680's the New England churches were packed every sabbath with as many as 1,500 attentive members. In 1689 Cotton Mather led the fervent colonists in a daring overthrow of the Andros regime, an act of which the founders would have been proud.[1]

But the spiritual transformation that occurred with the second generation was not so sudden nor so political as it may seem. The religious zeal and political confidence that were evident in the revolt of 1689 in New England were rooted in and nourished by new spiritual assurance that had emerged during the preceding decade.[2] With the shift

[1] For the best accounts of the events of the Andros regime and the effects of the Glorious Revolution on America, see T. H. Breen, *The Character of the Good Ruler: A Study of Puritan Political Ideas in New England, 1630-1730* (New Haven and London: Yale University Press, 1970), in particular pp. 134-179; Michael G. Hall, ed., *The Glorious Revolution in America* (Chapel Hill: Univ. of North Carolina Press, 1964); Miller, *From Colony to Province*, pp. 149-157; Bailyn, *New England Merchants*, shows the alliance of the merchants and the ministers against English control, pp. 167-177. On the Old South episode, see Hill, *Old South Church*, pp. 141-159. On the increased attendance at church during the 1680's, see Pope, *Half-Way Covenant*, pp. 175-188. On the young Winthrops, see Dunn, *Puritans and Yankees*, pp. 250-319.

[2] Cf. Miller, *From Colony to Province*, pp. 149-190, which stresses political motivations for the religious changes.

174

in the role of the second generation from enforced passivity to active leadership, the meaning of the Puritan sermon had also changed. Gradually, the ministers had ceased their lament of the lethargy of the rising generation and their exhortations to weep and mourn over New England's decline. To the people's question of what they might do to be saved the ministers had devised a new resolution: Be active, and do "GOOD WORKS," and be "Serviceable to His [God's] People. . . . The Great God Himself shall be the *gain* of such a man."[3] The reassuring message and language of the sermons of the 1680's had helped to alleviate the spiritual malaise of the second generation and to prepare its members for assertive action. Certainly the fears and doubts of the younger generations were never totally expunged; indeed, they made a dramatic reappearance in the witchcraft affair. But the works of Samuel Willard and Increase Mather had revitalized New England preaching, and ministers like Joshua Moodey, Edward Taylor, and Cotton Mather followed that lead in the late 1680's and into the 1690's.

While the 1660's and 1670's had been a time of intense inner searching to find evils the people unfairly assumed to be present, the last decade of the century brought a heightened concern with external enemies, such as the English king and the English governor, Satan and his witches, and eventually the French and Indians. The predominant message of the sermons of the late 1680's was social rather than personal. The preachers advocated community service and religious unity as a formula for peace, prosperity, and relief from the sufferings of a wounded conscience. To foster this spirit of harmony and confidence in the people, the ministers taught that a man who lived a morally upright life and believed in Christ could be fairly certain of salvation.

During these years the figure of God the Father became less threatening, and His actions appeared more explicable

[3] Cotton Mather, *Serviceable Man*, p. 14.

and benevolent. One minister explained that in all He does "God is a rational Agent aiming at a special mark . . . [and thus] we may understand much of the loving kindness of the Lord."[4] The difficulties God had sent His people were no longer interpreted as proof of God's departure but evidence of His special favor: "Crosses and troubles of themselves [are not] an Argument of God's hatred, but rather a token of his love, and a witness of our Adoption."[5] The ministers now preached that God had tested His people, and they had emerged victorious: "You have seen the worst days, the bitterness of death is over, the best are behind; and your present preservation is a pledge of your future salvation."[6] Leonard Hoar (1630-1675), who had planned to modernize and broaden Harvard's curriculum before he was forced to resign the presidency in 1675, had believed that God would soon fulfill His promise and a new time would come to New England "as the Sun riseth from under clogging Mists and obscuring Clouds."[7] Even as new political difficulties bore upon the colony, the ministers counselled: "Let not our Hearts be troubled . . . [or] dismayed with fear. . . . Cast not away your confidence" because "God as a Father cares for you and knows what you need."[8] The popular sermon of Richard Standfast assured: "The worst is past, the good is begun, the best is at hand."[9]

As the image of God the Father became more benign and abstract, the figure of Christ gained in splendor. In rich and ornate imagery the preachers presented Christ as the

[4] James Allen, *Serious Advice to Deliver One From Sickness* (Boston, 1679), p. 6.

[5] Richard Standfast, *A Little Handful of Cordial Comforts for a Fainting Soul* (Boston, 1690), p. 32.

[6] Allen, *Serious Advice*, p. 30.

[7] Leonard Hoar, *The Sting of Death and Death Unstung* (Boston, 1680), p. 2. For commentary on Hoar's tour as Harvard President, see Samuel Eliot Morison, *Harvard College in the Seventeenth Century* (Cambridge, Mass.: Harvard University Press, 1936), II, 392-414.

[8] Standfast, *Cordial Comforts*, pp. 24 and 44.

[9] *Ibid.*, p. 44.

hero who had interceded with the Father to win a Covenant of Redemption for His people in New England. The
ministers explained that in the past there had been "a controversy" between the people and God and "no possibility
on our part to pacify the Anger of God," but "Christ inter-
posed Himself as our Mediator . . . to reconcile and make
peace between God and us."[10] The ministers also frequently
imagined Christ as a princely lover who actively courted
His people. Joshua Moodey (1633-1697) elaborated upon
this popular metaphor: "There be two Seasons when especially men desire to be and appear to be beautiful, . . . in
their wooing *Time* and on their Espousal or *Marriage Day*.
So it is with Jesus Christ: Lord's Days and Lecture-days . . .
are Christ's *wooing days* and therefore doth he then deck
and array Himself with all his *Glory* and *Beauty* that he
may allure and prevail with men to have him, that being
ravished with his Beauty they may consent to his motion."[11]
In the sermons of the late 1680's the image of God the
Father was nearly eclipsed by the beauty and mercy of His
Son.

With the image of the fearful deity supplanted by the
figure of the merciful and gracious Son, the New England
churches began to lose their reputation as places to be
avoided by sinners and feared by children. Now the ministers tried to have the people think of religion as a refuge
from fears and trials. As Samuel Willard said, when "there
is little peace to be expected in or from the world . . . happy
[are] those Souls who are got into this Rock."[12] In His
church, John Higginson declared, Christ gives His people
"a Sovereign Cordial to preserve their hearts from the
malignities and venome and poison of all the troubles of

---

[10] John Higginson, *Our Dying Savior's Legacy of Peace* (Boston,
1686), p. 11.

[11] Joshua Moodey, *A Practical Discourse Concerning the Choice
Benefit of Communion with God* (Boston, 1685), p. 24. This sermon
was republished in 1746.

[12] Samuel Willard, "To the Reader," in Higginson, *Dying Savior.*

the world."[13] Those who were rooted securely in the church of Christ could expect "Peace in general [by which] we are to understand Prosperity, and Happiness, consisting in the absence of all Evil and presence all of good."[14] Not only did Christ protect His people against the threatening external enemies, but His peace calmed the inner forces as well; for those who abide with Him "the Conscience is pacified, the heart quieted, the will Satisfied, the Affections well pleased, and the whole soul at rest in *God*."[15] The members of Higginson's congregation could declare with him: "Oh, how great is this goodness!"[16]

To stress the special protection that Christ afforded His faithful in New England, the ministers described the continuing persecutions of protestants in Europe. Sermons preached by persecuted European ministers were published in Boston.[17] In his preface to one such sermon Cotton Mather emphasized the good fortune of the American Puritans as he gave a lurid account of the tortures the French protestants endured for their faith. According to Mather, the vile papists "stript others Naked, and pricked them with *Pins* and *Bodkins*. . . . Some they kept waking by cruel *Punches* and *Noises* . . . till they utterly thereby lost their Wits."[18] Also the cruel oppressors "bound Men and Ravished their *Wives* and *Daughters* before their eyes."[19] Unlike Mather, however, most ministers preferred with Higginson to preach about the advantages of true religion in America and the "merry and prosperous days that lie ahead for God's faithful."[20]

[13] Higginson, *Dying Savior*, p. 2.   [14] *Ibid.*, p. 3.
[15] *Ibid.*, p. 10.   [16] *Ibid.*, p. 36.
[17] See John Bailey, *Man's Chief End to Glorify God* (Boston, 1689); Gilbert Burnet, *A Sermon Preached before the House of Commons* (Boston, 1689); and Ezechiel Carré, *The Charitable Samaritan* (Boston, 1689).
[18] Cotton Mather, "Preface," Ezechiel Carré, *The Charitable Samaritan*, p. 3.
[19] *Ibid.*   [20] Higginson, *Dying Savior*, p. 4.

With such a spirit of optimism there was also a new emphasis upon action and upon Christian duty that was most fitting to the vigorous new role the second generation had come to play in the society. Now the ministers advised every Christian to "fill up his time with Duties and his Duties [will be filled] with Grace."[21] Richard Standfast urged "lift up therefore the Hands that hang down, and strengthen the feeble Knees, and run with Patience the Race set before us," for "a true Christian's life is not an idle Life but a busy one."[22] Just as an athlete develops the strength of his body, so the believer "*by the* Exercise of Grace *the soul is kept in a Holy, Healthful, and Cheerful frame.*"[23] The ministers promised that such holy conditioning would bring spiritual and emotional health to the whole being, for "there is comfort and sweetness in the exercise of any grace . . . *Comfort in love.*"[24]

As a renewed emphasis on the theme of Christian duty, the ministers refurbished the idea of the unity of the earthly and heavenly callings. Under the doctrine of the calling every action becomes sacred because the "*exercising* [of] *Grace will sublimate and spiritualize every action, turning natural affections into Graces.*"[25] The simplest activities— such as "a man's loving his Wife or Child"—become "gracious acts" and "his eating and drinking [are] acts of obedience and hence are of great account in the eyes of God."[26] Significantly, the sermons of John Cotton, who had stressed

[21] Nathaniel Mather, *A Sermon Wherein is Shewed That it is the DUTY and . . . CARE of Believers on CHRIST to Live in the Constant Exercise of GRACE* (Boston, 1684), p. 18. This sermon by the elder Nathaniel Mather, brother of Increase and pastor of a church in Dublin, Ireland, is another example of a sermon by a European preacher whose congregation was still living under Catholic persecution.

[22] Standfast, *Cordial Comfort*, p. 44.

[23] Nathaniel Mather, *CARE of Believers*, p. 26.

[24] *Ibid.*, p. 27.   [25] *Ibid.*

[26] *Ibid.*, pp. 27-28.

the calling, spiritual confidence, and the availability of Christ's grace, gained a new popularity in the 1680's.[27] And, as Cotton had done in the first decades of the century, the preachers of the 1680's returned to Martin Luther for words to inflame the hearts of the poor and the doubtful with self-respect and a love of Christ: "not the meanest, smallest act, but it hath a glory and excellency in it if grace be exercised: as *Luther* said, *a poor milk-maid milking, if done in Faith, is more glorious than the Conquests and Triumphs of Ceasar or Alexander.*"[28]

Along with this emphasis upon the spiritual value of a man's earthly activities there also came a modification in the attitude of the ministers toward the seeking of worldly profit. Instead of attacking an interest in material gain as an outright evil, the ministers borrowed metaphors from the market place. In *A Practical Discourse Concerning the Choice Benefit of Communion with God in His House* (1685), Joshua Moodey argued that experience had proved that God keeps an accurate record of the hours that each of His believers spends in church, and He is careful to reward each individual accordingly. God knows human nature too well for Him to let the efforts of men go unrewarded. As Moodey explained, "Gain smells sweet in most men's Nostrils. . . . So sweet and alluring a sound does Gain make that he who can *harp well upon* that *string* may hope for an attentive Auditory"; therefore, "God baits the net of his Gospel which he lets down in His House with a promise of a great Reward."[29] Moodey praised those who labored diligently at their earthly vocations: "It is Lawful,

27 For example, John Cotton's, *God's Promise to his Plantations* (London, 1634) was reprinted in Boston in 1686. There also seems to have been a new interest in the writings of William Perkins (1558-1602) as indicated by the reprinting of *The Foundation of Christian Religion* (Boston, 1682). These reprintings again indicate the effort to recapture the early Pauline spirit.

28 Nathaniel Mather, *CARE of Believers*, p. 28.

29 Moodey, *A Practical Discourse*, p. 5.

yea a Duty to be diligent in your particular callings; God has Commanded us in the sweat of our brows to get our Bread" (p. 13). And he pointed out that God offered His laborers a real bargain in church: "Your Time in the House of God will be found your best Time . . . [for] true Profit or Gain, real Honor, substantial Pleasure is here" (pp. 14-16). The shrewdest buyer would recognize that "as for Pleasures and Delights . . . no Cook dresses such meat, no Tavern sells such drink" as the Lord (pp. 17-18). In God's house will be found "such provision as abundantly exceeds what is to be found in any other . . . Soul Blessings, soul-profit, soul-pleasures" (p. 18).

The most difficult problem confronting the ministers throughout the 1680's continued to be that of bringing into full communion those people who were baptized church members but who felt unworthy of full membership. Although they had continued to attend religious services faithfully, many still believed that they had never experienced the true workings of God's grace in their hearts. The years of public lamentation and personal inner searching had failed to spark the fires of converting grace. As Cotton Mather observed, too many tormented souls still cried out: "*I Fear I have Committed the* UNPARDONABLE SIN, *and then I am utterly beyond the Reach of all Mercy for ever.*"[30] These doubtful souls looked to their ministers for help. The sermons of this period abound with the entreaties of wounded consciences such as this one from Richard Standfast's *A little Handful of Cordial Comforts for A Fainting Soul* (1690): "*I fear [that] I have not this Faith in Christ, and that I do not as yet believe in him. Show me therefore (I pray you) how I may be comforted against this fear, and how I may know whether I do believe in Christ? . . . How might I be so bold as to even begin to think that Christ may be willing to save such a creature as I?*"[31]

[30] Cotton Mather, *Balsamum Vulnerarium e Scriptura, or the Cause and Cure of a Wounded Spirit* (Boston, 1692), p. 78.

[31] Standfast, *Cordial Comforts*, pp. 10-12.

Some ministers like Standfast and Cotton Mather found it easy to formulate cordial responses to such doubts. Standfast, for example, answered that it is wrong "to think our own troubles [are] the worst when as indeed they are but common temptations" (p. 38). He showed that *"this very fear"* that one is not chosen should be a "comfort" and a "matter of Consolation," for it is proof of the workings of grace (p. 24). When the distressed supplicant insisted that he was undeserving because he had not a conversion experience, Standfast replied: "If our desires be with the Congregation, even that desire will be sufficient. . . . If it be so, then . . . you may say with *David, I have kept thy Word"* (pp. 39-43). Standfast believed that the love of God could not be judged by the laws of the church and that God's grace was not even limited to those in the church: "Neither is the Lord so confined to the Congregation, but that He is near to all that call upon him faithfully wheresoever they be" (p. 39). For other ministers, however, the problems of church membership could not be resolved so easily. For Edward Taylor the membership issue involved complex emotional and psychological questions.

The controversy over church membership that ensued between Edward Taylor (1645-1729) and Solomon Stoddard (1643-1729) in western Massachusetts during the last three decades of the century clearly delineated the two opposing solutions to the religious difficulties of the people of the second and third generations. The grandfather of Jonathan Edwards (1703-1758), Stoddard was the minister of the church at Northampton from 1672 until his death; there he married the widow of his predecessor, Eleazar Mather, and had two sons. As early as 1672 Stoddard had concluded that very few of the baptized members of the younger generation would ever have the conversion experience required by the churches for full church membership. Therefore, when he began his ministry in Northampton, Stoddard desired to admit all baptized church members to the Lord's Supper whether or not they felt the presence of God's con-

182

verting grace in their hearts. Stoddard hoped that the experience of receiving communion in itself might serve to
bring about the crisis of a conversion. Edward Taylor, pastor of the neighboring church in Westfield, and the father
of fourteen children by two marriages, was sympathetic
with Stoddard's aim of increasing the number of full members, but he could not condone Stoddard's method. Both
privately and publicly Taylor tried to convince Stoddard
of his error.[32]

Because he had been reared in England and had emi-
grated to the colony in his early twenties, Taylor graduated from Harvard in 1671 at the unusually late age of
twenty-six. He took up his ministry at Westfield a year
before Stoddard arrived at Northampton. Throughout his
career Taylor held tenaciously to his conviction that no
church member should approach the Lord's table unless he
felt the presence of converting grace. Most historians have
interpreted Taylor's firmness on this issue of church polity
as characteristic of a general theological conservatism in
Taylor's thought. However, Taylor's sermons of the 1680's
and 1690's are assuring in theme and unusually sensuous
in imagery, and they do not appear to be the work of a
religious conservative.[33]

[32] For some of the differences between Taylor and Stoddard on these
issues, see Norman S. Garbo's "Introduction," *Edward Taylor's Treatise
Concerning the Lord's Supper* (East Lansing, Mich.: Michigan State
University Press, 1966), pp. ix-xlvii; cf. Miller, *From Colony to Prov-
ince*, pp. 240 and 284. Miller tends to idolize Stoddard and slight the
serious thought of Taylor on these issues. For a biographical sketch of
Stoddard, see William B. Sprague, *Annals of the American Pulpit*
(New York: Robert Carter and Brothers, 1857), pp. 172-174.

[33] For the only full length biography of Taylor, see Grabo, *Edward
Taylor*. For commentary on the language of Taylor's sermons, see
Grabo's "Introduction" to *Edward Taylor's Christographia* (New Haven
& London: Yale University Press, 1962), pp. xi-xliv. Grabo views Taylor
as unique in preaching assurance and believes that even in 1702 Taylor's listeners were probably "not prepared" for the "positive assurance" of Taylor's preachings on Christ (p. xxiv). However, Grabo

Taylor's sermons do not present a conservative preacher's reiteration of the message of the 1660's and 1670's that few are saved and most are damned. On the contrary, he felt that in New England the figure of God the Father had become like a "Scare crow or a Bug-Bear to awe Children or Fools"[34] and that too many preachers had tended to "play the Hocus-Pocus with the Soul, promising without performing" (C, p. 28). Taylor's sermons are rich in the language of hope and assurance because he believed that most of his congregation was worthy of full membership. His purpose in his sermons was to arouse a compelling and irreversible desire to conversion in his listeners by making the Lord's Supper and Christ's love irresistible enticements. Like Willard and Cotton Mather, Taylor assured his people that a man need not be perfect to be one of God's chosen: "So long as thou art in the body, thou wilt have a body of sin in thee. . . . Truly this is the condition of God's children here in this life" (LS, pp. 152-153). He even held himself up as an example of one "overrun with evil and carnal thoughts" (LS, p. 153). At the same time he insisted that even those who think themselves the lowliest of men are held high in the Lord's regard because Christ's act of redemption had advanced human nature "Nigh to Deity" (C, p. 25). No man should "conclude . . . that thou hast not this wedding garment" (LS, p. 154) of God's grace, for men may even surpass the angels in their perfection: "Oh! admirable. Give place ye holy Angels of Light, Ye Sparkling Stars of the Morning. The brightest Glory, the Highest Seat in the Kingdom of Glory, the Fairest Colors in the Scutcheon of Celestial Honor belong to my nature" (C, p. 25).

---

endorses Miller's view that because of Taylor's policy on church admission he must be viewed as a theological conservative (pp. xii-xix).

[34] *Christographia*, p. 28. In this discussion of Taylor I shall be quoting from the two collections of Taylor's sermons, the *Christographia* and the *Treatise Concerning the Lord's Supper*; they will be designated as *C* and *LS*, respectively.

In order to lead his listeners to commit themselves totally to Christ, Taylor repeatedly focused attention upon the beauty of Christ, "the lovely rose of Sharon, and glorious lily of the valley" (*LS*, p. 170) and stressed the benefits of joy and peace to be gained from Christ: "O what Comfort. . . . It lets the Honey dews of heaven down into their Souls. Christ Conveys in Chariots of Grace the Sweet Consolations that are in heaven into their hearts. What Can be Sweeter?" (*C*, p. 431). Taylor also tried to describe the spiritual delight of the Lord's Supper that awaits believers: "Oh! the joy that spreads itself then over the soul. Oh! how it then is filled with singing" (*LS*, pp. 159-160). Yet Taylor did require his congregation to examine their hearts before entering into full church membership.

The key to this seeming contradiction in Taylor's thought lies in an understanding of the likely motive for his persistence on the issue of the Lord's Supper. Perhaps because of his late arrival to the colony, Taylor may have possessed special insight into the complex emotional lives of the people of his second- and third-generation congregation. He recognized that to bring scrupulous and uncertain people too quickly to the communion table might only expose their consciences to serious remorse if later they should fear that they had been victims of self-delusion. Such a one "is loathsome to himself if he find himself in any respect out of this wedden garment. . . . He hath the shame of his nakedness appear" (*LS*, p. 166). In the diary of Elizabeth White we have a record of such an episode.[35]

Taylor sought to bring church members into full communion with the same avidity as did Stoddard, but he wanted permanent communicants. He believed that the only safe and lasting way to bring a person to communion was through the outward ritual of a public confession (*LS*, pp. 162-163). But he also believed that some kind of exami-

[35] Elizabeth White, *The Experience of God's Gracious Dealings* (Boston, 1741).

185

nation was needed in order to prove to the communicant himself that he was a true believer and to prevent the "soul damage" that might otherwise result (*LS*, p. 162). Although he made no reference to Taylor at the time, Stoddard later admitted in 1714, in *A Guide to Christ*, the need for using caution and patience with each individual when he warned young ministers that each person must be led "through the whole work of *preparation* partly by *fear*, and partly by *hope* and that it is *extreamly dangerous* to tell him that *it is hopeful* GOD *has put the Seeds of Grace into him.*"[36] Through the reassuring themes and language of his sermons Taylor had tried to lead his people, albeit more gradually than did Stoddard, into a new era of spiritual confidence.

THE REVEREND COTTON MATHER

Without question the real virtuoso of the new themes and language of the sermons of the last decades of the century was the vigorous young minister, Cotton Mather (1663-1728). In the sermons he preached between 1686 and 1695, Mather was indefatigable in offering encouragement to his people. Against all of the trials New England endured during those years, Mather was unshakable in his conviction that God's people in America were destined for glory on earth and in heaven. Like the people of the second and of his own third generations, he had endured a period of self-doubt and searching; as a youth he had worried: "How shall I be able to Look my own Father in the Face at the Day of Judgment!"[37] In his personal life Mather always carried the burden of the great reputations of his father, Increase, and his illustrious grandfathers, Richard Mather and John Cot-

[36] Solomon Stoddard, *A Guide to Christ, or the way of directing Souls that are under the Work of CONVERSION* (Boston, 1735), pp. 2 and 4. The "Epistle to the Reader" by Increase Mather indicates that this work was first compiled for publication in 1714.

[37] Cotton Mather, "Paterna," unpublished ms, p. 6, as quoted in Shea, *Spiritual Autobiography*, p. 177.

ton, and he had to overcome the serious affliction of stammering speech that had threatened to deprive him of a career in the ministry. His diary testifies to his deep bitterness and to the agony of these private struggles.[38] But from the first-generation fathers Cotton Mather had learned the importance of self-assertion and perseverance, and in his writings he tried to inspire that tenacity in his people, particularly in the young.[39]

[38] *Diary of Cotton Mather*, pp. 2-3, 7-9, 35, 50-52.

[39] Cotton was, of course, New England's most astute student of the first-generation patriarchs as is testified to by his *Magnalia Christi Americana*. For the best examination of Cotton Mather as a thinker and man of letters, see Sacvan Bercovitch's essay, "Cotton Mather," in *Major Writers of Early American Literature*, ed. Everett Emerson (Madison, Wisc.: University of Wisconsin Press, 1972), pp. 93-149. The most sober biography of Cotton Mather remains Wendell's *Cotton Mather, The Puritan Priest*; cf. Ralph P. and Louise Boas, *Cotton Mather: Keeper of the Puritan Conscience* (New York: Harper and Brothers, 1928), and Phyllis Franklin, *Show Thyself a Man: A Comparison of Benjamin Franklin and Cotton Mather* (The Hague, Paris: Mouton Press, 1969). The best treatment of Cotton Mather as an intellectual is Middlekauf, *The Mathers*, pp. 191-367.

For good statements on Mather's thought and writing, see the following: David Levin, "Introduction," to Cotton Mather's *Bonifacius: An Essay Upon the Good*, ed. Levin (Cambridge, Mass.: Harvard University Press, 1966), pp. vii-xxviii; Kenneth Murdock, "Introduction," *Cotton Mather: Selections* (New York: Hafner, 1926), pp. ix-lviii; George H. Orians, "Introduction," to a collection of Cotton Mather's sermons, *Days of Humiliation, Times of Affliction . . . 1696-1727* (Gainesville, Fla.: Scholar Facsimiles, 1970), pp. iii-xxiv, Orians discovered the difficulty of finding fast-day sermons in the Cotton Mather canon; Josephine K. Piercy, "Introduction," to Cotton Mather's *The Christian Philosopher* (Gainesville, Fla.: Scholars' Facsimiles and Reprints, 1968), pp. v-xiii.

On Cotton Mather as a literary figure, see Austin Warren's essay on "Dr. Cotton Mather's *Magnalia*," in *Connections* (Ann Arbor, Mich.: University of Michigan Press, 1970), pp. 24-44, which shows Cotton Mather's conscious mastery of "the Baroque style"; cf. Bercovitch, "New England Epic," pp. 337-350. An invaluable reference for the study of Mather's work is the carefully annotated bibliography, Holmes, *Cotton Mather: A Bibliography of His Works*.

187

Except for the five years between his father's passing at the age of eighty-four in 1723 and his own death in 1728, Cotton Mather shared the pulpit of the Second Church of Boston with his father, Increase. During those years he established a reputation as a tireless pastor and public citizen, as a comforter of his people and defender of youth, and as an eminent scholar and prolific author; he also appears to have been a gentle and attentive father.[40] Yet even those biographers and historians who have approached him sympathetically have had only moderate success in creating a greater appreciation of his truly remarkable achievements.[41] Somehow Cotton has remained overshadowed in history, as he was throughout his life, by the towering figure of his father whom Professor Murdock has named "the foremost American Puritan."[42] Perhaps one of the reasons for an unwillingness to grant Cotton greater recognition is the seeming desperateness of his demand for it.

Cotton Mather carried the themes and language of assurance to their limits, limits he then tried to exceed with italics and exclamation points: "O What *Peace*! . . . O what *Joy*! even Joy *unspeakable and full of glory*. Oh what *Growth*, O what *Assurance*, O what *Perseverance*, in this Life will flow from these [fingers of God] unto the *saved* Believer!"[43] In answer to the message of decline he asserted

[40] On Mather's scientific learning, see Otho T. Beal and Richard H. Shyrock, *Cotton Mather: The First Significant Figure in American Medicine* (Baltimore: Johns Hopkins University Press, 1954), and George L. Kittridge, "Cotton Mather's Scientific Communications to the Royal Society," in *Proceedings of AAS*, 26 (1916), pp. 18-57. On Mather as a father, see Elizabeth B. Schlesinger, "Cotton Mather and His Children," *WMQ*, 3rd ser., 10 (1953), pp. 181-189; Samuel Mather, *Cotton Mather*, pp. 15-18, and Cotton Mather's *Diary*, pp. 534-537.

[41] For discussion of the problem of biographies of Cotton Mather, see David Levin, "The Hazing of Cotton Mather: The Creation of a Biographical Personality," in *In Defense of Historical Literature* (New York: Hill and Wang, 1967), pp. 34-57; cf. the essays on Cotton Mather by Katherine Anne Porter, *Collected Essays*, pp. 313-351.

[42] Murdock, *Increase Mather*.

[43] Cotton Mather, *The Call of the Gospel* (Boston, 1686), p. 14.

that his generation would see the coming of Christ. Perhaps as an unconscious response to his father's earlier attacks upon the young, Mather lashed out viciously at the old. The persistent shrillness and frequent self-righteousness of Mather's sermons, particularly of his early works, may have contributed to the emotional atmosphere that made possible the witchcraft delusion. And perhaps it is his presumptuous tone that continues to provoke modern readers. Yet in light of the historical and personal circumstances in which the young Mather found himself, it is not surprising that he erred by going to such extremes in his preaching of the themes of assurance.

Cotton Mather firmly believed that he had been sent on a special mission by God to lead his own and his father's generations out of their years of confusion and doubt and into a new time that would see the coming of Christ and the establishment of the New Jerusalem in America. The sermons of Mather's early years are charged with millenarian optimism as he tried to dazzle his listeners with a vision of promised glory for New England. In his view the people of New England had never been the cause of the colony's hardships. The forces of evil outside the garden had jealously attempted to wreck God's plan. But in spite of the efforts of all of New England's enemies, the people had triumphed: "The Vine which God here *Planted*" had taken "*deep root, and filled the land, so that it sent its Boughs unto the* Atlantic *Sea* Eastward, *and its Branches unto the* Connecticut *River* Westward, *and the Hills were covered with the Shadow thereof.*"[44] Thus Mather confidently told his people: "We shall soon Enjoy *Halcyon Days* with all the *Vultures* of Hell *Trodden under our Feet.*"[45] In the early years of the colony the ministers had frequently expressed the hope that New England might one day become the scene of Christ's triumphant descent to His New Jerusalem. But it was the chiliastic Cotton Mather who so

[44] Cotton Mather, *Wonders of the Invisible World*, pp. 13-14.
[45] *Ibid.*, p. 14.

clearly and emphatically expressed the belief that the glorious day was at hand and that New England was certain to be the site of the New Jerusalem: the coming of the Lord was not "a Metaphor," young Mather declared, it was "the Next Thing that is to be Look'd for."[46] The themes and language of Mather's early writings were designed to inflame all New Englanders with religious certainty and a new national pride.

Cotton Mather looked back upon the difficult years of New England's "decline" as a time when "all Debauchery was coming in among us like a mighty Flood. . . . We were in a *Sea of Fire* miserably scorched and scalded, and yet it was *mingled with Ice* . . . there was no getting out."[47] In those perilous days the people were right to fear God's departure and to cry out, "*Return we beseech thee O God!*" (*WW*, p. 43). But Mather was certain that the period of trials has passed for God's people: "And now behold He is *Returned* [to us]" (*WW*, p. 43). Cotton promised his congregation that "a Day" is soon to be expected when "*the*

[46] Cotton Mather, quoted in Miller, *From Colony to Province*, p. 188. For a general discussion of the theme of millennialism in New England writings, see Bercovitch, "Horologicals to Chronometricals."

For the view that Cotton Mather's chiliasm was a product of political crisis, see Miller, *From Colony to Province*, pp. 185-190; for an understanding of Mather's millennial hope as rooted in his eschatological view of history, see Bercovitch, "Cotton Mather," in *Major Writers of Early American Literature*, pp. 93-149, and Mason I. Lowance, "Typology and the New England Way: Cotton Mather and the Exegesis of Biblical Types," *EAL*, 4 (1969), pp. 15-37.

[47] Cotton Mather, *The Wonderful Works of God Commemorated* (Boston, 1690), p. 43. For the following discussion of Cotton Mather's early sermons, I shall be drawing upon several works that shall be cited in the text by the following designations: *OM—Addresses to Old Men, Young Men, and Little Children* (Boston, 1690); *BV—Balsamum Vulnerarium* (Boston, 1692); *CC—A Companion for Communicants* (Boston, 1690); *CG—Call of the Gospel* (Boston, 1686); *SM—The Serviceable Man* (Boston, 1690); *SO—Small Offers toward the Service of the Tabernacle in the Wilderness* (Boston, 1689); *WW—The Wonderful Works of God* (Boston, 1690).

Son of Man shall appear . . . [when] *The Lord shall con-
sume that wicked one with the breath of his mouth, . . .
with the brightness of his coming"* (*WW*, pp. 3-4). When
Governor Andros was overthrown and the Glorious Revolution had ended the reign of the popish James II in England,
Mather took these events as signs of "the *Dawnings* of
that day" (*WW*, p. 4).

In this exuberant tone of millennial hope Mather introduced the members of the established second generation
and the young people of his own third generation to a new
theme of national salvation. In the preface to one of his
sermons that he dedicated "To my Country," he declared,
"Our *Good God* will not *ever* . . . Remove the People
which is now enriching this part of the New World, for
Another Nation to succeed in the room thereof" (*SM*, p. 2
of preface). Whenever Cotton Mather compared America
to the other countries of the world, he always found that
"there is no Land in the Universe more free from the de-
bauching and the debasing Vices of Ungodliness" than his
own.[48] Only New England "enjoys these Dews of Heaven
when the rest of the world is dry" (*CG*, p. 24), for the people on this "little spot of Ground . . . *have known* [Christ's
love] *above all the Families of the earth"* (*CG*, p. 24).

Because of his conviction of God's love for New England,
Mather suggested that the days of fasting and humiliation
be replaced by days of thanksgiving and song: "It is an *excellent thing* indeed that we may have a *Day of Thanksgiving* [when] we might all *stir up ourselves* . . . to *Sing*
and *Spread* the *praises* due to the Eternal God for the
excellent things which He has done" (*WW*, p. 20). God
the Father, as Cotton Mather imagined Him, responded
more favorably to thanksgiving than to lament: "As for
days of Thanksgiving . . . all men have seen the wonderful
successes of them" (*WW*, p. 21). In the opening lines of his
first published sermon, *The Call of the Gospel*, Mather

48 Cotton Mather, *Wonders of the Invisible World*, p. 11.

formulated what he believed to be a proper statement of thanksgiving from a grateful people: "Yea, who among us all . . . can forebear joining with the rapturous shouts of Heaven, with that *Angelical* and *Evangelical* Outcry in Luke 2: 14: *Glory to God in the highest, on earth peace, good will towards men!*" (*CG*, pp. 1-2).

In spite of his words of comfort and assurance, the most compelling problem for Cotton Mather, as well as for his fellow ministers, continued to be those "half-way" members of the church who still felt themselves unworthy of full membership. He believed "God hath sent me to Heal the Broken Hearted" (*BV*, p. 2), and he worked tirelessly to do so. As one who frequently suffered the pangs of doubt and shame himself, he could empathize with those who cried out, "*Alas, I am wretched and poor and miserable and Blind and Naked! . . . I am now condemned already!* And *The Great God is Angry with me, every Day!*" (*BV*, p. 8). And he could respond to the misery of those who believed, "*I Fear I have Committed the* UNPARDONABLE SIN, *and then I am utterly beyond the reach of all Mercy forever*" (*BV*, p. 78). Through his sermons Mather tried to "lay Open the Manifold and Amazing WOUNDS of a TROUBLED CONSCIENCE and Pour the *Balsam* of Seasonable *Counsels* and *Comforts* into those Terrible WOUNDS" (*BV*, title page), and he attempted to enlighten such sufferers about the inner workings of their consciences.

From his considerable study Mather had learned that "the Prophets would sometimes put *words* into the *Mouths* of them that they were travailing for the *Salvation* of" (*CG*, p. 33), and so in his sermons he also tried "something of that kind . . . by the Bringing of those Thoughts into your minds which may Comfort" (*CG*, p. 33). In this spirit he encouraged his listeners to "say now with yourselves . . . 'God may become *my Friend*, and *His Foe* may become *His Child*'" (*CG*, p. 35). Even the most heinous sinner may argue to himself and to Christ: "*A Dog may have crumbs; It seems I am a Dog*; Therefore . . . *I may have crumbs too*"

(*CG*, p. 29). Cotton Mather was certain that Christ "will deny no part of the *Syllogism* which shall thus be Framed by a wrestling *Faith*" (*CG*, p. 29).

To those who were still unable to conquer their fear, Mather explained that "the voice of a wounded Conscience is that of our Affrighted Father" (*BV*, p. 7), who reprimands out of affection for his child. Although the sinner should heed this inner voice, he should not fear it: the presence of the voice alone is a sign of redemption. Mather declared that it was "absurd" for such men "to have their Hearts wounded, sinking, swooning, with Imaginations about the *Election* of God" (*BV*, p. 82), for these fears in themselves "render it undubitably clear that you are among the *Elect*" (*BV*, p. 82). Mather also understood that those who labor under an over-scrupulous conscience "sometimes get a contracted or habitual *peevishness* of Soul which makes them Love to *wound* themselves" (*BV*, p. 18). And he had observed that once people acquired this habit of self-loathing they would often "have an unaccountable *pleasure* in their own *Torment* and, like madmen, it gratifies them to be cutting of themselves with all sorts of gross Arguments against their own good Estate" (*BV*, p. 18). Although Mather found these wounds of doubt and shame upon the hearts of the second- and third-generation people to be most grievous, he continued to counsel against despair: "Don't let your Imaginations be, *That there is no hope!*" (*CG*, p. 35).

In a *Companion for Communicants* (1690) Mather made his most complete statement on the acute problem of church membership and the Lord's Supper. "Assurance is not Absolutely Necessary in order to a *worthy Coming* unto the Holy Supper" (*CC*, p. 131), he told his congregation. And he extended his invitation for them to "Come with all your involuntary and unavoidable Infirmities . . . with all your Hated and your Loathed Plagues," for "you shall be welcome here though you have but Faith enough to say with Tears, *Lord, help my Unbelief!*" (*CC*, p. 77). In another of his comforting arguments, Mather reasoned that every member of the church had a right to partake of communion: all who attended services must have some interest in Christ; and since an interest in Christ is all that is required for full membership, then it is the privilege of every member to partake of the Lord's Supper (*CC*, p. 5). In fact, the young Mather argued that it was the duty of every church member to attend the sacrament because at the Last Supper Christ ordered His followers to "THIS DO" in memory of Him. For a church member not to come to the Lord's banquet "is a *Disobedience* to the *Commands* of the Lord Jesus Christ" (*CC*, p. 63).

On the question of the need for the communicant to make a public testimony of his faith, Mather observed that "Every Good man has not such a courage and presence of mind" (*CC*, p. 52). Therefore, all he required was that the believer write a note to the minister or tell him in private "*what Impressions the Word of God has had upon his Immortal Soul*" (*CC*, p. 53). Though they "may stand not like *Olive-plants about the Table of the Lord*, but rather like *Bruised Reeds*" (*CC*, p. 130), nevertheless the Lord will accept the weakest of plants. True faith need only be as great "*as a Grain of Mustard Seed*, and yet it is a *True Faith*" even if "almost Invisible" (*CC*, p. 130).

As a pastor, Cotton Mather had striking success with the young people of Boston. Under his guidance "many scores of *young* persons" had "taken upon them a more serious profession of Religion," and in meetings conducted by Mather in his home they endeavored "to quicken and strengthen one another in it" (*OM*, p. 46).[49] During his years of preparation for the ministry, he had implored God to "let me *write* something that may do good unto *young Persons* when I shall be dead and gone."[50] He always recalled that "our Lord Jesus Christ gave the most sensible

[49] See Mather's comments on these youth groups in his *Diary*, pp. 24, 80, 101, 179, 209, 370, 399, 420-421, 575.

[50] Cotton Mather, *Diary*, p. 9, and see similar comment, p. 7.

and pathetic manifestations of his *Love* to the *Youngest* of his Disciples" (*OM*, p. 46). In his *Addresses to Old Men, Young Men, and Little Children* in 1690 Mather declared openly his alliance with the young and attacked the older people for their unwillingness to release their hold upon the younger generation.

Cotton Mather's approach to the relationship between the generations was in direct contrast to that of his father, Increase, who had spent so much rhetoric berating the young. Now with Increase in England for four years, Cotton presented a stinging attack upon the ignorance, selfishness, and pride of the elders. Of course, it was too late for him to undo what his father had done, and ironically many of the elders Mather now attacked were the same men whom Increase had castigated in their youth. But with Mather the generational conflict became metaphor, and he assailed his symbolic fathers with vehemence that equaled if not surpassed that of his own father's sermons to the young of the 1670's.

After an opening apology in which he expressed his "filial Affection" for his seniors, Mather announced, "Fathers . . . I do . . . entreat you to attend unto a few Directions" (*OM*, p. 19). He had been shocked to discover that "there is a lamentable ignorance about the Lord Jesus Christ in many that have lived unto old Age"; in fact, it was a "scandal . . . how little many *old men* among ourselves do understand about *The Covenant of Redemption*" (*OM*, p. 21). To illustrate his charge, he told of one *"old man* who had enjoyed the constant Preaching of the Word, and yet when he lay on his Death-bed, he still thought: *Jesus Christ was an amiable Youth*, and other things too ridiculous to be recited" (*OM*, p. 21). Mather might have added that this deficiency in the religious knowledge of the elders had resulted from the lack of emphasis upon Christ or the Redemption in the Puritan sermons during the decades between 1650 and 1680. But he was not disposed to recognize these mitigating circumstances.

A central theme of Cotton Mather's address to the old men was the issue of the patriarchal control of property and power by the elders. He observed that as men grow older, "the fear of want comes upon them and they are then most anxious about living in the world," and they become "infinitely *sparing* and *sordid*, and they scrape to lay up, without any Bounds" (*OM*, p. 42). He found such acquisitiveness despicable: "You are at . . . pains to hoard up Legacies and Portions. . . . *Fathers*, you dishonor yourselves" (*OM*, p. 42). He predicted that those fathers who claimed to be gathering wealth for their children's inheritance would only discover by the time that they would pass on these legacies that the young people, "will not thank you for them" (*OM*, p. 42). Mather further urged the elders to loosen their control over the society of New England in order to allow the young people to play a more significant role. "Since you are past the doing of anything in the Field," he advised, "be much in *prayer* for the Rising generation" (*OM*, p. 37). Instead of trying to direct the young people, "get into the *Mount*, that you may there procure for us the Salvations of the Lord" (*OM*, p. 37).

To those older men who might feel that they are yet vigorous enough to play an active role in the society, Mather recommended, "Look often into your *Coffins*" and "Remember *that you are now marching off apace*" (*DM*, p. 39). Perhaps to make the elders more concerned with their own health than with the society, Cotton drew upon his medical knowledge for a morbid description of the aging process: "Your parts are under a Decay, your Fancy, your Judgment, your Memory are now failing. . . . You can't lie long asleep; nor sleep late in a Morning. . . . You become Deaf and thick of Hearing; . . . *Desire fails*; that is, to Meat or Drinks, or the other Delights of human Life. . . . It can't be long before the *Silver Cord* of your spinal marrow will be *snap't* . . . ; that it can't be long before the *pitcher* of your Arterious Vein be crackt at the right ven-

196

tricle of your heart. . . . Before the *Wheel* of your great
Artery be split at the left ventricle" *(OM*, pp. 40-41). The
imagery of decay and doom was still present in the New
England sermon, but with Cotton Mather that imagery no
longer applied to the members of the younger generations.

Perhaps it was Mather's effort to appeal to the young
people of Boston that led him to present religious doctrines
in generational terms. When Mather wanted to emphasize
the meaning of the Covenant of Redemption, he preached
that before Christ's act of Redemption the people had owed
God the Father *"meritorious Obedience"* (*SO*, p. 5), just
like that which a child owes his father when he lives under
his father's roof. Under the New Dispensation, however,
"this Duty is to be paid in a way of *ingenuous* Gratitude"
(*SO*, p. 5), just as a mature adult who has established his
own home need only demonstrate his gratitude to his father.

Mather also taught that the Covenant was not a bond
of submission and obedience. The individual who joined
the church or declared his belief in Christ became free and
independent. He urged his listeners to *"run away from
your old masters.* Come away poor souls, come away from
your land of your Captivity" (*SO*, p. 23). Since only those
outside the Covenant were shackled, Mather urged his listeners to release themselves and toil no longer for "those
Task-masters which have hitherto been torturing your soul"
(*SO*, p. 23). Join with Christ and escape tyranny like a poor
apprentice who flees an oppressive Master: "Look upon the
grim face of the *Patrons* under which you groan; say to
them all, *Farewell, you malicious, you bloody, you sordid
Masters, Farewell; We hope you shall* never *have any of our*
Service *more"* (*SO*, p. 24). To young people who felt they
had labored under an unfairly demanding father or master,
Cotton Mather must have had strong appeal when he
shouted defiantly from the pulpit: *"Tis enough!* Say, *The
time past may suffice!* Thus take ye the *Wings of a Dove*
and flee away!" (*SO*, p. 24). It is no wonder that Mather's

197

house was frequently filled with young people who had "taken upon them a more serious profession of Religion" (*OM*, p. 46).

One of Mather's most effective techniques for enticing the young into the church was his emphasis upon the greatest enemy of youth, the Devil. During the 1660's and 1670's, when the ministers had placed the blame for all of New England's troubles upon the people themselves, the figure of Satan had occupied a secondary position to the rising generation as the cause of evils in the colony. With the shift in the message of the sermon toward assurance of the young in the 1680's, Satan reemerged as the principal foe. More than any of his fellow preachers, the young Cotton Mather found the image of the Devil a useful one.

Although even John Calvin had thought of the Devil only as a metaphor, a "sphere of atrocity and horror under the name of a person,"[51] Cotton Mather gave the figure of Satan great imaginative power. He encouraged the people of New England to project all of their inner fears and doubts upon this "accursed enemy" and to redirect their abhorrence away from themselves and each other and toward this ancient villain. Mather insisted that Satan had caused all of New England's trials and had tried to persuade the Father that there had been a decline of piety among God's people. Because Satan is "to *young* men a particular Enemy" (*OM*, p. 55), he maligned the reputation of the rising generations before the Lord: "There is a *Court* somewhere kept in the *invisible world* at which the Devils prefer as many complaints as they can against us. It is in this *Court* that they represent us as doing the *things for which the wrath of God should come upon the Children of Disobedience*" (*OM*, p. 55). Mather also believed the Devil to be responsible for much of the inner doubt and anguish of conscience of many of his church members: "The

51 John Calvin, quoted in Roland Frye, *God, Man and Satan* (Princeton, N.J.: Princeton University Press, 1960), p. 22.

EVIL SPIRIT has his marvelous *Energy* in wounding of
our Consciences" (*BV*, p. 14).

To appeal to the imaginations of the young, Mather portrayed Satan as an old man whose special interest was to
capture and enslave young people. In the invisible world
there was a *"grand Segniour* among [all the devils]: *One*
of peculiar Dignity and Influence, this *chief* Devil we may
call *the* Devil" (*OM*, p. 54), and it is he who is the "cursed
Enemy which all *young* men are to contend withal" (*OM*,
p. 52). Like a shrewd elder, this senior devil uses *"counsel,*
and *study*, and labor in the *doing*" (*OM*, p. 54) of his evil
work to young people. All who are not safe with Christ are
"Bond Slaves and *Captives* of the devil" (*OM*, p. 60). They
become servants in the family of the Devil and are forced
to labor under Satan's commands because "he is a sort of a
Prince and a *God* unto them" (*OM*, p. 60). When a person
does manage to overcome this enemy and come to Christ,
that believer achieves a new freedom: "He gets rid of his
former *Taskmaster* like *Israel* escaped from *Pharaoh*" (*OM*,
p. 60).

With this renewed emphasis upon the figure of Satan in
the colonies in the late 1680's, it is not surprising that the
witchcraft episode occurred during the brief period of confusion and doubt after the political crisis of 1689-1690. Cotton Mather and the other preachers of the 1680's had taught
the colonists that they should not blame themselves when
things did not seem to go well for New England. And in
1692 the people found a new scapegoat to blame for their
sudden turmoil: the Devil's earthly allies. Although it may
not have been the result only of Cotton Mather's tendency
to present the Devil as a ruling elder, the witchcraft trials
saw young people accusing older people and even prominent authorities of heinous crimes.[52]

[52] For studies of the witchcraft episode as the result of political and
religious change, see George L. Kittredge, *Witchcraft in Old and New
England* (Cambridge: Harvard University Press, 1929), in particular

An observer at the Salem trials, Mather clearly agreed with Michael Wigglesworth "that innocent blood has been shed, and that many have had their hands defiled therewith."[53] But he did not speak out vigorously enough.[54] Perhaps he was silently considering the part his own sermons may have played in stirring the profound and complex emotional forces that erupted in the summer of 1692. After these events the figure of Satan appeared much less frequently in Cotton Mather's sermons. In his biography of his father, Samuel Mather (1706-1785) reported that at home Cotton Mather would tell his children of the *"good Angels* who love them, help them, [and] guard them," but "he would not say much to them of the *evil Angels* because he would not have them entertain any frightful Fancies about the Apparitions of *Devils.*"[55] The lessons of Salem were not wasted on Cotton Mather. Throughout the rest of his career he sought to bring a new era of religious confidence to New England.

---

pp. 372ff; Wesley Frank Craven, *The Colonies in Transition, 1660-1713* (New York: Harper & Row, 1968), especially pp. 250-252; H.R. Trevor-Roper, *Crisis of the Seventeenth Century,* in particular p. 128, where he sees the "social fear . . . of a different kind of society" as the underlying cause of the terrors.

For the best studies of the witchcraft delusion as a psychological phenomena, see Chadwick Hansen, *Witchcraft at Salem,* and Starkey, *The Devil in Massachusetts,* in particular, p. 32, where Starkey notes the frustration endured by young women in New England, where the marriages were delayed. See also Kai T. Erikson, *Wayward Puritans,* pp. 137-159.

On Cotton Mather's involvement in the witchcraft episode, see Thomas J. Holmes, "Cotton Mather and His Writings on Witchcraft," in *The Papers of the Bibliographical Society of America,* 18 (1924), pp. 31-59; Charles W. Upham, *Salem Witchcraft* (Boston, 1867, reprinted New York: F. Ungar Pub. Co., 1959); and especially Hansen, *Witchcraft at Salem,* pp. xiv and 220-221.

[53] As quoted in Hansen, *Witchcraft at Salem,* p. 274.

[54] *Ibid.,* p. 265.

[55] Samuel Mather, *Cotton Mather,* pp. 17-18.

E P I L O G U E

DURING and after the witchcraft delusion there occurred a
brief revival of the old themes of decline as a few of the
ministers suddenly shifted the blame for New England's
struggles back to the people themselves. However, there is
a touch of nostalgia in these later chastisements that sets
them apart from the blistering attacks of the 1670's, and
the image of the benevolent God the Father is present even
in the less assuring sermons of the 1690's.[1] The direction
toward hope and assurance in Puritan theology and preaching had been well established after the period of searching
and doubt of the late 1670's and early 1680's, particularly
in the writings of Samuel Willard and Increase Mather.
Cotton Mather and the young men like Ebenezer Pemberton and Thomas Prince who entered the ministry in the
early eighteenth century under Cotton's guidance would
continue to preach a message of hope. That course would
not be seriously altered until the brilliant fourth-generation
minister, Jonathan Edwards (b. 1703), would restore the

[1] See, for example, Joshua Scottow, *Old Men's Tears for their Own
Declensions* (Boston, 1693) and *Narrative of the Planting of the Massachusetts Colony* (Boston, 1694) reprinted in the *Collections of the Massachusetts Historical Society*, 4th ser., 4 (1858), pp. 279-330; see also
Increase Mather, *A Discourse Concerning the Uncertainty of the Times
of Men and the Necessity of Being Prepared for Sudden Changes and
Death* (Boston, 1697), in particular pp. 35-37.

figure of an angry God and place the people of New England again in His hands.

Between 1720 and 1750 many of the young people who had migrated from their homes in the eastern towns were caught up in the sudden wave of powerful religious revival that swept the western sections of New England. These revivals affected most the young men in those areas so that the increase in church membership of males during this period was more than twice that of women.[2] Of course, the interrelationships between the people and their religion cannot have been precisely the same as they had been in the later seventeenth century. Much was changing in the society: Puritan child-rearing practices seem to have been mollified in the early eighteenth century, new philosophical attitudes toward authority had begun to take hold in America, and a different, if still precarious, relationship to England had been established. Even the fairly isolated western communities had to be touched by such important developments. However, in the sermons, particularly those of Edwards, the figure of the wrathful God the Father again became the central image, and, as Edwards reported: "It was a time of joy in families on the account of salvation's being brought unto them; parents rejoicing over their children as new born, and husbands over their wives, and wives over their husbands. . . . every hearer eager to drink in the words of the minister as they came from his mouth; the assembly in general were, from time to time, in tears while the word was preached; some weeping with sorrow and distress, others with joy and love, others with pity and concern for the souls of their neighbors."[3] Clearly, there continued to be a vital connection between the emotional lives of the people and the language of their ministers.

It is significant that another major religious revival oc-

[2] See Cowing, "Sex and Preaching in the Great Awakening," *AQ*, 20 (1968), pp. 624-644.

[3] *The Works of President Edwards in four volumes* (New York: Leavitt, 1843), III, 235.

curred in America during the critical years between 1820 and 1850, when the second and third generations of the revolutionary founding fathers were attempting to define themselves as members of a new nation. During that Second Great Awakening men like Charley Finney, Lyman Beecher, and Nathaniel William Taylor created from the theology and symbolism of American Protestantism the message and imagery of manifest destiny that combined an awe of the founding fathers with the confidence in the ultimate greater victory of the sons.

Perhaps in a time of disruption in human affairs, when old customs and continuity are undermined, religious language inevitably becomes dynamic and assumes new symbolic meanings. The poets, linguists, philosophers, and theologians of our own day have made us more conscious of the difficulties of communication. We have come to see that it is through language that we define and understand our existence and that those who shape the language are truly unacknowledged legislators of the world. With our knowledge of American religious history we should not be surprised, then, that in our present period of economic uncertainty, public distrust, and generational tension many young people are seeking reassurance of their roles and identities from religion. After the past two decades, during which the threat of sudden and total destruction from nuclear attack was constant and the lament of the failure and decay of America's holy mission was a recurrent motif of the national rhetoric, young people are now seeking a message of hope and inner peace. In the countryside and on the campuses hundreds of thousands of the young are studying the Bible, forming religious and quasi-religious groups, and searching for charismatic and reassuring religious leaders.

In the case of New England in the later seventeenth century, the deep psychosocial crisis wrought by the rapidly changing milieu and by a unique generational struggle created a serious need for a language by which the members

203

of the younger generations could understand and cope with their cultural situation and with historical events that threatened to overwhelm them. Although the Puritan sermon certainly spoke to important political and social issues of the day, the power of the sermon was in its symbolic and metaphorical meaning, which resulted from a dynamic interaction between the clergy and their people.

I. Primary Works

ALTHOUGH my study has led me to examine all the works published in America before 1700, those which are quoted directly or which have had a significant bearing upon my analysis are cited here.

A. Sermon Literature

Adams, William. *God's Eye on the Contrite*. Boston, 1685.
————. *The Necessity of Pouring Out of the Spirit from on High upon a Sinning Apostatizing People*. Boston, 1679.
Allen, James. *New Englands Choicest Blessing*. Boston, 1679.
Allin, James. *Serious Advice to Deliver Ones from Sickness*. Boston, 1679.
Allin, John. *Animadversions upon the Antisynodalia Americana*. Cambridge, 1664.
————. *The Spouse of Christ Coming Out of Affliction, Leaning upon Her Beloved*. Cambridge, 1672.
Arnold, Samuel. *David Serving His Generation*. Cambridge, 1674.
Bailey, John. *Man's Chief End to Glorify God*. Boston, 1689.

Burnet, Gilbert. *A Sermon Preached before the House of Commons*. Boston, 1689.

Carré, Ezechiel. *The Charitable Samaritan*. Boston, 1689.

Cobbett, Thomas. *A Fruitful and Useful Discourse touching the Honour due from Children to Parents and the Duty of Parents towards their Children*. London, 1656.

Cotton, John. *Covenant of God's Free Grace*. London, 1645.

———. *God's Mercie Mixed with His Justice*. London, 1641. ed. Everett Emerson. Reprinted, Gainesville, Florida: Scholars' Facsimiles, 1958.

———. *God's Promise to His Plantations*. London, 1634.

———. *The Way of Life*. London, 1641.

Danforth, Samuel. *A Brief Recognition of New-Englands Errand into the Wilderness*. Cambridge, 1671.

———. *The Cry of Sodom Enquired into*. Cambridge, 1674.

Davenport, John. *Another Essay for Investigation of the Truth. In Answer to Two Questions*. Cambridge, 1663.

———. *Gods Call to His People to Turn unto Him; Together with His Promise to Turn unto Them*. Cambridge, 1669.

Eliot, John. *A Brief Answer to a Small Book written by John Norcot against Infant-Baptism*. Boston, 1679.

Firmin, Giles. *The Real Christian; or A Treatise of Effectual Calling*. London, 1670.

Fitch, James. *A Holy Connexion*. Cambridge, 1674.

Higginson, John. *The Cause of God and His People in New-England*. Cambridge, 1663.

———. *Our Dying Savior's Legacy of Peace*. Boston, 1686.

Hoar, Leonard, M.D. *The Sting of Death and Death Unstung*. Boston, 1680.

Hooker, Samuel. *Righteousness Rained from Heaven*. Cambridge, 1677.

Hooker, Thomas. *Redemption: Three Sermons (1637-1656)*, ed. Everett H. Emerson. Reprinted, Gainesville, Florida: Scholars' Facsimiles, 1956.

———. *The Souls Implantation*. London, 1637.

Hubbard, William. *The Benefit of a Well-Ordered Conversation.* Boston, 1684.

———. *The Happiness of a People.* Boston, 1676.

Keith, George. *The Presbyterian and Independent Visible Churches in New-England.* London, 1691.

Ker, Patrick. *The Map of Man's Misery.* Boston, 1692.

Mather, Cotton. *Addresses to Old Men, Young Men, and Little Children.* Boston, 1690.

———. *Balsamum Vulnerarium e Scriptura, or the Cause and Cure of a Wounded Spirit.* Boston, 1691.

———. *Baptismal Piety.* Boston, 1727.

———. *Best Ornaments of Youth.* Boston, 1707.

———. *The Call of the Gospel.* Boston, 1686.

———. *Cares About the Nurseries.* Boston, 1702.

———. *Coderius Americanus.* Boston, 1708.

———. *A Companion for Communicants.* Boston, 1690.

———. *Days of Humiliation, Times of Affliction, 1696-1727.* ed. George Orians. Gainesville, Florida: Scholars' Facsimiles, 1970.

———. *The Duty of Children.* Boston, 1719.

———. *Early Piety Exemplified.* London, 1689.

———. *Early Religion Urged.* Boston, 1694.

———. *Family Religion Urged.* Boston, 1709.

———. *A Family Sacrifice.* Boston, 1703.

———. *A Family Well-Ordered.* Boston, 1699.

———. *Help for Distressed Parents.* Boston, 1695.

———. *Manuductio ad Ministerium.* Boston, 1726.

———. *The Minister, A Sermon.* Boston, 1722.

———. *Ornaments of the Daughters of Zion, or the Character and Happiness of Virtuous Women.* Boston, 1691.

———. *Parental Wishes and Changes.* Boston, 1705.

———. *The Present State of New England.* Boston, 1690.

———. *The Pure Nazarite.* Boston, 1721.

———. *Religion of the Closet.* Boston, 1705.

———. *Repeated Warnings.* Boston, 1712.

———. *The Resort of Piety.* Boston, 1716.

Mather, Cotton. *The Serviceable Man*. Boston, 1690.

―――. *Small Offers toward the Service of the Tabernacle in the Wilderness*. Boston, 1689.

―――. *Successive Generations*. Boston, 1715.

―――. *Things Young People Should Think Upon*. Boston, 1700.

―――. *Thoughts for a Day of Rain*. Boston, 1712.

―――. *Wayes and Joyes of Early Piety*. Boston, 1712.

―――. *Weaned Christian*. Boston, 1704.

―――. *Will of a Father Submitted To*. Boston, 1713.

―――. *The Wonderful Works of God Commemorated*. Boston, 1690.

―――. *A Young Man's Preservative*. Boston, 1699.

―――. *Youth Advised*. Boston, 1719.

Mather, Cotton and Others. *A Course of Sermons on Early Piety*. Boston, 1721.

Mather, Eleazar. *A Serious Exhortation to the Present and Succeeding Generation in New England*. Cambridge, 1671.

Mather, Increase. *A Call from Heaven to the Rising Generation*. Boston, 1679.

―――. *The Day of Trouble Is Near*. Cambridge, 1674.

―――. *A Discourse Concerning the Danger of Apostasy*. Boston, 1679.

―――. *A Dissertation . . . to Encourage Unsanctified Persons to Communion*. Boston, 1708.

―――. *The Divine Right of Infant Baptism*. Boston, 1681.

―――. *The Doctrine of Divine Providence Opened and Applyed*. Boston, 1684.

―――. *An Earnest Exhortation to the Children of New England*. Boston, 1700.

―――. *An Earnest Exhortation to the Inhabitants of New-England, to Harken to the Voice of God*. Boston, 1676.

―――. *The Glorious Kingdom of Christ now approaching*. Boston, 1710.

———. *The Greatest Sinner Exhorted and Encouraged to Come to Christ and that Now Without Delaying.* Boston, 1686.

———. *Heavens Alarm to the World.* Boston, 1681, reprinted in 1682.

———. *The Mystery of Christ Opened and Applyed.* Boston, 1686.

———. *Practical Truths Tending to Promote the Power of Godliness.* Boston, 1682.

———. *Pray for the Rising Generation.* Boston, 1678, reprinted in 1679.

———. *Remarkable Providences Illustrative of the Earlier Days of American Colonisation.* London: J. R. Smith, 1856.

———. *Renewal of Covenant the Great Duty Incumbent on Decaying and Distressed Churches.* Boston, 1677.

———. *Returning Unto God the Great Concernment of a Covenant People.* Boston, 1680.

———. *A Sermon wherein is shewed that the church of God is sometimes a subject of Great Persecution.* Boston, 1682.

———. *Some Important Truths about Conversion.* Boston, 1684.

———. *The Times of Men Are in the Hand of God.* Boston, 1675.

———. *The Wicked Mans Portion.* Boston, 1675.

———. *Wo to Drunkards.* Cambridge, 1673.

Mather, Nathaniel. *A Sermon Wherein is Shewed That It Is the DUTY and . . . CARE on Believers of CHRIST to Live in the Constant Exercise of GRACE.* Boston, 1684.

Mather, Richard. *A Disputation Concerning Church-Members and their Children.* London, 1659.

———. *Farewel-Exhortation To the Church and People of Dorchester.* Cambridge, 1657.

Mather, Samuel. *A Testimony from the Scriptures against Idolatry & Superstition.* Cambridge, 1670.

Mitchell, Jonathan. *Nehemiah on the Wall in Trouble-som Times.* Cambridge, 1671.

Moodey, Joshua. *A Practical Discourse Concerning the Choice Benefit of Communion with God in His House.* Boston, 1685.

———. *Souldiery Spiritualized or the Christian Souldier Orderly, and Strenuously Engaged in the Spiritual Warre, and So Fighting the Good Fight.* Cambridge, 1674.

Norton, John. *The Orthodox Evangelist.* London, 1657.

———. *Three Choice and Profitable Sermons.* Cambridge, 1664.

Nowell, Samuel. *Abraham in Arms.* Boston, 1678.

Oakes, Urian. *New-England Pleaded with.* Cambridge, 1673.

———. *A Seasonable Discourse.* Cambridge, 1682.

———. *The Soveraign Efficacy of Divine Providence.* Boston, 1682.

———. *The Unconquerable, All-Conquering, & More-Than-Conquering Souldier.* Cambridge, 1674.

Oxenbridge, John. *New-England Freeman Warned and Warmed, To Be Free Indeed.* Cambridge, 1673.

———. *A Quickening Word.* Cambridge, 1670.

Pemberton, Ebenezer. *A Funeral Sermon, on the Death of the Rev. Mr. Samuel Willard.* Boston, 1707.

———. *A Sermon Preached in the Audience of the General Assembly.* Boston, 1706.

Rogers, Daniel. *Matrimonial Honour.* London, 1642.

Rowlandson, Joseph. *The Possibility of Gods Forsaking a People.* Boston, 1682.

Scottow, Joshua. *Old Men's Tears for their Own Declensions.* Boston, 1691.

Shepard, Thomas. "Election Sermon in 1638" in *New England Historical Register,* 24 (1870), pp. 361-366.

———. *The Sincere Convert.* London, 1650.

———. *The Sound Believer.* London, 1664.

———. *Three Valuable Pieces.* Boston, 1747.

Shepard, Thomas Jr. *Eye-Salve, or a Watch-Word . . . to Take Heed of Apostasy.* Cambridge, 1673.

————. *Wine for Gospel Wantons: or, Cautions against Spiritual Drunkenness.* Cambridge, 1668.

Standfast, Richard. *A Little Handful of Cordial Comforts for a Fainting Soul.* Boston, 1690.

Stoddard, Solomon. *An Answer to Some Cases of Conscience Respecting the Country.* Boston, 1722. In *The Magazine of History*, No. 55, pt. 2, 14 (1917), pp. 191-207.

————. *A Guide to Christ, Or the way of directing Souls that are under the Work of CONVERSION.* Boston, 1714.

————. *Safety in Appearing at the Day of Judgement in the Righteousness of Christ.* Boston, 1687.

————. *The Tryal of Assurance.* Boston, 1698.

————. *The Way for a People To Live Long in the Land that God Hath Given Them.* Boston, 1703.

Stoughton, William. *New-Englands True Interest.* Cambridge, 1670.

Taylor, Edward. *Christographia*, ed. Norman Grabo. New Haven and London: Yale University Press, 1962.

Thatcher, Thomas. *A Fast of Gods Choosing.* Boston, 1678.

Torrey, Samuel. *A Plea for the Life of Dying Religion.* Boston, 1683.

Wadsworth, Benjamin. *Invitations to the Gospel Feast or free offer of salvation through Christ.* Boston, 1715.

————. *Mutual Love and Peace Among Christians.* Boston, 1701.

————. *The Well-Ordered Family.* Boston, 1712.

Wakeman, Samuel. *A Young Man's Legacy to the Rising Generation.* Cambridge, 1673.

Walley, Thomas. *Balm in Gilead to Heal Sions Wounds.* Cambridge, 1669, reprinted 1670.

Whiting, John. *The Way of Israels Welfare.* Boston, 1686.

Willard, Samuel. *A Brief Discourse on Justification.* Boston, 1686.

————. *A Child's Portion: or the Unseen Glory.* Boston, 1684.

Willard, Samuel. *A Compleat Body of Divinity*, eds. Thomas Prince and Joseph Sewall. Boston, 1726.

———. *Covenant-Keeping the Way to Blessedness*. Boston, 1682.

———. *The Doctrine of the Covenant of Redemption*. Boston, 1693.

———. *The Duty of a People That Have Renewed Their Covenant*. Boston, 1680.

———. *The Fiery Tryal No Strange Thing*. Boston, 1682.

———. *The Heart Garrisoned*. Cambridge, 1676.

———. *Heavenly Merchandize; or the Purchasing of TRUTH Recommended and the Selling of It Disswaded*. Boston, 1686.

———. *The High Esteem Which God Hath of the Death of His Saints . . . Occasioned by the Death of the Worshipful John Hull*. Boston, 1683.

———. *Mercy Magnified on a Penitent Prodigal*. Boston, 1684.

———. *A Remedy against Despair*. Boston, 1700.

———. *A Sermon . . . Occasioned by the Death of the Much Honoured John Leveret*. Boston, 1679.

———. *Spiritual Desertions Discovered and Remedied . . . for the Help of Dark Souls*. Boston, 1699.

———. *Useful Instructions for a Professing People in Times of Great Security and Degeneracy*. Cambridge, 1673.

Wilson, John. *A Seasonable Watch-Word unto Christians against the Dreams & Dreamers of This Generation*. Cambridge, 1677.

B. Diaries, Journals, and Autobiographies

Adams, William. "Memory of the Reverend William Adams of Dedham, Massachusetts," *Collections of the Massachusetts Historical Society*, 4th ser., 1 (1852), pp. 8-22.

Bradstreet, Simon. "Diary, 1664-83," *New England Historical and Genealogical Register*, 8 (1854), pp. 325-333 and 9 (1855), pp. 43-51.

Bullivant, Dr. Benjamin. "Diary, 1690," in *Massachusetts Historical Society Proceedings*, 1st ser., 16 (1878), pp. 103-108.

Clapp, Roger. *The Memoirs of Captain Roger Clapp.* Boston, 1731.

Coit, Mehitable Chandler. *Mehitable Chandler Coit, Her Book, 1714.* Norwich, Conn., 1895.

"The Correspondence of John Woodbridge, Jr. and Richard Baxter," ed., Raymond P. Stearns, *New England Quarterly*, 10 (1937), pp. 577-583.

Cotton, John. "Diary of the Honorable John Cotton, 1694-1698," *Publications of the Colonial Society of Massachusetts*, 26 (1925), pp. 277-280.

Davenport, John. *The Letters of John Davenport, Puritan Divine.* ed. Isabel M. Calder. New Haven: Yale University Press, 1937.

Easton, Peter. "Diary, 1631-1678," *Newport Mercury*, Dec. 26, 1857 and Jan. 2, 1858.

Eliot, John. "Description of New England in 1650," *Massachusetts Historical Society Proceedings*, 2nd ser., 2 (1886), pp. 46-50.

————. Diary, 1643-1677," *New England Historical and Genealogical Register*, 35 (1881), pp. 21-24, 241-247.

Flynt, Josiah. "Diary of Rev. Josiah Flynt, 1653-1674," in *Dedham Historical Register*, 10 (1899), pp. 19-25.

Green, Joseph. "The Diary of the Reverend Joseph Green," *Essex Institute Historical Collections*, 8 (1866), pp. 215-224; 10 (1869), pp. 73-104; 36 (1900), pp. 325-330.

Grove, John. "The Diary of John Grove, 1669-1794," in *Connecticut Magazine*, 10 (1906), pp. 18-24.

Hamond, Lawrence. "Diary of Captain Lawrence Hammond, 1677-94," *Massachusetts Historical Society Proceedings*, 2nd ser., 7 (1891-1892), pp. 144-172.

Hobart, David. "Diary of David Hobart, 1679-1740," in the *Diary of Rev. William Bentley.* Salem, 1911, III, pp. 284-286.

Hobart, Peter. "Diary of Rev. Peter Hobart, 1635-1678," in the *Diary of Rev. William Bentley*. Salem, 1911, III, pp. 282-284.

Homes, William. "Diary, 1689-1746," *New England Historical and Genealogical Register*, 48 (1894), pp. 446-453; 49 (1895), pp. 413-416; 50 (1896), pp. 155-166.

Hull, John. "The Diaries of John Hull," in *Transactions and Collections of the American Antiquarian Society*, 3 (1857).

Keayne, Robert. "The Apologia of Robert Keayne," ed. Bernard Bailyn, *Publications of the Colonial Society of Massachusetts, Transactions*, 43 (1964).

Lechford, Thomas. *Note-book . . . June 27, 1638 to July 29, 1641*, ed. Edward Everett Hale. Cambridge: J. Wilson and Son, 1885.

Mather, Cotton. *Diary of Cotton Mather*, ed. C. W. Ford. 2 vols. New York: Frederick Ungar Publishing Co., 1957. Also published as "Diary of Cotton Mather, 1681-1708," *Collections of the Massachusetts Historical Society*, 7th ser., 7-8 (1911-1912).

————. *The Diary of Cotton Mather, D.D., F.R.S. for the Year 1712*, ed. William R. Manierre, II. Charlottesville: University Press of Virginia, 1964.

————. *Selected Letters of Cotton Mather*, ed. Kenneth Silverman. Baton Rouge: Louisiana State University Press, 1971.

Mather, Increase. "The Autobiography of Increase Mather," ed. M. G. Hall. *Proceedings of the American Antiquarian Society*, 71, pt. 2 (1962), pp. 271-360.

————. "Diary of the Rev. Increase Mather, 1674-1687," *Proceedings of the Massachusetts Historical Society*, 2nd ser., 13 (1899-1900), pp. 340-374; "Another Version, 1674-1687," pp. 398-411.

Mourt, G. and others. *A Relation or Journal of . . . the English Plantation settled at Plymouth in New England*. London, 1622. Reprinted and edited, Dwight B. Heath. New York: Corinth Books, 1963.

Paine, John. "Diary of Deacon John Paine, 1695-1718" in *Mayflower Descendant*, 8 (1906), pp. 180-184, 227-231; 9 (1907), pp. 49-51, 97-99, 136-140.

———. "John Paine's Journal," *Publications of the Colonial Society of Massachusetts*, 18 (1917), pp. 188-191.

Pierpont, Jonathan. "Diary of Reverend Jonathan Pierpont, 1682-1707," *New England Historical and Genealogical Register*, 13 (1859), pp. 255-258.

Randolph, Edward. "Diary and Letters, 1675-1700," *Massachusetts Historical Society Proceedings*, 1st ser., 18 (1880-1881), pp. 258-261.

Russell, Noahdiah. "Diary of the Reverend Noahdiah Russell, 1682-1688," *New England Historical and Genealogical Register*, 7 (1853), pp. 53-60.

Scottow, Joshua. "Journal, 1675," *New England Historical and Genealogical Register*, 43 (1889), pp. 68-70.

Sewall, Samuel. *The Diary of Samuel Sewall, 1674-1729, Collections of the Massachusetts Historical Society*, 5th ser., 5-7 (1878-1882).

Shepard, Thomas. "Autobiography of the Rev. Thomas Shepard," *Publications of the Colonial Society of Massachusetts*, 27 (1932), pp. 345-400.

———. *God's Plot: The Paradoxes of Puritan Piety, Being the Autobiography and Journal of Thomas Shepard*, ed. with an introduction, Michael McGiffert. Amherst: University of Massachusetts Press, 1972.

Taylor, Edward. "Diary of Edward Taylor, 1668-72," *Massachusetts Historical Society Proceedings*, 1st ser., 18 (1880-1881), pp. 5-18.

———. "Spiritual Relation," ed. Donald E. Sanford in *American Literature*, 35 (Jan., 1964), pp. 467-473.

Vaughan, Major William. "Diary of Major William Vaughan, 1684," in George E. Hodgdon, *Reminiscence and Genealogical Record of the Vaughan Family*. Rochester, New York, 1918.

White, Elizabeth. *The Experience of God's Gracious Dealings*. Boston, 1741.

Wigglesworth, Michael. *The Diary of Michael Wigglesworth: 1653-1657*, ed. Edmund S. Morgan. New York: Harper & Row, 1965.

Winthrop, John. *Journal of John Winthrop*. Lincoln, Mass.: Sawtells of Somerset, 1969.

C. Histories, Records, and Additional Works

Becon, Thomas. *The Catechism of Thomas Becon*, ed. the Reverend John Ayre. Cambridge: University Press, 1844.

Boston Town Records from 1642 to 1729, in *Report of the Records Commission*, Vol. 8. Boston: Rockwell and Churchill, 1882.

Bradford, William. "First Dialogue, or The Sum of a Conference between Some Young Men . . . and Sundry Ancient Men" (w. 1648) in *Old South Leaflets*, Vol. 2, Number 49. Boston, 1893.

———. *Of Plymouth Plantation, 1620-1657*, ed. Samuel Eliot Morison. New York: Knopf, 1966.

Bradstreet, Anne. *The Works of Anne Bradstreet*, ed. Jeannine Hensley. Cambridge: Harvard University Press, 1967.

Browne, Robert. *The Writings of Robert Harrison and Robert Browne*, ed. Albert Peel and Leland H. Carlson. London: G. Allen & Unwin, 1953.

Calvin, John. *Institutes of the Christian Religion*, trans. Ford Battles. Philadelphia: Westminster Press, 1960.

Chronicles of the First Planters of the Colony of Massachusetts Bay, ed. Alexander Young. Boston: Little, Brown, 1846.

Edwards, Jonathan. *Images or Shadows of Divine Things*, ed. Perry Miller. New Haven: Yale University Press, 1948.

———. *The Works of President Edwards in four volumes*. New York: Leavitt, 1843.

Hubbard, William. *A General History of New England From the Discovery to 1680*, in *Collections of the Massachusetts Historical Society*, 2nd ser., 5-6 (1848), and Cambridge: Hilliard and Metcalf, 1815.

————. *A Narrative of the Troubles with the Indians in New-England.* 2 vols. Boston, 1677, ed. Samuel G. Drake, Roxbury, Massachusetts, 1865.

Hutchinson, Thomas. *The History of the Colony of Massachusetts Bay*, ed. Lawrence S. Mayo. 3 vols. Cambridge, Massachusetts: Harvard University Press, 1936.

Janeway, James. *A Token for Children.* London, 1672, reprinted Boston, 1702.

Lechford, Thomas. *Plain Dealing, or News from New England.* London, 1642, reprinted and ed. Darret B. Rutman. New York: Johnson Reprint Corp., 1969.

Mather, Cotton. *Bonifacius: An Essay Upon the Good*, ed. David Levin. Cambridge, Mass.: Harvard University Press, 1966.

————. *The Christian Philosopher*, ed. Josephine K. Piercy. Gainesville, Florida: Scholars' Facsimiles, 1968.

————. *Cotton Mather: Selections*, ed. Kenneth Murdock. New York: Hafner, 1926.

————. *Magnalia Christi Americana.* 2 vols. Hartford: Silas Anclaus & Son, 1853.

————. *Parentator.* Boston, 1724.

————. *The Wonders of the Invisible World.* Boston, 1693, reprinted London: J. R. Smith, 1862.

Mather, Increase. *A Brief History of the War with the Indians in New-England.* London, 1676.

————. *The Life and Death of that Reverend Richard Mather.* Cambridge, 1670, reprinted Athens, Ohio: Ohio University Press, 1966.

Mather, Samuel. *The Life of the very Reverend Cotton Mather.* Boston, 1729.

New England's First Fruits. London, 1643, in *Old South Leaflets*, Vol. 3, Number 51. Boston, 1894.

Perkins, William. *The Foundation of Christian Religion.* Boston: 1682.

Plymouth Church Records, 1620-1859. Boston: *Publications of the Colonial Society of Massachusetts*, 1920-1923.

217

Prince, Thomas. *A Chronological History of New England . . . 1602 to . . . 1730.* Boston, 1736.

Robinson, John. *Observations Divine and Moral for the Furthuring of Knowledge and Virtue.* Leyden, 1625.

―――. *The Works of John Robinson,* ed. Robert Ashton. 3 vols. Boston, 1853.

Scottow, Joshua. "A Narrative of the Planting of the Massachusetts Colony Anno 1628," *Collections of the Massachusetts Historical Society,* 4th ser., 4 (1858), pp. 279-330.

Shepard, Thomas. *The Works of Thomas Shepard.* New York: Ams Press, 1967.

The Synod. *The Necessity of Reformation.* Boston, 1679.

Thompson, Benjamin. *New Englands Crisis, Or a Brief Narrative, Of New-Englands Lamentable Estate at present, compar'd with the former (but few) years of Prosperity.* Boston, 1676.

Wigglesworth, Michael. *Day of Doom,* ed. Kenneth B. Murdock. New York: Spiral Press, 1929.

Winthrop, John. *History of New England.* ed. James Savage. 2 vols. Little, Brown and Company, 1853.

―――. *Winthrop Papers.* 5 vols. *Massachusetts Historical Society.* Boston: Merrymount Press, 1929-1947.

Wood, William. *New England Prospect.* London, 1634.

II. Secondary Works

Ahlstrom, Sydney E. *A Religious History of the American People.* New Haven: Yale University Press, 1972.

―――. *Theology in America. The Major Protestant Voices from Puritanism to Neo-Orthodoxy.* Indianapolis and New York: The Bobbs-Merrill Co., Inc., 1967.

Andreasen, N.J.A. *John Donne: Conservative Revolutionary.* Princeton, N.J.: Princeton University Press, 1967.

Ariès, Philippe. *Centuries of Childhood: A Social History of Family Life.* trans. Robert Baldick. New York: Knopf, 1962.

Bailyn, Bernard. *Education in the Forming of American*

Society. Chapel Hill: University of North Carolina Press, 1960.

———. *The New England Merchants in the Seventeenth Century*. Cambridge: Harvard University Press, 1955.

Bailyn, Bernard and John Clive. "England's Cultural Province," *William and Mary Quarterly*, 3rd ser., 11 (1954), pp. 200-213.

Baritz, Loren. *City on a Hill, A History of Ideas and Myths in America*. New York: Wiley Publishers, 1964.

———. "The Idea of the West," *American Historical Review*, 66 (1961), pp. 618-640.

Battis, Emery John. *Saints and Sectaries; Anne Hutchinson and the Antinomian Controversy in the Massachusetts Bay Colony*. Chapel Hill: University of North Carolina Press, 1962.

Beall, Otho T. Jr. and Richard H. Shyrock. *Cotton Mather, First Significant Figure in American Medicine*. Baltimore: Johns Hopkins Press, 1954.

Benton, Robert M. "The American Puritan Sermon before 1700," unpublished dissertation, University of Colorado Graduate School, 1968.

———. "An Annotated Check List of Puritan Sermons Published in America before 1700," *Bulletin of the New York Public Library*, 74 (1970), pp. 286-337.

Bercovitch, Sacvan, ed. *The American Puritan Imagination: Essays in Revaluation*. New York and London, Cambridge University Press, 1974.

———. "Cotton Mather," in *Major Writers of Early American Literature*, ed. Everett Emerson. Madison and London: University of Wisconsin Press, 1972.

———. "The Historiography of Johnson's *Wonder Working Providences*," *Essex Institute Historical Collections*, 104 (1968), pp. 138-161.

———. "Horologicals to Chronometricals: The Rhetoric of the Jeremiad," in *Literary Monographs*, ed. Eric Rothstein, vol. 3. Madison: University of Wisconsin Press, 1970.

Bercovitch, Sacvan, ed. "New England Epic: Cotton Mather's *Magnalia Christi Americana,*" *English Literary History*, 33 (1966), pp. 337-350.

————. "New England Epic: A Literary Study of Cotton Mather's *Magnalia Christi Americana,*" unpublished dissertation, Claremont Graduate School, 1965.

————, ed. *Typology and Early American Literature.* Amherst: University of Massachusetts Press, 1972.

————. "Typology in Puritan New England: The Williams-Cotton Controversy Reassessed," *American Quarterly*, 19 (1967), pp. 166-191.

Black, Robert C. III. *The Younger John Winthrop.* New York: Columbia University Press, 1966.

Blench, J. W. *Preaching in England in the Late Fifteenth and Sixteenth Centuries; A Study of English Sermons, 1450-c. 1600.* New York: Barnes and Noble, 1964.

Boas, Ralph and Louise. *Cotton Mather, Keeper of the Puritan Conscience.* New York and London: Harper & Bros., 1928.

Bodkin, Maud. *Archetypal Patterns in Poetry; Psychological Studies of the Imagination.* London: Oxford University Press, 1934, reprinted 1965.

Boorstin, Daniel J. *The Americans: The Colonial Experience.* New York: Random House, 1958.

————. "The Puritan Tradition: Community above Ideology," *Commentary*, 26 (1958), pp. 288-299.

Breen, T. H. *The Character of the Good Ruler; A Study of Puritan Political Ideas in New England, 1630-1730.* New Haven: Yale University Press, 1970.

Bridenbaugh, Carl. *Cities in the Wilderness: The First Century of Urban Life in America, 1625-1742.* New York: The Ronald Press Co., 1938.

————. *Vexed and Troubled Englishmen, 1590-1642.* New York: Oxford University Press, 1968.

Brown, B. Katherine. "Freemanship in Puritan Massachusetts," *American Historical Review*, 59 (July, 1954), pp. 865-883.

Brown, John. *Puritan Preaching in England; A Study of Past and Present*. New York: C. Scribner's Sons, 1900.

Brumm, Ursula. *American Thought and Religious Typology*, trans. John Hooglund. New Brunswick, N.J.: Rutgers University Press, 1970.

Bultmann, Rudolf Karl. *The Presence of Eternity: History and Eschatology*. New York: Harper, 1957.

Burke, Kenneth. *The Rhetoric of Religion; Studies in Logology*. Boston: Beacon Press, 1961, reprinted Berkeley, Calif.: University of California Press, 1970.

Bushman, Richard L. *From Puritan to Yankee: Character and the Social Order in Connecticut, 1690-1765*. Cambridge, Mass.: Harvard University Press, 1967.

Calhoun, Arthur W. *A Social History of the American Family from Colonial Times to the Present*. 2 vols. Cleveland: The Arthur H. Clark Co., 1917-1919.

Campbell, Joseph. *The Masks of God*. New York: Viking Press, 1959.

———, ed. *Myths, Dreams, and Religion*. New York: E. P. Dutton, 1970.

Carroll, Peter N. *Puritanism and the Wilderness: The Intellectual Significance of the New England Frontier, 1629-1700*. New York: Columbia University Press, 1969.

Clark, Charles E. *The Eastern Frontier; The Settlement of Northern New England, 1610-1763*. New York: Knopf, 1970.

Clark, Elmer T. *The Psychology of Religious Awakening*. New York: The Macmillan Co., 1929.

Cohn, Norman. *The Pursuit of the Millennium; Revolutionary Millenarians and Mystical Anarchists of the Middle Ages*. Revised and expanded edition. New York: Oxford University Press, 1970.

Coolidge, John S. *The Pauline Renaissance in England: Puritanism and the Bible*. Oxford: Clarendon Press, 1970.

Cowing, Cedric B. "Sex and Preaching in the Great Awakening," *American Quarterly*, 20 (1968), pp. 624-644.

Craven, Wesley Frank. *The Colonies in Transition, 1660-1713.* New York: Harper & Row, 1967.

Cremin, Lawrence A. *American Education: The Colonial Experience, 1607-1783.* New York: Harper & Row, 1970.

Crowder, Richard. *No Featherbed to Heaven: A Biography of Michael Wigglesworth, 1631-1705.* East Lansing, Mich.: Michigan State University Press, 1962.

Danielou, Jean. *From Shadows to Reality: Studies in the Biblical Typology of the Fathers,* trans. Wulstan Hibberd. London: Oates, 1960.

Davies, Horton. *Worship and Theology in England: From Cranmer to Hooker, 1534-1603.* Princeton, N.J.: Princeton University Press, 1970.

————. *Worship and Theology in England: From Watts and Wesley to Maurice, 1690-1850.* Princeton, N.J.: Princeton University Press, 1961.

Degler, Carl N., ed. *Pivotal Interpretations of American History.* 2 vols. New York: Harper & Row, 1966.

DeJong, Peter Y. *The Covenant Idea in New England Theology, 1620-1847.* Grand Rapids, Mich.: William B. Eerdmans Publishing Co., 1945.

Demos, John. *A Little Commonwealth: Family Life in Plymouth Colony.* New York: Oxford University Press, 1970.

————. "Families in Colonial Bristol, R.I.," *William and Mary Quarterly,* ser. 3, 25 (1968), pp. 40-57.

————. "Notes on Life in Plymouth Colony," *William and Mary Quarterly,* ser. 3, 22 (1965), pp. 264-286.

————, ed. *Remarkable Providences: 1600-1760.* New York: George Braziller, 1972.

Dollar, George W. "The Life and Works of The Reverend Samuel Willard, 1640-1707," unpublished dissertation in modern history, Boston University Graduate School, 1960.

Doten, Dana. *The Art of Bundling.* New York: Farrar & Rinehart, 1938.

Downey, James. *The Eighteenth Century Pulpit; A Study of the Sermons of Butler, Berkeley, Secker, Sterne, Whitefield and Wesley.* Oxford: Clarendon Press, 1969.

Dunn, Richard S. *Puritans and Yankees; The Winthrop Dynasty of New England, 1630-1717.* Princeton, N.J.: Princeton University Press, 1962.

———. "The Social History of Early New England," rev., *American Quarterly*, 24 (1972), pp. 661-679.

Earle, Alice Morse. *Child Life in Colonial Days.* New York: The Macmillan Co., 1899.

———. *Customs and Fashions in Old New England.* New York: C. Scribner's Sons, 1894.

———. *Home Life in Colonial Days.* New York: The Macmillan Co., 1900.

Eggleston, Edward. *The Transit of Civilization from England to America in the Seventeenth Century.* New York: D. Appleton and Co., 1901.

Eliade, Mircea. "The Yearning for Paradise in Primitive Tradition," *Daedalus*, 88 (1959), pp. 255-267.

Elliott, Emory. "*Persona* and Parody in Donne's *The Anniversaries*," *The Quarterly Journal of Speech*, 58 (Feb., 1972), pp. 48-57.

Emerson, Everett H. "Calvin and Covenant Theology," *Church History*, 25, No. 2 (June, 1956), pp. 136-144.

———. *English Puritanism from John Hooper to John Milton.* Durham, N.C.: Duke University Press, 1968.

———. *John Cotton.* New York: Twayne Publishers, 1965.

Erikson, Erik H. *Childhood and Society.* 2nd edition. New York: W. W. Norton and Co., 1963.

———. "Ego Development and Historical Change," *The Psychoanalytic Study of the Child*, 2 (1946), pp. 359-396.

———. *Identity, Youth, and Crisis.* New York: W. W. Norton, 1968.

Erikson, Kai T. *Wayward Puritans; A Study in the Sociology of Deviance.* New York: Wiley and Co., 1966.

Esler, Anthony. *The Aspiring Mind of the Elizabethan Younger Generation.* Durham, N.C.: Duke University Press, 1966.

Feinstein, Howard M. "The Prepared Heart: A Comparative Study of Puritan Theology and Psychoanalysis," *American Quarterly*, 22 (1970), pp. 166-176.

Fleming, Sanford. *Children and Puritanism: The Place of Children in the Life and Thought of the New England Churches, 1620-1847.* New Haven: Yale University Press, 1933.

Forbes, Harriette, comp. *New England Diaries, 1602-1800, A Descriptive Catalogue of Diaries, Orderly Books and Sea Journals.* New York: Russell & Russell, 1967.

Ford, Worthington Chauncey. *The Boston Bookmarket: 1679-1700.* Boston: The Club of Odd Volumes, 1917.

Franklin, Phyllis. *Show Thyself a Man. A Comparison of Benjamin Franklin and Cotton Mather.* The Hague, Paris: Mouton Press, 1969.

Frederick, John T. "Literary Art in Thomas Hooker's *The Poor Doubting Christian,*" *American Literature,* 40 (1968), pp. 1-8.

————. "Literary Art in Thomas Shepard's *Parable of the Ten Virgins,*" *Seventeenth Century News,* 26 (1968), p. i, item 7.

Fromm, Erich. *Escape from Freedom.* New York: Farrar & Rinehart, Inc., 1941.

Frye, Roland Mushat. *God, Man, and Satan; Patterns of Christian Thought and Life in Paradise Lost, Pilgrim's Progress and the Great Theologians.* Princeton, N.J.: Princeton University Press, 1960.

Fussel, Edwin. "Benjamin Thompson, Public Poet," *New England Quarterly,* 26 (1953), pp. 494-511.

Gilsdorf, Aletha Joy. "The Puritan Apocalypse: New England Eschatology in the Seventeenth Century," unpublished dissertation, Yale University Graduate School, 1965.

Goodsell, Willystine. *A History of the Family as a Social and Educational Institution.* New York: The Macmillan Co., 1915.

Grabo, Norman. *Edward Taylor.* New York: Twayne Publishers, 1961.

————. "John Cotton's Aesthetic: A Sketch," *Early American Literature,* 3 (1968), pp. 4-10.

————. "Puritan Devotion and American Literary Theory," *Themes and Directions in American Literature*, eds. Ray B. Browne and Donald Pizer. Lafayette, Ind.: Purdue University Press, 1969.

————. "The Veiled Vision: The Role of Aesthetics in Early American Intellectual History," *William and Mary Quarterly*, 3rd ser., 19 (1962), pp. 493-510.

Greven, Phillip J. *Four Generations: Population, Land and Family in Colonial Andover, Massachusetts*. Ithaca, N.Y.: Cornell University Press, 1970.

Hall, David D. *The Faithful Shepherd: A History of the New England Ministry in the Seventeenth Century*. Chapel Hill: University of North Carolina Press, 1972.

————, comp. *Puritanism in Seventeenth-Century Massachusetts*. New York: Holt, Rinehart & Winston, 1968.

Hall, G. S. "Marriage and Fecundity of Colonial Men and Women," *Pedagogical Seminary*, 10 (1903), pp. 275-314.

Hall, Michael G., ed. *The Glorious Revolution in America: Documents on the Colonial Crisis of 1689*. Chapel Hill: University of North Carolina Press, 1964.

Haller, William. *The Puritan Frontier: Town Planting in New England Colonial Development, 1630-1600*. New York: Columbia University Press, 1951.

————. *The Rise of Puritanism*. New York: Columbia University Press, 1938.

Hanscom, Elizabeth D., ed. *The Heart of the Puritans; Selections from Letters and Journals*. New York: The Macmillan Co., 1917.

Hansen, Chadwich. *Witchcraft at Salem*. New York: George Braziller, 1969.

Haroutunian, Joseph. *Piety Versus Moralism: The Passing of the New England Theology*. New York: H. Holt and Co., 1932.

Heimert, Alan E. "Puritanism, the Wilderness, and the Frontier," *New England Quarterly*, 26 (1953), pp. 361-382.

Heimert, Alan E. *Religion and the American Mind, from the Great Awakening to the Revolution.* Cambridge: Harvard University Press, 1966.

Hill, Christopher. *Society and Puritanism in pre-Revolutionary England.* New York: Schocken Books, 1964.

Hill, Hamilton A. *History of the Old South Church (Third Church) Boston, 1669-1884.* 2 vols. Boston and New York: Houghton Mifflin & Co., 1890.

Hinton, R.W.K. "Husbands, Fathers, and Conquerors: Patriarchalism in Hobbes and Locke," *Political Studies,* 16 (1968), pp. 55-67.

Holland, Norman. *The Dynamics of Literary Response.* New York: Oxford University Press, 1968.

Holmes, Thomas James. *Cotton Mather: A Bibliography of His Works.* 3 vols. Cambridge: Harvard University Press, 1940.

———. "Cotton Mather and His Writings on Witchcraft," in *The Papers of the Bibliographical Society of America,* 18 (1924), pp. 31-59.

James, William. *The Varieties of Religious Experience; A Study in Human Nature.* New York: Longmans, Green and Co., 1902.

Jantz, Harold S. "The First Century of New England Verse," *Proceedings of the American Antiquarian Society,* 53 (1943), pp. 219-508.

Johnson, Frederick Ernest. *Religious Symbolism.* New York and London: Harper and Brothers, 1955.

Jones, James W. *The Shattered Synthesis: New England Puritanism before the Great Awakening.* New Haven: Yale University Press, 1973.

Kaufmann, U. Milo. *The Pilgrim's Progress and Traditions in Puritan Meditation.* New Haven: Yale University Press, 1966.

Kirkpatrick, Clifford. *The Family as Process and Institution.* New York: The Ronald Press Co., 1955.

Kittredge, George L. "Cotton Mather's Scientific Communications to the Royal Society," in *American Antiquarian Society Proceedings*, 18 (1907), pp. 148-212.

——. "Notes on Witchcraft," in *American Antiquarian Society Proceedings*, 18 (1907), pp. 148-212.

——. *Witchcraft in Old and New England*. New York: Russell & Russell, 1956.

Lane, William C. "Early Harvard Broadsides," *Proceedings of the American Antiquarian Society*, New Series, 24 (1914), pp. 264-304.

Lesser, Marvin X. "All for Profit: The Plain Style and the Massachusetts Election Sermons of the Seventeenth Century," unpublished dissertation, Columbia University Graduate School, 1967.

Lesser, Simon O. *Fiction and the Unconscious*. Boston: Beacon Press, 1957.

Levin, David. *In Defense of Historical Literature*. New York: Hill & Wang, 1967.

Levy, Babette M. *Preaching in the First Half Century of New England History*. Hartford, Conn.: The American Society of Church History, 1945, reprinted New York: Russell & Russell, 1967.

Littlefield, George Emery. *Early Boston Booksellers, 1642-1711*. Boston: The Club of Odd Volumes, 1900.

——. *The Early Massachusetts Press, 1638-1711*. 2 vols. Boston: The Club of Odd Volumes, 1907.

——. *Early Schools and School-Books of New England*. Boston: The Club of Odd Volumes, 1904.

Lockridge, Kenneth A. "The Population of Dedham, 1636-1736," *Economic History Review*, 19 (1966), pp. 318-344.

——. *A New England Town: The First Hundred Years, Dedham, Massachusetts, 1636-1736*. New York: Norton, 1970.

——. "The History of a Puritan Church, 1637-1736," *New England Quarterly*, 40 (1967), pp. 399-424.

Lowance, Mason I. Jr. "Images and Shadows of Divine Things: Puritan Typology in New England from 1660-1750," unpublished dissertation, Emory University Graduate School, 1968.

——. "Typology and the New England Way: Cotton Mather and the Exegesis of Biblical Types," *Early American Literature*, 4 (1969), pp. 15-37.

McClelland, David C. *The Achieving Society*. Princeton, N.J.: Van Nostrand, 1961.

McGiffert, Michael, comp. *Puritanism and the American Experience*. Reading, Mass.: Addison-Wesley, 1969.

Mead, Margaret. "The Implications of Culture Change for Personality Development," *American Journal of Orthopsychiatry*, 17 (1947), pp. 633-646.

Mead, Margaret and Martha Wolfenstein, eds. *Childhood in Contemporary Cultures*. Chicago: University of Chicago Press, 1956.

Meserole, Harrison T., ed. *Seventeenth-Century American Poetry*. New York: W. W. Norton and Company, 1968.

Middlekauff, Robert. *The Mathers: Three Generations of Puritan Intellectuals, 1596-1728*. New York: Oxford University Press, 1971.

Miller, Perry. *Errand into the Wilderness*. Cambridge: Harvard University Press, 1956.

——. "The Half-Way Covenant," *New England Quarterly*, 6 (1933), pp. 676-715.

——. "The Marrow of Puritan Divinity," *Publications of the Colonial Society of Massachusetts, Transactions*, 32 (1935), pp. 247-300.

——. *The New England Mind*. 2 vols. Boston: Beacon Press, 1953, reprinted 1966.

——. *Orthodoxy in Massachusetts, 1630-1650*. Gloucester, Mass.: P. Smith, reprinted 1965.

——. "Preparation for Salvation in Seventeenth-Century New England," *Journal of History of Ideas*, 4 (June, 1943), pp. 253-286.

Miller, Perry and Thomas Johnson, eds. *The Puritans.* New York: Harper & Row, reprinted 1963.

Minnick, Wayne C. "The New England Execution Sermon, 1639-1800," *Speech Monographs*, 35 (1968), pp. 77-89.

Mitchell, William Fraser. *English Pulpit Oratory from Andrewes to Tillotson; A Study of Its Literary Aspects.* New York and Toronto: The Macmillan Co., 1932.

Moller, Herbert. "Sex Composition and Correlated Culture Patterns of Colonial America," *William and Mary Quarterly*, 3rd ser., 2 (1945), pp. 113-153.

Morgan, Edmund S. "New England Puritanism: Another Approach," *William and Mary Quarterly*, 3rd ser., 18 (1961), pp. 236-242.

——. *The Puritan Dilemma: The Story of John Winthrop.* Boston: Little, Brown, 1958.

——. *The Puritan Family: Religion & Domestic Relations in Seventeenth-Century New England.* New York: Harper & Row, New Edition, 1966.

——, ed. *Puritan Political Ideas, 1558-1794.* Indianapolis: Bobbs-Merrill, 1965.

——. *Visible Saints: The History of a Puritan Idea.* New York: New York University Press, 1963.

Morison, Samuel Eliot. *Builders of the Bay Colony.* Boston and New York: 1930.

——. *The Founding of Harvard College.* Cambridge: Harvard University Press, 1935.

——. *Harvard College in the Seventeenth Century.* 2 vols. Cambridge: Harvard University Press, 1936.

——. *The Intellectual Life of Colonial New England.* New York: New York University Press, 1956, reprinted 1965, 1970.

Murdock, Kenneth B. "Clio in the Wilderness: History and Biography in Puritan New England," *Church History*, 24 (1955), pp. 221-238, revised and reprinted in *Early American Literature*, 6 (Winter, 1971-1972), pp. 201-219.

——. *Increase Mather: The Foremost American Puritan.* Cambridge: Harvard University Press, 1925.

Murdock, Kenneth B. *Literature and Theology in Colonial New England.* Cambridge: Harvard University Press, 1949.

———. "William Hubbard and the Providential Interpretation of History," *Proceedings of the American Antiquarian Society,* 52 (1943), pp. 15-37.

Murrin, John M. "Review-Essay [new Puritan histories]," *History and Theory,* 11 (1972), pp. 226-275.

Nash, Roderick. *Wilderness and the American Mind.* New Haven: Yale University Press, 1967.

Nuttall, Geoffrey F. *Visible Saints: The Congregational Way, 1640-1660.* Oxford: B. Blackwell, 1957.

Nye, Russel B. *American Literary History: 1607-1830.* New York: Knopf, 1970.

Oberholzer, Emil Jr. *Delinquent Saints: Disciplinary Action in the Early Congregational Churches of Massachusetts.* New York: Columbia University Press, 1956.

Ong, Walter J., ed. *In the Human Grain, Further Explorations of Contemporary Culture.* New York: The Macmillan Company, 1967.

———. *Ramus: Method and the Decay of Dialogue; From the Art of Discourse to the Art of Reason.* Cambridge: Harvard University Press, 1958.

Palfrey, John G. *History of New England.* 5 vols. Boston: Little, Brown, and Co., 1860-1890.

Pettit, Norman. *The Heart Prepared: Grace and Conversion in Puritan Spiritual Life.* New Haven: Yale University Press, 1966.

Piercy, Josephine K. *Studies in Literary Types in Seventeenth Century America (1607-1710).* New Haven: Yale University Press, 1939.

Pinchbeck, Ivy. "The State and the Child in Sixteenth Century England," *British Journal of Sociology,* 7 (1956), pp. 273-285; 8 (1957), pp. 59-74.

Plumstead, A. W., ed. *The Wall and the Garden: The Massachusetts Election Sermons, 1670-1775.* Minneapolis, Minn.: University of Minnesota Press, 1968.

Pope, Robert G. *The Half-Way Covenant: Church Membership in Puritan New England.* Princeton, N.J.: Princeton University Press, 1969.

Porter, Katherine Anne. *The Collected Essays and Occasional Writings of Katherine Anne Porter.* New York: Delacorte Press, 1970.

Powell, Chilton L. "Marriage in Early New England," *New England Quarterly,* 1 (1928), pp. 323-334.

Powell, Sumner Chilton. *Puritan Village, The Formation of a New England Town.* Middletown, Conn.: Wesleyan University Press, 1963.

Reinitz, Richard. "Symbolism and Freedom: The Use of Biblical Typology as an Argument for Religious Toleration in Seventeenth Century England and America," unpublished dissertation, University of Rochester Graduate School, 1967.

―――, ed. *Tensions in American Puritanism.* New York: Wiley, 1970.

Rosenberg, Bruce A. *The Art of the American Folk Preacher.* New York: Oxford University Press, 1970.

Rutman, Darrett B. *American Puritanism; Faith and Practice.* Philadelphia: Lippincott and Co., 1970.

―――. "God's Bridge Falling Down: Another Approach to New England Puritanism Assayed," *William and Mary Quarterly,* ser. 3, 19 (1962), pp. 408-421.

―――. *Husbandmen of Plymouth; Farms and Villages in the Old Colony, 1620-1692.* Boston: Beacon Press, 1967.

―――. "The Mirror of Puritan Authority," in *Law and Authority in Colonial America,* ed. George A. Billias. Barre, Mass.: Barre Publishers, 1965.

―――. *Winthrop's Boston; Portrait of a Puritan Town, 1630-1649.* Chapel Hill, N.C.: University of North Carolina Press, 1965.

Sanford, Charles L. *The Quest for Paradise: Europe and the American Moral Imagination.* Urbana, Ill.: University of Illinois Press, 1961.

Sasek, Lawrence A. *The Literary Temper of the English Puritans.* Baton Rouge, La.: Louisiana State University Press, 1961.

Sargant, William W. *The Battle for the Mind, A Physiology of Conversion and Brainwashing.* Garden City, N.Y.: Doubleday & Co., 1957.

Schlesinger, Elizabeth B. "Cotton Mather and his Children," *William and Mary Quarterly*, 3rd ser., 10 (1953), pp. 181-189.

Schneider, Herbert W. *The Puritan Mind.* New York: H. Holt & Co., 1930.

Schücking, Levin L. *The Puritan Family: A Social Study from Literary Sources,* trans. Brian Battershaw. New York: Schocken Books, 1970.

Seybolt, Robert F. *Apprenticeship and Apprenticeship Education in Colonial New England and New York.* New York: Columbia University Press, 1917.

Shea, Daniel B. Jr. *Spiritual Autobiography in Early America.* Princeton, N.J.: Princeton University Press, 1968.

Shipton, Clifford K. "The New England Clergy of the 'Glacial Age,'" *Publication of the Colonial Society of Massachusetts, Transactions,* 32 (1933), pp. 24-54.

———. "The New England Frontier," *New England Quarterly,* 10 (1937), pp. 25-36.

Silverman, Kenneth, ed. *Colonial American Poetry.* New York: Hafner, 1968.

Simpson, Alan. *Puritanism in Old and New England.* Chicago: University of Chicago Press, 1955.

Spencley, Kenneth J. "The Rhetoric of Decay in New England Writing, 1665-1730," unpublished dissertation, University of Illinois Graduate School, 1967.

Sprague, William D. *Annals of the American Pulpit,* vol. 1. New York: Robert Carter & Brothers, 1857.

Starbuck, Edwin D. *The Psychology of Religion.* New York: C. Scribner's Sons, 1903.

Starkey, Marion L. *The Devil in Massachusetts: A Modern*

Inquiry Into the Salem Witch Trials. New York: Knopf, 1949.

Stearns, Raymond P. and David H. Brawner. "New England Church 'Relations' and Continuity in Early Congregational History," *Proceedings of the American Antiquarian Society,* 75 (1965), pp. 13-45.

———. *Science in the British Colonies of America.* Urbana, Ill.: University of Illinois Press, 1970.

Stiles, Henry R. *Bundling.* New York: Book Collectors Ass'n, 1934.

Stone, Lawrence. "Social Mobility in England: 1500-1700," *Past and Present,* 33 (1966), pp. 16-55.

Swift, Lindsay. "The Massachusetts Election Sermons," *Publications of the Colonial Society of Massachusetts, Transactions,* 1 (1892-1894), pp. 388-451.

Trevor-Roper, H. R. *The Crisis of the Seventeenth Century: Religion, the Reformation and Social Change.* New York: Harper & Row, reprinted 1968.

Tuveson, Ernest L. *Redeemer Nation: The Idea of America's Millennial Role.* Chicago: University of Chicago Press, 1968.

Tyler, Moses Coit. *A History of American Literature: 1607-1765.* New York: G. P. Putnam's Sons, 1878, reissued Ithaca, N.Y.: Cornell University Press, 1949.

Upham, Charles W. *Salem Witchcraft; with an Account of Salem Village and a History of Opinions on Witchcraft and Kindred Subjects.* Boston, 1867, reprinted New York: F. Ungar Publishing Co., 1959.

Van Dyken, Seymour. *Samuel Willard, 1640-1707: Preacher of Orthodoxy in an Era of Change.* Grand Rapids, Mich.: William B. Eerdmans Publishing Co., 1972.

Von Rohr, John. "Covenant and Assurance in Early English Puritanism," *Church History,* 34, No. 2 (June, 1965), pp. 195-203.

Walzer, Michael L. *The Revolution of the Saints; A Study in the Origins of Radical Politics.* Cambridge: Harvard University Press, 1965.

Warren, Austin. *Connections*. Ann Arbor: University of Michigan Press, 1970.

Weeden, William B. *Economic and Social History of New England, 1620-1789*. New York: Hillary House Publishers, 1963, reprint of 1890 edition.

Welch, D'Alté A. "A Bibliography of American Children's Books Printed Prior to 1821," *Proceedings of the American Antiquarian Society*, 73 (1963), pp. 121-324.

Wendell, Barrett. *Cotton Mather, The Puritan Priest*. New York: Dodd, Mead, and Company, 1891, reprinted 1963.

Wilder, Amos N. *The Language of the Gospel: Early Christian Rhetoric*. New York: Harper & Row, 1964.

Williams, George H. *Wilderness and Paradise in Christian Thought*. New York: Harper & Row, 1962.

Wright, Louis B. *The Cultural Life of the American Colonies: 1607-1763*. New York: Harper, 1957.

———. *Culture on the Moving Frontier*. Bloomington, Ind.: University of Indiana Press, 1955.

Wright, Thomas G. *Literary Culture in Early New England, 1620-1730*. New Haven: Yale University Press, 1920, reprinted New York: Russell & Russell, 1966.

Ziff, Larzer. *The Career of John Cotton: Puritanism and the American Experience*. Princeton, N.J.: Princeton University Press, 1962.

———. *Puritanism in America; New Culture in a New World*. New York: Viking Press, 1973.

———. "The Social Bond of the Church Covenant," *American Quarterly*, 10 (1958), pp. 454-462.

Zuckerman, Michael. *Peaceable Kingdoms: New England Towns in the Eighteenth Century*. New York: Knopf, 1970.

INDEX

Absalom, biblical story of, 67, 121
Adams, William, 42, 45
Allen, James, 140, 154; *New England's Choicest Blessing*, 155f
Allin, James, 43-45, 151
Ames, William, 20
Andover, Massachusetts, 34
Andros, Edmund, 11, 170, 173, 191
Anglican, 127-128, 174
Antinomian episode, 39, 41
Arminianism, 151
Arnold, Samuel, 89, 96; *David Serving His Generation*, 95f
attire and fashion, 118-119
audience response, 11n
autobiographies, 7, 9, 63, 78-79, 84

baptism, 40, 43, 70, 125; see also Half-Way Covenant
Becon, Thomas, 63-64
Beecher, Lyman, 203
Bradford, William, 26, 35
Bradstreet, Anne, 69
Bradstreet, Simon, 173
Brown, Edmund, 23
Brown, Thomas, 28

bundling, 36

Calhoun, Arthur, 65
calling, 25, 41, 72-74, 83-84, 131, 179-181
Calvin, John, 68, 198
Cambridge Church, 142
Cambridge platform, 38
child-rearing, 7, 63f, 153-154, 161; adolescence, 72f, 80-81, 83-85, 92 (separation from parents in, 75-76); apprenticeship, 34, 74f, 197; children's literature, 66; early doubt, 80; early piety, 69f; home discipline, 23, 64, 69, 148; latency period, 82; obedience and disobedience, 71, 76, 78, 81, 86, 112, 120-121, 160; puberty, 83; religious training, 153, 156, 161 (secret prayer, 82, 84, 99); shaming, 66, 69, 72, 80, 85, 89, 99, 101, 103, 193
church membership, 13, 24, 29, 42-43, 52, 57, 90, 125, 155, 159, 167, 181-185, 192-193, 202; tests for, 24, 37-40, 53-54, 85-86, 140; see also Baptism and Half-Way Covenant

235

101, 112, 116, 120-121, 148,
160, 179, 197; perfectionism,
24, 166; predestination, 40,
165; preparation of the heart,
40-47; reason, use of, 153;
salvation, 151 (assurance of,
133-134); see also calling,
church membership, commu-
nion, conversion experience,
covenant, Half-Way Covenant,
New Dispensation, Pauline
spirit

Quakers, 59, 86, 92

Randolph, Edward, 90
religious apostasy, 90, 92, 97-98,
107
Restoration of Charles II, 60,
79, 119
Robinson, John, 25, 68
Rogers, Daniel, 64
Ruddock, John, 29

St. Paul, 20-22, 146, 166
Satan, 73, 107, 175, 198, 200;
as scapegoat, 79, 107, 198-200
Second Church of Boston, 126,
163-164, 188
sermons:
    forms: artillery election, 89,
110, 146; execution, 66, 120,
135, 169; funeral, 101, 110-111,
166
    rhetorical art of ministers,
10n
sermon imagery: benevolent God,
56, 95, 125, 134, 136, 169, 175,
193, 201; candlestick, loss of,
100, 123; Christ as Savior, 14,
55-56, 129, 132, 134, 141, 147,
158, 160, 176f, 185; Christian
soldier, 147; comets, 118;
corrupt vine, 132, 160; darkness
and light, 108-109, 155-156;

death, 68, 111; death of
founders, 115; decay and ruin,
59, 88, 98, 124, 150-151, 196-
197; drought, 109-110, 113, 124,
141, 155; family order, 133;
family separation, 3, 13, 67, 78,
101, 105, 107, 122; garden and
wall, 59, 105, 107-108, 110,
112, 114, 131, 147, 150, 153, 158,
164, 167; Indians as threat, 66,
107, 175; loss, 88, 99, 103, 108;
marketplace, 171, 180-181;
master and servant, 120-121,
123, 197, 199; plagues, 144;
planting and growth, 91, 102,
108-110, 112, 115, 131-132,
150-151, 158, 167, 189, 194;
serpents, 108, 152; sickness and
health, 88, 92, 97, 112, 144,
151, 155, 158, 176n, 179, 196;
sleeping, 94, 106, 119, 133;
storms, 110, 113-115, 119, 124,
141, 153, 170f; wilderness, 59,
105, 107, 109-110, 149 (explication of, 108); wrathful God,
13, 59, 66, 88, 97, 99, 105-106,
110, 114, 116-120, 136, 141, 144,
150, 184, 202
sermon themes:
    assurance, 13, 54-55, 70, 87,
99, 104; as central message,
173-186; shift toward, 136-157;
Mather, Cotton, 186-204;
Mather, Increase, 125-135;
Willard, Samuel, 158-172
    fear of external attack, 103,
105, 108-117, 147, 150, 170f,
175, 189, 198; impending doom,
39, 114, 172; Last Judgment,
66-68, 119, 130, 186; millennialism, 39, 124, 128, 189, 190n,
191; see also decline, myth of
Sewell, Joseph, 17

Library of Congress Cataloging in Publication Data

Elliott, Emory, 1942-
 Power and the pulpit in Puritan New England.

 Bibliography: p.
 Includes index.
 1. Preaching—History—New England. 2. Puritans—
New England. I. Title.
BV4208.U6E43   285'.9'0974   74-29093
ISBN 0-691-07206-X